More Praise for *White House Warriors*

"This insightful and compelling book helps make sense of how the White House's powerful National Security Council staff works and also why it often doesn't—sometimes helping presidents make sound foreign policy but all too frequently getting the policy wrong with terrible human consequences. Richly detailed from interviews with White House staffers, the book disproves Donald Trump's feverish claims of a 'deep state' out to undermine the presidency."

—Gary J. Bass, author of *The Blood Telegram: Nixon, Kissinger, and a Forgotten Genocide*

"In the White House briefing room, I was often asked about the power of the National Security Council. John Gans was one of my best sources to help explain the ways this unique and elusive institution has served the American president, including the one I worked for. In *White House Warriors*, Gans proves as good a guide for readers as he was for me, taking all of us inside the staff's daily work as well as the debates and decisions that continue to transform America's relationship with the world."

—Josh Earnest, former White House press secretary

"When it comes to US national security policy, some of the most powerful and consequential people in Washington are also the least well known. John Gans shines a bright light on these National Security Council staffers and shows how they have influenced presidential decisions on war for decades. *White House Warriors* is must-read for anyone interested in how Washington really works."

—Ivo H. Daalder, former US ambassador to NATO and coauthor of *In the Shadow of the Oval Office*

"In *White House Warriors*, John Gans provides a clear-eyed and pro-vocative account of what it's like to serve a president. Anyone who wants to work in a White House or understand one should read this essential new book."

—Jennifer Palmieri, former White House communications advisor and *New York Times* best-selling author of *Dear Madam President*

"A fine new book about the National Security Council, and particu-larly the NSC staff. John Gans brings us into the NSC world through lively accounts of the roles played by key senior aides, from Mike For-restal under John F. Kennedy to Meghan O'Sullivan under George W. Bush. The result is a lively, credible analysis that brings the policy process alive. *White House Warriors* is a splendid read for students, scholars, and policy practitioners alike."

—I. M. Destler, professor at Maryland School of Public Policy and coauthor of *In The Shadow of the Oval Office*

White House Warriors

White House Warriors

How the National Security
Council Transformed the
American Way of War

JOHN GANS

Liveright Publishing Corporation
A Division of W. W. Norton & Company
Independent Publishers Since 1923
New York London

For information about permission to reproduce selections from this book, write to
Permissions, Liveright Publishing Corporation, a division of W. W. Norton & Company, Inc.,
500 Fifth Avenue, New York, NY 10110

For information about special discounts for bulk purchases, please contact
W. W. Norton Special Sales at specialsales@wwnorton.com or 800-233-4830

Manufacturing by Lake Book Manufacturing
Book design by Daniel Lagin
Production manager: Julia Druskin

Library of Congress Cataloging-in-Publication Data

Names: Gans, John (John A.), author.
Title: White House warriors : how the National Security Council transformed the American way
   of war / John Gans.
Other titles: How the National Security Council transformed the American way of war
Description: New York : Liveright Publishing Corporation, a division of W. W. Norton & Company,
   [2019] | Includes bibliographical references and index.
Identifiers: LCCN 2018054255 | ISBN 9781631494567 (hardcover)
Subjects: LCSH: National Security Council (U.S.)—History. | National security—United States—
   Decision making. | United States—Military policy—Decision making. | Strategic culture—United
   States. | Civil-military relations—United States. | United States—Foreign relations—1945–
Classification: LCC UA23 .G356 2019 | DDC 355/.033573—dc23
LC record available at https://lccn.loc.gov/2018054255

Liveright Publishing Corporation, 500 Fifth Avenue, New York, N.Y. 10110
www.wwnorton.com

W. W. Norton & Company Ltd., 15 Carlisle Street, London W1D 3BS

1 2 3 4 5 6 7 8 9 0

To Anjuli, who loves with all her heart.

The greatest trust between man and man is the trust of giving counsel.   —FRANCIS BACON, "OF COUNSEL"

Excuse me, darling. . . . I want you to remember this face here, okay? This is the guy behind the guy, behind the guy.

—TRENT, *SWINGERS*

CONTENTS

White House Warriors

INTRODUCTION

The President's "Personal Band of Warriors"

The grandfather clock by the door in the Oval Office was ticking.

The president, years into a divisive war, was about to announce the biggest decision of his time in the White House. Facing resistance from senior military officers and hesitation from his secretary of state, the commander in chief had made a controversial and risky choice. In a speech later that day, he would tell the American people of a plan to send tens of thousands of additional US troops to a bloody conflict where thousands of American service members had already been killed and dozens of attacks were occurring each day.

Disagreeing with his advisors and isolated from a public pessimistic about the war, the president was far out on a limb when a member of the National Security Council staff, known in Washington simply as "the NSC," joined him in the Oval Office. After giving the president a quick briefing before the speech and starting to walk out of the room, the young aide turned to say one more thing. Trying to buck up the war-weary president, she said: "I know you feel really alone right now, but I want you to know that you are not alone. I am standing there with you."[1]

Of course, this NSC staffer was down the hall and back behind the scenes by the time the president faced the nation all alone and gave his televised speech that evening. Her name was not mentioned, she did not get called before Congress to explain the strategy, nor was the staffer charged with traveling the country explaining the choice to the public. Technically, she did not even work in the White House itself but instead labored far from the eyes of the public she served in the building next door.

The Executive Office Building looks important, a six-story mountain of Virginia and Maine granite, all columns and mansard rooftops, and protected by an iron fence. Completed in 1888, the State, War, and Navy Building was rechristened when its eponymous and growing tenants departed for new confines in the years before and after World War II. Still the plaque that bears the Executive Office Building's generic name* is no help to tourists and other passersby wondering what all the badged and busy men and women, who hustle up the building's imposing staircases early each morning, do all day and often late into the night.

Today, those toiling on the third floor are the staffers of the National Security Council,† the forum where the president meets with cabinet secretaries and senior military leaders. The NSC staff has evolved since its creation seven decades ago. What began as a collection of the council's administrative clerks has become the president's "personal band of warriors," as George W. Bush, the commander in chief making the decision to send a surge of troops to Iraq, called the staffer Meghan O'Sullivan, who briefed him before the announcement speech, and her colleagues.[2]

Just as housing the NSC was not the original purpose of the Executive Office Building itself, presidential warriors were not the plan when Congress created the staff in a single line of law in 1947. But every president needs help, whether it is with little questions (what is the name of a foreign leader's wife?) or the big ones (should we go to war?). As the NSC staff has helped with the

---

* The Executive Office Building has gone by many names and abbreviations over the years: the State, War, and Navy Building; the EOB; the Old Executive Office Building, or OEOB; and now the Eisenhower Executive Office Building, or EEOB. For simplicity's sake, the name "Executive Office Building" will be used throughout this book.

† In Washington, "NSC" and "National Security Council" are applied to the NSC staff and the Council itself. For clarity, the "NSC" will be used for the staff while the National Security Council will be applied to the forum where the president meets with cabinet officials.

inane tasks and the near-impossible challenges, each commander in chief has, in his own way, trusted and empowered the dedicated staffers sitting right next door.

In return, though the War Department left the Executive Office Building decades ago, the NSC's warriors have kept up the fight. Shielded in secrecy and driven by a responsibility to the president as well as the country's security, the staff works, and sometimes battles, to get answers and ideas, often in the face of opposition from secretaries of defense and state. From the Executive Office Building's third floor and in one-on-one conversations with the commander in chief, the NSC has exerted more influence over presidential decisions than any single institution or individual over the last seventy years, transforming not just America's way of war but also the way Washington works.

The men and women walking the hushed corridors of the Executive Office Building do not look like warriors. Most are middle-aged professionals with penchants for dark business suits and prestigious graduate degrees, who have spent their lives serving their country in windowless offices, on far-off battle-fields, or at embassies abroad. Before arriving at the NSC, many joined the military or the nation's diplomatic corps, some dedicated themselves to teach-ing and writing about national security, and others spent their days working for the types of politicians who become presidents. By the time they joined the staff, each had shown the pluck—and the good fortune—required to end up staffing a president.

O'Sullivan might have started her journey to the Executive Office Build-ing earlier than any NSC staffer in history. As an elementary school student in Massachusetts, the precocious second grader wrote a paper on what she believed to be the state of Palestine.[3] After her teacher patiently explained that it was not an independent nation, the seven-year-old O'Sullivan, ashamed her research had missed such a critical fact, was driven to learn more. She went on to college in Washington, then a job on Capitol Hill, a doctorate at the Univer-sity of Oxford, and later a role at a prominent think tank before she joined the government a month after the attacks of September 11, 2001.

In Washington and books about it, individuals are often referred to by the name of their institution, so a three-star general comes to represent all of the "Pentagon" just as an assistant secretary of state serves as the entire department's voice. The NSC is no different, and in conversations in Washington, especially on the war, O'Sullivan was considered a representative of the staff and even the White House. Yet the NSC's members have come from different places—rich and poor; registered Democrats, Republicans, and independents; some were wonks in second grade and others bloomed much later—and they have chosen to serve in the Cold War, the war on terror, and the decade in between.

When the crimson-haired O'Sullivan first joined the NSC in 2004, she was a striking presence for more than just her hair color in the Executive Office Building's checkered hallways and on the wider Bush national security team. The 34-year-old O'Sullivan was a rare young woman in meetings when the business of national security, especially at the highest levels, was still dominated by middle-aged men. Having worked in her career's earliest days for a Democratic senator, O'Sullivan was also not a dyed-in-the-wool conservative, let alone a hawk, in the Republican administration. And unlike many in Washington, she had gone to war, as a civilian who arrived in Baghdad in the first few days of the 2003 invasion.

Even if O'Sullivan stood out in discussions, it is relatively hard to see her and other NSC staffers in news coverage or in the history books. Presidents get most of the credit, blame, and attention, often followed by the cabinet secretaries on the National Security Council, military leaders, and the staff's boss, the national security advisor. Staffers instead are found often just out of the news camera's frame and just below historians' radars, usually sitting, listening, watching, and taking notes on the backbench of meetings in the White House Situation Room, the Oval Office, and elsewhere.

There are few paths to those rooms and the NSC itself. Because the staff's budget is relatively small, it can only hire so many people directly: O'Sullivan was a rare expert appointee whose tenure was tied to the president's. Most of the hundreds and hundreds of staffers who have served on the NSC have been loaned temporarily, usually for a year or two, paid, and given security clearances by the military, the diplomatic corps, or the intelligence community. But that is all it takes. Staff members like their boss, the national security advisor, are not required to be confirmed or even questioned by Congress, and the press and public are rarely alerted to their hire.

When each NSC staffer first walks up the steps to the Executive Office Building, he or she joins an institution like no other in government. Compared to the Pentagon and other bureaucracies, the staff is small, hierarchically flat with only a few titles like directors and senior directors reporting to the national security advisor and his or her deputies. Compared to all those at the agencies, even most cabinet secretaries, the staff are also given unparalleled access to the president and the discussions about the biggest decisions in national security.

Yet despite their access, the NSC staff was created as a political, legal, and bureaucratic afterthought. The National Security Council was established both to better coordinate foreign policy after World War II and as part of a deal to create what became known as the Defense Department. Since the army and navy only agreed to be unified under a single department and a civilian cabinet secretary if each still had a seat at the table where decisions about war were expected to be made, establishing the National Security Council was critical to ensuring passage of the National Security Act of 1947. The law, as well as its amendments two years later, unified the armed forces while also establishing the Joint Chiefs of Staff and the Office of the Secretary of Defense, as well as the CIA.

At first the council itself got all the attention due to the novelty and importance of its charge; indeed, one headline billed its members "The Men Who Guard the Nation's Security."[4] Though the council's makeup evolved over the years, inviting different officials to its meetings and allowing more than a few women like O'Sullivan to do the guarding, its members, called "principals" in Washington, still include the president, the vice president, the secretaries of defense and state, and some others of cabinet rank. The national security advisor, a White House position, runs its meetings, and the chairman of the Joint Chiefs of Staff and leading intelligence officials attend only as advisors to, not as members of, the council.

Everyone in Washington—Congress, the White House, the military, and the State Department—agreed that a forum of such stature, considering decisions of such consequence, needed administrative staff to keep it productive and push its paper. But the agreements stopped there. The State Department did not want a "director" for the new team, the first defense secretary wanted the staff to sit at the newly built Pentagon, and the president's advisors pre-ferred they become a "further enlargement of the presidential staff."[5]

The White House won the argument. The NSC executive secretary—so named as a concession to the secretary of state—and his team were treated as a part of the president's executive office, housed in the Executive Office Building and charged with serving the "presidential position."[6] From those first choices, subsequent presidents empowered the NSC to meet their own needs as the gov-ernment grew, as technology shrank the distances between the commander in chief and the frontlines, and as the nation's interests and their defense went global during the Cold War.

As a result, O'Sullivan joined an NSC that, though hidden from the public's view and Congress's reach in the Executive Office Building, was expected and empowered to serve the commander in chief rather than the council itself, which lost influence as presidents used it less and less for advice and more for photo opportunities. Along the way, the staff transformed from adjunct presidential staffers to aides to all-powerful national security advisors before becoming managers of the policy process and eventually drivers of the policy itself. Through this evolution, president after president came to rely on the staff to pursue the foreign policy responsibilities bestowed by the Constitution and born amid a changing world.

Understanding just how the staff *staffs* the president requires knowing the way Washington's national security policymaking is supposed to work on paper—and how it has worked in practice since 1947.

At the beginning of each new presidential administration, the recently sworn-in commander in chief issues a memorandum detailing the way he wants to manage national security. This document establishes the bureaucratic rules of the road for the running discussion about national security that is sometimes called the interagency process: who from the agencies will come to meetings, chair them, and be responsible for assignments. These memoranda are not enacted by Congress or even expected to last long, since the guidelines can be altered as situations and presidents require; but the memo establishes what is supposed to be the regular order and, in some cases, a pecking order, which is why more than a few times the document has led to disagreements.

The staff is only mentioned fleetingly, if at all, in these memoranda. Instead, the NSC's role has been developed over decades of what should be considered Washington "common law," as one former White House official called it.[7] Rather than legislation, custom and tradition have established the unwritten dos and don'ts of NSC staffing. The staff is trusted to serve the president with briefings, policy papers, and talking points and to support the national security advisor and policy process by organizing, taking notes at, and sharing the outcomes of its meetings.

Although the staff works in secret, the common law that governs its behavior is well known in Washington. The unwritten code came into force in the 1980s and has been passed down from staffer to staffer and administration to administration. It has also been blessed without objection by Congress as well as Washington's foreign policy establishment, who expect NSC colleagues and the national security advisor to make sure the common law is followed.

More important than what is allowed by common law is what is forbidden. The staff is not supposed to go "operational." The NSC's staff members are not expected to join the real battles on the frontlines, develop tactical plans, or issue direct orders to commanders there or anyone else at the Departments of Defense and State, in the intelligence community, and elsewhere. Legally and practically, the NSC is not in the chain of command, so staffers can review operations at the White House Situation Room, sometimes in great frustration and even despair, but actual execution must remain in the hands of the nation's military, diplomats, and spies.

The NSC staff are also not expected to be go-it-alone advocates for their own ideas, working around official channels or subverting their colleagues and counterparts in Washington. They are to serve as so-called "honest brokers" who fairly relay to the president the views of all his advisors but also can give their own advice. That last part of honest brokering is a delicate, if not impossible, practice in Washington, where trust is fragile, passion about policy drives careers, and "honesty" is often in the eye of, and defined by, one's rivals.

There is no formal introduction to these rules for NSC staffers like O'Sullivan. The common law is not posted in the Executive Office Building's hallways, emailed on first days, or formally policed by the national security advisor.

The staffers in one of the most secured buildings in the world—where emails, phone calls, and meetings are guarded—operate on an honor system.

Still, on most days, it is relatively easy to follow the rules, even those left unwritten. Staffers like O'Sullivan simply support their boss. They get the president ready for phone calls, trips, and visits with foreign leaders. They draft talking points and contribute to speeches. They prepare him for deliberations and decisions with his advisors and the National Security Council. And once the president makes a choice, they measure how the policy is working.

Yet the world, and certainly war, rarely work according to plan. Despite the clear organizational charts delineated in the early administration memoranda and the decision directives written to limit ambiguity, national security is hard, and far less precise than many would hope. Enemies have a say, strategy X does not always lead to result Y, Murphy's Law can trump the art of war, and often Washington is simply proven wrong about what to do and how to do it.

Yet despite access to the latest intelligence, few know for sure if a plan is working or not. Policymakers from the president down sometimes can feel what some in Washington call "drift," the sense that events are out of the control of people who are used to feeling just the opposite. Even then, commanders in chief, busy and eager to appear confident, are slow to question the chosen course, and most of the senior civilian and military advisors, who developed—and thus remain invested in—the original plan, believe they will make it work in time.

As a result, Washington can take a while to figure out just what is going on and what the United States should do instead. After all, a change of course requires acknowledging that the first plan was wrong, an admission few seasoned politicians and policymakers are eager to make. It requires deciding more time will not help. And in the case of some of the most strenuous, detailed, and expensive of national undertakings, it can require fundamentally rethinking and revising the way America thinks about and wages war.

None of this is easy, which is why change is so hard in Washington and often requires a fight. Every day in the nation's capital, thousands of men and women work to shape national security policy. Each of them, from the cabinet secretaries on the National Security Council to the desk officers at the agencies, especially the Departments of State and Defense, believe they know what is best and deserve to have a say. Yet at a moment of crisis and drift, the president often looks to those who also have his best interests in mind.

When a member of the NSC staff like O'Sullivan is called to see the president, there is little time to waste. Every minute counts in national security and a president's day. After racing down the steps to the Executive Office Building and crossing the driveway, the staffers hustle into the West Wing's basement below a nondescript awning, and race either down the steps to the Situation Room on the right or upstairs to the Oval Office.

Once in the room, the NSC staff rarely has a place on the official agenda and little real power to decide a matter or even issue an order, which is left to the president. But the NSC staff has the choice to speak up. As they decide whether to stay quiet, members of the NSC must weigh their dedication to the president and country, worry about violating Washington common law, and weather the frustration of defense secretaries and others in Washington, who would often prefer the staff keep their ideas to themselves.

Time and again, in the decades since its creation, members of the NSC staff, like O'Sullivan, have chosen to speak up in conversations with the president and in the memos and meetings before and after. As a result, staffer by staffer and president by president, the NSC has taken greater responsibilities from the agencies and become the intellectual engine of national security, fighting for policies that have been triumphs as well as terrible tragedies. Through it all, the NSC has shaped today's world, and America's relationship with it, in good ways and bad.

When O'Sullivan turned to say one more thing to President Bush before the speech announcing the surge, he barely reacted as the minutes ticked away. It was the end of a long fight over a war gone bad, and neither the commander in chief nor his NSC warrior were in particularly good form: Bush's poll numbers were down and his advisors divided, while O'Sullivan was the target of criticism and questions about her competency from some in government and out. As the president said a rushed, "Thanks, thanks," he was likely talking less about the awkward pep talk than about their work together for the decision he was about to announce.[8]

Like O'Sullivan that day, most on the NSC staff choose to say their piece, ask a hard question, or propose a new idea. Their voice is not always heeded or even heard. But by simply speaking up, NSC staffers have changed the course of their own lives and history, even as they transformed how America fights its wars and how Washington works. In return for their fights, most staffers, like O'Sullivan in the Oval Office, have received the thanks of a grateful president.

Yet the names of these staffers, let alone their voices and impact, are hardly ever known outside of the Oval Office or the third floor of the Executive Office Building. You deserve to know who they are and what they fight for. And at a time when many Americans have doubts about government and questions about a so-called deep state of unelected officials controlling policy, you must decide if you want the NSC to keep up the fight, because the staff are not only the president's warriors. They are yours.

CHAPTER ONE

The "Bright Young Men" on the NSC

"Somber and Shaken"

On November 2, 1963, Michael Forrestal was one of a dozen or so NSC staffers serving President John F. Kennedy.[1] After walking into a White House meeting that Saturday, Forrestal handed a "flash" message to Kennedy, who had aspired since taking office to play a hands-on role managing foreign policy like President Franklin Roosevelt. With the help of NSC staffers like Forrestal and National Security Advisor McGeorge Bundy, the young president realized that ambition in Vietnam and elsewhere around the world, as the note in his hand made clear.

Forrestal, who was thirty-four when he began at the White House, had been raised to be in that room. The son of the first secretary of defense, a product of Princeton University and Harvard Law School, and a protégé of the US foreign policy establishment, Forrestal had been preparing to advise a president almost since he was old enough to talk. After Kennedy telephoned to recruit him to join the White House team, a precocious Forrestal demanded to know, "To do what, Mr. President?" The commander in chief replied: "That's not important. Just get down here."

Once Forrestal arrived at the White House, he pushed harder than many of his peers for the United States to take a more aggressive stand in the Vietnam War. Wearing horn-rimmed glasses and an overconfident air even for an administration that many considered arrogant, the staffer eventually encouraged the president, without the advice of most of the National Security Council, to acquiesce to a coup d'état against Ngo Dinh Diem, the beleaguered South Vietnamese president. Now Forrestal had come to the Cabinet Room to deliver the message that Diem was dead, news which left Kennedy, according to one observer's memory, "somber and shaken."[2]

Forrestal's fight for the removal of Diem was a sign of how far the NSC had come since the young staff member's own father, James Forrestal, the first secretary of defense, had himself fought to design and then control the National Security Council—including, most consequentially, the staff his son later joined. To the frustration of then-secretary Forrestal, President Harry Truman tied the staff not to the Defense Department or the National Security Council alone but to the presidency. As each of his successors, including Dwight Eisenhower, Kennedy, and Lyndon Johnson, treated the NSC as his own, staffers like the younger Forrestal had the opportunity if not the necessary power to fight for their own ideas, good and bad, for how to win the Cold War and the era's hot wars.

The "Presidential Position"

Of course, Roosevelt had not needed an NSC to win World War II. Despite the establishment of the White House's professional staff, known as the Executive Office of the President in 1939, and some informal military and diplomatic coordinating committees, the thirty-second president preferred hands-on, ad hoc war management. Roosevelt issued orders directly to a loose collection of senior military leaders, used his personal advisors as envoys to the world and Washington, and personally communicated with allies like British prime minister Winston Churchill.

Roosevelt's was, according to one biographer, a "deliberately organized—or disorganized" approach.[3] The president, who described himself as "a juggler . . . perfectly willing to mislead and tell untruths if it will help win the war," kept his cards close, his options open, and just about everyone else, including his last vice president Harry Truman, in the dark.[4] Although it worked and World War II was won, Roosevelt's juggling drove Washington mad and worried the senior officials, uniformed and civilian, who were charged with protecting the nation's security. With the president's death, the ascension of Truman, and the end of the war, those in the bureaucracy and military services sought to establish some semblance of regular order.

Concerned about Roosevelt's ad-hocracy and the American public's potential retreat into isolationism, many policymakers believed it was time, in Truman's words, to establish a "closely knit, cooperating and effective machinery" for national security in a changing Washington and world.[5] The government had grown during the war; technology, like nuclear weapons, had advanced; and the United States had increasingly global interests and cooling relations with the Soviet Union to manage. The new president also believed the moment required, among other reforms, the unification of the separate armed forces, such as the army, which was then part of the War Department—a step the individual military services resisted.

Few fought harder or longer than Secretary of the Navy James Forrestal, a former Wall Street financier. He was all in favor of better war management, but Forrestal also doubted his own and his service's interests would benefit from unification, which would likely take the military service secretaries out of the president's cabinet. Rather than reject reform outright, Forrestal sought to control the plan that would produce it, and he enlisted Ferdinand Eberstadt, a friend and former government official who was working in business in New York at the time, to help.

Eberstadt admitted up front the impossibility of the job. He wrote, since it was "unlikely that any one form of military organization would equally meet" all the nation's needs and traditions, it would be best to come up with a plan that would advance "the more essential ones."[6] To do so, Eberstadt recommended the creation of a national security council and the establishment of a "permanent secretariat, headed by a full-time executive" to prepare agendas, provide data, and distribute the council's conclusions.[7] If the plan was done right, the council and its staff could improve national security decisions while also allowing for Forrestal's true ambition: a seat at the table for each of the country's military services.[8]

Truman was willing to accept a council if it meant Forrestal, and his and the navy's many friends on Capitol Hill, would get on board with unification; but some at the White House smelled trouble when the service secretary sent Eberstadt's plan directly to Congress.[9] The president's team worried the navy was hijacking the unification process and that any legislation based on its secretary's blueprint would pull power from the president.[10] To counter Forrestal, the White House drafted legislation and lobbied to ensure the final product was acceptable to Truman.[11]

In the end, the White House's language dominated the final, passed text. Any law, of course, is still subject to interpretation, and the National Security Act of 1947 was no different. Forrestal, named the first secretary of defense, was not done fighting to get his way. He wanted the principals on the National Security Council to be able to make decisions without the president, and he tried to gain control of its new staff by having most of the members work out of offices at the Pentagon.[12]

The White House, however, kept protecting the president's interests even after the bill's signing. Truman's personal staff, in a memorandum of "suggestions," explained that the National Security Council was a presidential instrument. Accordingly, the new NSC leader should be considered an "administrative assistant to the president"; and the NSC staff "housed as near to other Executive Office units as possible, preferably in the Executive Office Building." The staff members themselves, though mostly loaned or detailed by the agencies and military, were to be considered additions to the presidential staff and dedicated to the "presidential position."[13]

Truman accepted this interpretation, and the suggestions were presented at the first National Security Council meeting in September 1947.[14] According to one White House official, Forrestal, a council member as the first secretary of defense, was so frustrated by the turn of events he promptly threw the memo "in the wastebasket."[15] Far from his ambition to decentralize authority, the National Security Council gave the White House the opportunity, especially after a disappointed Forrestal left government in 1949, and the dedicated staff to manage national security matters, and even wars, from the White House.

Truman's "Broker of Ideas"

The *New York Times* ran a photograph of one early meeting of the National Security Council with the headline "The Men Who Guard the Nation's Security."[16] Seated across the table from the president in the White House Cabinet Room was Sidney Souers, the first ever NSC "executive secretary," a title

Truman chose to mollify a concerned secretary of state.[17] The picture in the *Times* was a rarity for the low-key Souers: he placed a premium on his and the new staff's anonymity.

The NSC executive secretary, who had been promoted to rear admiral in the navy at the end of World War II before moving into the business world, worked out of the Executive Office Building with thirty staffers, half of whom were detailed by the armed services or sent over from the new Main State Building in the Foggy Bottom neighborhood of Washington.[18] According to Souers, he and his team were only to serve the president and as a "broker of ideas in crisscrossing proposals" from around the national security agencies.[19]

The new staff was made up of three teams. The secretariat prepared agendas, recorded minutes, and circulated drafts of policy papers. Separately, the NSC staff included junior detailees from the agencies, who were led by a "captain" (usually a senior Foreign Service officer from the State Department) and drafted policy papers. And third, the NSC "consultants," top-level members of the various departments, came to the White House occasionally to provide quality control and then to secure buy-in from senior-level officials back at their home agencies.[20] George Kennan, America's leading Sovietologist at the time and the State Department's first director of policy planning, was an early NSC consultant.[21]

Souers believed this structure helped avoid what he called the "ivory tower" problem: policy that was too divorced from the military's and diplomats' operational needs and too inflexible to deal with a rapidly changing world.[22] In those days of limited communications and technology, national security policy was still driven by papers on matters broad and narrow. Once the agencies and the staff wrote, the National Security Council principals reviewed, and the president approved the papers, each was then distributed around government as well as to embassies and military installations around the world for reference and implementation.

Max Bishop, a member of State's Policy Planning Staff, was one staffer writing on the Truman NSC. Born in Arkansas and raised in the Midwest, Bishop had been inspired as a prep school student to serve his country when he read a *Saturday Evening Post* article about the newly created Foreign Service, the nation's diplomatic corps.[23] He was so intrigued that while on a family trip in Washington, Bishop went to the front desk at the then–State, Navy, and War

Building and asked for "all the dope on the Foreign Service."[24] After being told about the entrance exam, the aspiring diplomat grew so nervous he wrote to the secretary of state to ask what happened to failures.

During his senior year at the University of Chicago, Bishop proved he had no reason to worry, passing the test on his first try in 1932. The young diplomat went on to serve in Asia and at State's Foggy Bottom headquarters before he was assigned to the NSC at age thirty-nine and given an office in the Executive Office Building, where he had inquired about government service decades before. Even though Bishop maintained some responsibilities, an office, and a boss (Kennan) at the State Department, the NSC staffer appreciated that his second assignment gave him face time with National Security Council principals like the secretary of state and the opportunity to think about global issues.[25]

Despite the work of Bishop and other staffers, the early NSC did not function to Truman's satisfaction.[26] It could take months for a paper to reach the president after being drafted, reviewed, and approved for his decision. As a busy president waited, early staffers were also spending a lot of time at their home agencies where they still had operational responsibilities. The entire arrangement contributed, one early council principal said of the process, to policy that too often fell victim to the "foul-up factor" resulting from personal rivalries and parochial interests.[27]

Although Congress made some reforms to the national security system, including the removal of service secretaries from the National Security Council in 1949, it was war itself, including the new Cold War and Korean War, that began to really empower the staff. For the United States, a reluctant belligerent in the two world wars, both the standoff with the Soviet Union and the fight against North Korea were new types of conflict for the country, the military, and the president. The Cold War was a global ideological struggle in a war-weary and increasingly nuclear-armed world after the Soviet Union first secured the bomb in 1949. Meanwhile, the Korean War was America's first hot war, even if it was euphemistically called a police action, of the new era.

World Wars I and II were what are known as total wars. During the second world war every citizen was asked to sacrifice and every tool in the country's arsenal, including eventually nuclear weapons, was used to try to not just defeat the opposition but destroy its ability and desire to make war in the future. Even though some believed the confrontation with the Soviet Union could become World War III, another total war, many in the US government, including on the Truman NSC, sought to deter such an outcome. As they did, conflagrations like North Korea's invasion of the South in 1950 had the potential to expand into a broader war, which is why Truman and his team, including the NSC, sought early on to keep the war limited, both in its objectives and its means.

Meanwhile, a government study on "United States Objectives and Programs for National Security," completed in April just before the outbreak of the war in Korea and better known in Washington as NSC-68, sought to put the United States on a Cold War footing. The paper most consequentially called for a massive increase in defense spending to ensure conventional and nuclear deterrence; but NSC-68 also had a profound, if less widely appreciated, impact on the staff in the Executive Office Building.[28] On its last page, the authors suggested the president establish a "revised and strengthened" NSC, which the White House tried to do by adding staff, and more senior staffers at that, who were detailed full-time from the agencies.[29]

The start of the Korean War in June reinforced the need for NSC-68's recommended buildups to the nation's defenses as well as to the president's NSC staff. Truman, who had mostly avoided National Security Council meetings, reengaged, chairing more meetings of the National Security Council, and the NSC staff were there to help.[30] With the world and Washington both rapidly changing, the president demanded that his decisions on Korea and other issues be channeled through—and coordinated by—the stronger, senior NSC staff, which had begun meeting twice weekly.[31] Truman also brought on W. Averell Harriman, the investment banker and ambassador, to serve as special assistant to the president, adding a senior manager to the White House national security team to wrangle an unwieldy government and disagreeing cabinet secretaries.[32]

"Planning Board"

Regardless of these changes, Dwight Eisenhower spent a great deal of time on the campaign trail in 1952 criticizing *how* Truman made national security policy. Eisenhower, a devotee of strategic planning from his days in the army, thought Truman was not using the NSC staff and system well enough and promised to take the National Security Council "from shadow to substance."[33] But because candidate Eisenhower's complaints were based on a dated understanding of Truman's process, President Eisenhower wound up— despite some spin—actually using much of the structure his predecessor had put in place.

Once Eisenhower won the White House, the new president found out just what Truman had been doing—because he asked, or at least one of his campaign aides did. Robert Cutler, a Republican lawyer and banker, interviewed many of the Truman players and proposed a series of changes that sounded more sweeping than they were in practice.[34] The biggest and most consequential reform was a formalization of Harriman's position. Cutler recommended in a memorandum that Eisenhower appoint a "special assistant to the president for national security affairs." After reading Cutler's proposal, the new president gave him the job, one that would eventually become known as the "national security advisor" and grow into one of the most well-known positions in Washington.[35]

Eisenhower's other changes to the NSC amounted to a rebranding. Cutler recommended a "Planning Board" be dedicated to long-term strategy and synchronization. Though it was announced to considerable fanfare, Cutler admitted this was merely a renaming of what was by then called the NSC Senior Staff.[36] As one of Cutler's successors as Eisenhower's special assistant eventually wrote, the Planning Board was just an "interdepartmental group which in one form or another has functioned" since the staff's creation.[37]

As on the Truman NSC, the "new" board was made up of senior planners from various departments doing double duty at the staff. Robert Bowie, a native of Baltimore, Maryland, and a graduate of Princeton University and Harvard Law School, had been Maryland's assistant attorney general before serving in the army during World War II. In 1953, he joined the Eisenhower State Department's Policy Planning Staff and quickly found he was also assigned to the NSC's Planning Board. He was forty-three when he walked into the Executive Office Building.[38]

Bowie was later joined by Army Major General Francis W. Farrell. Born in Chicago, Illinois, Farrell had been an instructor at West Point, where he had graduated in 1920, before commanding the Eleventh Airborne Division Artillery in the Pacific during World War II. He became chief of staff of the Eighty-Second Airborne Division before serving in the Korean War, first in the infantry and then training the army of the Republic of Korea. Farrell, at age fifty-five, was named an assistant to the chairman of the Joint Chiefs of Staff and to a dual role as the chairman's representative on the NSC's Planning Board.[39]

Eisenhower believed Bowie's and Farrell's second job on the Planning Board—developing short-, medium-, and long-term strategies for every possible issue—was critical to national security at a time of dramatic change in the world. The Soviet Union had changed leaders with the death of Joseph Stalin, European countries were growing stronger even as they shed their colonies, and postimperial convulsions roiled Asia, the Middle East, and Latin America. Because there were finite US resources to respond to all of this change, the president wanted to figure out—and plan for—how to protect America's interests without undermining its economy.

The thirty-fourth president put the Planning Board to the task. Bowie, Farrell, and the rest of the staff met twice a week, and their NSC business and planning were supposed to take priority over their day jobs at State, the Pentagon, and elsewhere.[40] The team drafted papers on various topics for consideration and debate, and sometimes edits, by the National Security Council. These included detailed studies of various topics, from the general (for example, the "basic" national security policy) to the far more specific (such as "US action in [the] event of unprovoked communist attack against US aircraft"), with recommendations for action that could be approved by Eisenhower.[41]

"Policy Hill"

As time went on, Eisenhower realized any improvement in planning needed to be matched by better management of a policy's implementation. In September 1953, the president created the Operations Coordinating Board (OCB) to figure out how the nation's military and diplomats could best implement a decision and to monitor their performance.[42] The OCB had a separate staff of fifty-five and its own offices near the Executive Office Building.[43] Truman staffer Bishop, who had gone on from his NSC assignment to a consul general post in Saudi Arabia before returning to Washington for another position at State Department headquarters, found himself again doing some work for the NSC, this time as a representative to the OCB.[44]

In addition to drafting papers and monitoring the performance of the bureaucracy, Eisenhower wanted to ask hard questions about the American strategy in the Cold War.[45] The NSC staff Planning Board did the asking, as well as much of the thinking and drafting, behind a big paper on the topic, known as NSC 162/2. The 1953 report, a massive intellectual and bureaucratic effort, helped refine US military strategy for the Cold War, as well as a conventional war, and the limited conflicts being fought around the world in the wake of receding colonial empires.[46]

French Indochina was home to one of these limited wars as the nationalist rebellion, led by Ho Chi Minh, sought to end France's colonial rule. Reluctantly, Eisenhower and the United States had provided financial aid but no military forces to France in the fight and then supported a 1954 agreement that split Vietnam into two territories. The United States installed Ngo Dinh Diem, a fierce anti-Communist, as prime minister in the South (he soon became president) and funded his government and military. But as both South Vietnamese institutions struggled to counter a growing insurgency supported by the North, Eisenhower resisted sending combat troops, in part due to the thinking about limited war in NSC 162/2.[47]

As American support for Diem continued, Eisenhower's former special assistant Cutler tried to explain what all the NSC staffers on the Planning Board and OCB were doing at such a busy time in the world. In 1956, he wrote about how recommendations traveled up one side of the "Policy Hill," via the Planning Board, where Bowie, Farrell, and their colleagues served as an "acid bath" for ideas. At the top, in the National Security Council meetings, any Planning Board papers were reviewed and any disagreements exposed by the staff were "thrashed out." [48] Once the president had made a decision, it would travel, as designed, "down the other side of Policy Hill to the departments and agencies responsible for its execution," to be monitored by the OCB.[49]

Despite all this process, some in Washington worried that the NSC and the entire national security system were not as effective as necessary at a time when the Soviet Union appeared on the march with the launch of the Sputnik satellite and other gains. The president was one of those concerned. Eisenhower, knowing there were inefficiencies and that National Security Council meetings had become laborious, had moved to make reforms behind the scenes; but one prominent member of Congress still took his concerns about the system public.[50] In April 1959, Senator Henry "Scoop" Jackson, a Democrat from

Washington state, said the Eisenhower procedure and the so-called policy hill were "pretty as a picture," but all of it was a "dangerously misleading façade."[51]

Jackson worried that the NSC's broad policy papers forced compromises and took decisions out of the president's hands by establishing precooked responses to global events.[52] Jackson's concerns and fears about the United States falling behind the Soviet Union in the Cold War helped launch a multiyear congressional inquiry, one of several the NSC would face in its history, into how best to organize for national security. Although Jackson's review did not lead to many significant changes to the National Security Council or NSC, his criticisms of Eisenhower were helpful to a young presidential candidate seeking any advantage available in a tight election: Senator John F. Kennedy of Massachusetts.

A "Tight Group of Very Able General Utility Assistants"

After defeating Eisenhower's vice president Richard M. Nixon in November 1960, Kennedy got right to business. Dean Acheson, a secretary of state under Truman who met with Kennedy after the election, remembered the president-elect said that he "had spent so much time in the last few years on knowing people who could help him become president that he found he knew very few people who could help him be president."[53] Kennedy was not short of advice for long, Eisenhower offered his two cents, Jackson's committee churned out reports, and every so-called wise man in Washington, like Acheson, was a phone call away.[54]

But it was a far lesser-known advisor who had the greatest impact on the Kennedy national security team and the NSC staff. Richard Neustadt, a Columbia University professor and former Truman White House staffer, had the president-elect's ear. Neustadt, who had just published a book, *Presidential Power and the Modern Presidents*, began writing memoranda for Kennedy on how to think about and organize his presidency. It was Neustadt, the author-turned-advisor, who recommended that the young commander in chief take a cue from Roosevelt and be his own "chief of staff"—the ultimate decider of matters large and small as the Cold War evolved.[55]

Although the National Security Council had been established specifically to limit presidents from aspiring to Rooseveltian juggling of foreign policy, Neustadt came up with a cunning way for Kennedy to reassert control. With a simple executive order, the new president could make the NSC staffers not servants of the larger National Security Council but instead a "tight group of very able general utility assistants" to the president himself and to Kennedy's pick for national security advisor, McGeorge Bundy, a dean at Harvard who, like others in the president's orbit, had grown up in and been raised to lead the elite establishment.[56]

Without going to Congress for funding or fighting with the cabinet, Kennedy, following Neustadt's advice, made sure the NSC "were his men," as one staffer recalled.[57] The resulting staff was small, with only a dozen policy staffers at the start; its members, like the rest of Kennedy's team, were young, and the staff included some "very high-powered, strong-minded people."[58] In practice, it was all a rather clubby affair, with staffers empowered by access and free-wheeling conversations with an informal president who distrusted and distanced himself from the more bureaucratic National Security Council and acted at times, according to one on the team, less like a commander in chief than a "desk officer."[59]

Although it took a year to get a call from the president and join this team at the White House, Michael Forrestal fit right in. Even among a bold, and some argued cocky, White House, Forrestal carried himself with the confidence of a man who knew better and had been discussing foreign policy with those who had made it for years. Born in New York, his Ivy League education was punctuated by World War II service in the navy his father helped lead. In the service, young Forrestal rose to the rank of lieutenant and served in posts as a defense attaché in Moscow under Ambassador and future Truman advisor Averell Harriman.

It was Harriman who all but adopted Forrestal after his father, by then a former defense secretary and suffering from depression, committed suicide in 1949 by hanging himself and then falling out a window at the Bethesda Naval Hospital in Maryland. Guided by Harriman and other members of the foreign policy establishment, the younger Forrestal began a law career, fed his interest in international affairs, and mingled in the same social circles as Kennedy. At one Harriman-hosted lunch in New York weeks after the 1960 election, the president-elect off-handedly asked Forrestal, "When are you coming down?"

Though interested, Forrestal had just become partner at a law firm, so he confidently asked, "Could I have a rain check?"[60]

The "Worst One We've Got"

As Forrestal labored at the firm, Kennedy and his team got to work on Vietnam. Within days of the young president's inauguration, he said the war in Southeast Asia was "the worst one we've got, isn't it?"[61] Despite the US-backed Diem regime's inability to establish popular support, effective governance, and control over the military, the Kennedy team embraced Diem tightly without demanding reforms in return. Instead, Kennedy and his team tried to better use American military advisors—some of whom the new president dispatched to Vietnam—to get the South Vietnamese armed forces prepared and dedicated to fight the growing insurgency.

The war was the type of problem Kennedy wanted in his hands when he became president. He and others on his team thought it was time for the United States to shift from defense to offense in the Cold War, which was settling into an uneasy stasis between two nuclear superpowers. To compete, without risking atomic catastrophe, the Kennedy team believed the United States required a steady hand at the helm and a stronger capacity to fight the limited wars, often between Cold War proxies battling among the ruins of collapsing colonial empires, which were becoming the hallmark of the era.

The White House was skeptical of the traditional way of fighting such wars. The Kennedy team was uninspired by both the massive retaliation that Eisenhower had developed, which relied on a huge conventional and even nuclear response to any kind of Cold War challenge, and the attrition warfare, which relied on wearing out an adversary through persistent, punishing combat, recommended by traditional military strategists. Each path felt clunky and potentially catastrophic to the Kennedy team, who wanted to develop a more "flexible response," both in the methods, like counterinsurgency tactics, and means, including establishing the Army Special Forces or Green Berets, to win wars like Vietnam.[62]

But playing offense in the Cold War was easier said than done, in part because the Kennedy NSC flattened Eisenhower's policy hill. Out were the formal planning board and operations control board, and in were what one reporter called the "cream of [Kennedy's] academic harvest."[63] Young and smart staffers with degrees from the Ivy League and a willingness to question authority wanted to help Kennedy do "his business," as Bundy explained.[64] Still, this informal system caused some quiet concerns in Washington. One staffer held over from the Eisenhower team said of the new approach and the author who recommended it, "Neustadt recommended dismantling the NSC machinery. Then he . . . left all the broken crockery around the White House."[65]

Those internal concerns became public after the disastrous April 1961 Bay of Pigs operation, in which CIA-trained Cuban exiles failed to overthrow the Communist regime in Cuba. A *New York Times* headline read simply, "How Cambridge Flunked the First Test."[66] But rather than being chastened in the wake of the disaster, Kennedy and the White House used the resulting outcry to strengthen the president's grip on the NSC. Bundy and some of the staff were moved from the Executive Office Building to the White House, where a high-tech command post, called the Situation Room, was established with a dedicated staff. Instead of having to rely on the agencies to share cables and communications, the White House could now put the "raw stuff" unfiltered into the hands of the increasingly hands-on president.[67]

The changes were noticed in turf-conscious Washington where the increasingly empowered NSC, which one observer called a "foreign office in microcosm," caused concerns, particularly at the State Department.[68] At one point, even Kennedy, who had cautioned against the national security advisor and NSC substituting for the secretaries of state and defense, wanted to know what his staffers were doing.[69] Bundy, in a memorandum on the staff's rules of the road, explained to the president that the NSC served as a "center of initiative and energy" and an extension of Kennedy "himself—as his eyes and ears," but the staff was "not . . . a place for men trying to peddle their own remedies without Presidential backing."[70]

"Have You Thought That Out?"

Such was the NSC Forrestal found when he finally took Kennedy up on his invitation in February 1962. Upon Forrestal's arrival at the White House, Bundy assigned him to work on the "Far East," which included China as well as Southeast Asia. But the new staff member confessed to the president: "I don't know anything at all about the Far East. I've never studied it; I've never been there."

Kennedy simply replied: "That's fine. That's just what we want. Somebody without preconceptions and prejudices." Kennedy was so unconcerned about Forrestal's lack of regional knowledge, the president quickly asked where his new assistant for Far Eastern affairs had gotten his tie.[71]

Even without Asia expertise, Forrestal brought more than neckwear to the NSC. Reflecting his upbringing, Forrestal had strict anti-Communist views and a strong belief in what the United States could accomplish around the world with the right decisions in Washington. Like many at the White House, the NSC staffer also thought a chance to shape history had finally arrived, as his fathers had in World War II. Yet as journalist and Kennedy chronicler David Halberstam observed, Forrestal, like many of his generation in the White House, who had been the "company commanders" in that war, came across as a bit too eager to replace the generals.[72]

At the White House, Forrestal was assigned to serve as an extension of another World War II veteran, Kennedy. The president dispatched his staffer to Vietnam and Southeast Asia on fact-finding trips to get a clearer picture of what was really going on. Kennedy also used Forrestal as a go-between with senior members of the administration, like the staffer's mentor Harriman, who was then serving in the State Department, as well as Vice President Lyndon Johnson who had been close to Forrestal's father when serving in the navy during World War II.

During the Kennedy administration, Johnson was not engaged deeply in foreign policy or Vietnam. But the president still wanted his vice president kept in the loop, and the job often fell to Forrestal. Briefing Johnson often proved a far different exercise than sessions with the urbane and engaged Kennedy. At one meeting, Forrestal arrived to find the vice president already prone and naked on a table in mid-massage. In between the masseur's smacks and rubs, and Johnson's grunts, Forrestal unsuccessfully tried to draw the vice president's attention to the policy details at hand.[73]

In addition to making trips to the field and briefing Johnson, the opinionated Forrestal also took the initiative on Vietnam strategy. The NSC staffer was not afraid to disparage a colleague's idea or to tell Bundy and the president exactly what was on his mind. The staffer's candor was one reason why Kennedy liked and gave him so much access, which worried the national security advisor. To Forrestal's continuing frustration, Bundy demanded to know what he planned to tell the president in their meetings and asked, "Have you thought that out?"[74]

Few issues seemed to animate Forrestal as much as counterinsurgency, which had become the Kennedy administration's strategy in Vietnam in 1961. As revolutions sprouted up all over the postimperial world, militaries from Asia to Africa were contending with guerrilla tactics and learning the hard-earned lessons for how best to handle them, including the need to separate, support, and protect the local population. The staffer shared with others in the administration a generational conviction that if they robustly applied integrated political, military, and economic plans, then they could isolate and defeat insurgencies like the one growing stronger in South Vietnam.

Working with like-minded colleagues, Forrestal peddled counterinsurgency to anyone who would listen or read. At one point, he insisted that a book on counterinsurgency by a French army officer, Roger Trinquier's *Modern Warfare*, should be studied by all American military leadership in Vietnam, where advice was not always welcome.[75] Forrestal explained the dynamic between the inquisitive staffer and the engaged warfighter on the frontlines. "It's like talking to the quarterback of a football team in the middle of the game," he said, "I mean, they were optimistic. They had to be. They also had a tendency to select those facts which would be most favorable to their cause and to the thought that it was winning."[76]

To break through the optimism, Forrestal got his ideas considered subtly. For as much informal time as the Kennedy NSC spent with the president, policy proposals about national security matters large and small were still supposed to be considered through a formal interagency process of meetings and memoranda that made sure everyone's issues and concerns were aired and considered. Because the staff had little formal standing in this process and no official seat at the table, Forrestal recalled, the NSC could "not attempt to introduce brand new ideas by force into the governmental machinery." Instead, Forrestal and his colleagues "tried to find somebody else in the other departments who had similar ideas and encouraged him to surface them, so that they could get to the President in the normal course."[77]

"Pussy-Footing"

In those days, Forrestal found many allies, particularly at the State Department, committed to counterinsurgency. The US "Strategic Hamlet" program sought to help pacify the South Vietnamese countryside and win popular support for the central government, and for a while and in data reports from the field, the plan, along with the thousands of Americans on the ground advising South Vietnam's military, appeared to be making progress. After Forrestal returned from one trip to South Vietnam in early 1963, he and a colleague reported the war was "clearly going better than it was a year ago."[78]

Still Forrestal believed the corrupt and incompetent Diem regime was an impediment to the program to win over the South Vietnamese population. After less than a year working on Vietnam, Forrestal had come to believe the United States had been "pussy-footing with Diem for too long."[79] Despite the progress in the countryside, each day the South Vietnamese government in Saigon seemed to give the NSC staffer more reason to fret and feel events there were drifting out of his, and the rest of Kennedy's team's, control. When Diem's special forces began cracking down on political opponents in May 1963 and support for the regime cratered, Forrestal looked for a way to change the South Vietnamese president's approach.

Then in August another option presented itself. Disaffected Vietnamese military officers approached American representatives with a proposal for a coup against Diem. The generals wanted, according to one Pentagon report, an indication of the US position on the idea and tacit support for it.[80] When the American team in Saigon cabled Washington for a decision, Forrestal, working with allies at the State Department like his mentor Harriman, wrote a supportive response and on Saturday, August 24, cabled the draft for approval to Kennedy, who was vacationing in Hyannis Port, Massachusetts.

Since even before he became president and Neustadt designed his NSC, Kennedy had wanted this type of decision in his hands. Forrestal's draft cable said, "If . . . Diem remains obdurate and refuses, then we must face the possibility that Diem himself cannot be preserved."[81] When Forrestal cabled it to Kennedy, the NSC staffer promised support was being "obtained" by others at State and Defense, and argued for haste since the "situation in Saigon may not remain fluid for long." It was, Forrestal argued to the president, "desirable [to] transmit this message tonight."[82] A few hours later, Kennedy approved the message, and it was dispatched to Saigon.[83]

Although nothing transpired immediately in South Vietnam, when the president and his team returned to work in Washington on Monday, August 26, it became clear the cable had not been formally approved by the national security advisor, the secretary of defense, or the chairman of the Joint Chiefs of Staff. Many on the Kennedy National Security Council complained internally about both the policy (several on the team outright opposed undermining Diem and what Vice President Johnson later called "this coup shit") and the process (one military advisor thought Forrestal's move had been an "egregious end run").[84]

On reflection, Kennedy was blunt, "We fucked that up."[85] Although some questioned how National Security Advisor Bundy, who was also away, had allowed such a consequential cable to go with so little review and discussion, his NSC staffer rightly took the brunt of the blame.[86] Even then Forrestal believed the decision was the right one, but how it had been made was "a mistake because the government did not reach a formal consensus." As a result, Forrestal, who admitted it had been *his* mistake, offered his resignation to the president, but Kennedy only replied: "You're not worth firing. You owe me something, so you stick around."[87]

Though Kennedy did not renege on the tacit approval given to the plotters of the coup, the conspiracy appeared to fizzle, and the president's team, including Forrestal, renewed calls for reforms in South Vietnam. Then on November 1, American representatives in Saigon were alerted that the plot was under way.[88] According to notes, Forrestal said at the time, it was a "well-executed coup, much better than anyone would have thought possible"; but matters quickly got out of hand.[89] Diem surrendered on the condition that his safety be guaranteed, only to be promptly killed in the back of an armored personnel carrier. When Forrestal informed Kennedy of the news the next day, the president went white and left the room distraught.[90]

A few weeks later, Forrestal traveled to South Vietnam to review the aftermath and meet with the recently recognized military junta. Before he departed, the NSC staffer visited with Kennedy, who had recently agreed to begin withdrawing troops from the country the next year. On the trip, the president wanted Forrestal to again be his eyes and ears and report back. According to him, Kennedy also suggested that on the NSC staffer's return, "We've got to sit down and do a rather more careful job than we have in the past in assessing what the role of the United States really is in Southeast Asia."[91]

"The Curtain Is Slowly Descending"

The conversation between the president and his NSC staffer never happened. On November 22, the president was shot in Dallas, Texas. Kennedy was declared dead at 1:00 p.m. local time. At 2:38 p.m., Johnson took the oath of office aboard *Air Force One*. When he did, Johnson also took leadership of a nation in shock, America's involvement in South Vietnam, and the late president's foreign policy team, including Bundy and Forrestal.

As the new president received his first briefing on Vietnam, the NSC staffer responsible for the country was half a world away. Forrestal had been awoken at 4 a.m. in Saigon to the news that Kennedy had been killed. When the staffer spoke by phone with Bundy at the White House, the national security advisor told him Kennedy would have wanted Forrestal to press on with the trip, and Johnson "agreed that this was the thing to do."[92] The president who sent him may have been dead, but Forrestal continued his trip and returned to Washington in early December to brief the new commander in chief on the war.

The NSC staffer, like many others, was surprised that Johnson asked him and other Kennedy men to continue their service.[93] The new president, who brought more traditional opinions about government (he wanted Congress involved, cabinet secretaries empowered, and staff to be staffers rather than advisors), did make some modest changes to reflect his style. He all but abandoned formal National Security Council sessions for Tuesday lunches with principals and without staff. Johnson also relied on the NSC less for advice than for intelligence and gossip, for which he had a voracious appetite, usually picked up from reports in the Situation Room and around government.[94]

Forrestal had returned from South Vietnam with a great deal of information. He was worried about the war and told Johnson directly that the "most urgent current problem" was the collapse of the counterinsurgency program, the perceived success of which had turned out to have been based on bogus progress reports by South Vietnam and some on the American team there. Still, Forrestal felt it best to not push too hard for a change of course but instead to give Johnson time. "My Gosh, we have a new president," the staffer recalled thinking. "Let's not propose anything new, really. Let's just try to keep the thing on an even keel."[95]

As weeks became months, Forrestal, unbowed by the criticism of his role in the Diem coup or what he had seen of its aftermath in Southeast Asia, had a difficult time keeping his patience or his concerns on an even keel. In March 1964, he said of Vietnam, "This is a Greek tragedy, and the curtain is slowly descending."[96] To avoid such a fate, Forrestal pushed Bundy and Johnson for decisions to change the US team in Saigon, reemphasize counterinsurgency as American and South Vietnamese policy, and launch a formal government review to find a new path forward.

Most of Forrestal's urgency was in vain. Johnson made a few minor decisions that spring, but his main concern was, as he asked, whether time was "working with us or against us, and if against us, how fast?" It fell to Forrestal to answer the president's question in May 1964. Although the NSC staffer did not think a military crisis was likely in the near term, he wrote, "What I think is needed fairly soon (i.e. within the next month or 6 weeks) is action by the United States in some part of Southeast Asia which gets across forcefully to the Vietnamese a sense that . . . we will do whatever is required to insure" the insurgency is contained.[97]

Over the next few months, the still new president took a few isolated actions, including reprisal bombings after the Gulf of Tonkin attacks in August, but nothing like what Forrestal thought was necessary. Neither he, the rest of the NSC staff, nor Bundy and others on the National Security Council could force Johnson to make a major decision one way or another on the war. With time not yet against the United States, Johnson was able to punt on any significant actions until after his election campaign concluded in November 1964.

The president was so desperate to avoid mistakes on Vietnam during the presidential campaign that he approved Forrestal's request to leave the NSC and become the secretary of state's special assistant for Vietnam affairs. Despite the president's continued desire to keep the Kennedy team together, he approved the plan but told the staffer he had a "double job" at State.[98] Not only was he to keep working on the war, but Forrestal was to "keep the lid on [it at State]" and make sure there were no screwups. If the headlines were bad, the president warned, "Forrestal, it will be your fault."[99]

Although Vietnam had only occasionally drawn the public's attention before Johnson's victory in November, Forrestal remained in close touch with Bundy and with his two replacements on the NSC, Chester Cooper, a

CIA detailee, and James Thomson, a State employee. When Cooper, who was forty-seven and had a doctorate from American University, was given the Asia assignment, Bundy called it a "difficult, thankless task."[100] At least he would have help: the thirty-three-year-old Thomson, "gifted young man, but not perfectly suited to the bureaucracy," was assigned to the Far East team.[101]

"You May Well Be Right"

Even though the two new staffers continued to help Johnson and Bundy prepare for meetings and decisions, Cooper and Thomson, along with Forrestal when still doing NSC work, were mostly support players for those with the real influence: getting data and answering questions. When insurgents attacked a US air base in South Vietnam in February 1965, Bundy, with help from Cooper who was with the national security advisor in Saigon at the time of the attack, urged Johnson to approve Operation Flaming Dart I, which led to more attacks, reprisals, and a sustained bombing campaign.

Yet few associated with the NSC were comfortable with how fast Vietnam was escalating. At State, Forrestal, who still had residual influence at the White House, believed some military action was needed but that political and economic progress were more important for long-term stability in South Vietnam.[102] Cooper, who had been in Vietnam right before the reprisals were ordered, began to ask Bundy shortly afterward, "Where are we going?" He argued the team needed "more walking and less running" and "perhaps a bit of just plain sitting" to contemplate what the United States should be doing in South Vietnam.[103] Thomson, who had voiced his concerns many times to Bundy, wrote a February 1965 memorandum with the subject line, "One Dove's Lament."[104]

However, as Forrestal had found with his pitch on counterinsurgency, the NSC staff only had so much power to get their ideas and concerns heard. Most on the National Security Council, as well as Bundy, felt the United States needed to do something—and the indecisive Johnson needed to decide on something—before South Vietnam was lost for good. After training the South Vietnamese military, trying counterinsurgency, and commencing sustained bombing only to come up short—and with Republicans like former vice president Richard Nixon calling for a more aggressive response—ground troops seemed like the option to try next. In July, Johnson approved the deployment of ground troops, and by the end of 1965, almost 180,000 Americans had been dispatched to South Vietnam.

Well before Johnson gave the order, one NSC staffer had explained why all those troops would prove futile. After Bundy showed Thomson a proposed bombing plan, the skeptical NSC staffer said he was "not sure this is going to work." The North Vietnamese, Thomson explained, were only too aware "that we will have to go home, someday, quite soon." [105] Bundy simply replied: "Well, James, that's a good point. You may well be right. Thank you so much." [106]

In the years ahead, the United States would find out how right the NSC staffer was. As the number of American troops increased in Vietnam to almost 500,000 in the next few years, and the fight became more conventional, the fundamental dynamics of the war did not change. [107] Though strategies evolved, the Johnson team believed that a gradual escalation of the fight, and the restraint it showed in not using nuclear weapons or sending a massive invasion into North Vietnam, were communicating a sophisticated message to America's adversaries there. Yet the North Vietnamese, and their insurgents in the South, remained committed to simply outlasting the United States. [108]

"Bright Young Men"

By the time they did, Forrestal, Cooper, Thomson, and Bundy were out of the White House. Forrestal left the State Department on March 1, 1965, never to return to government. An increasingly disenchanted Cooper decided to leave the staff later that year, though he continued his government service away from the NSC. [109] Thomson soon returned to Harvard.

To finally replace Bundy, who left to run the Ford Foundation in early 1966, Johnson appointed another Kennedy man. Walt Rostow, a former MIT professor who had joined the Kennedy NSC only to move on to State in the administration's first year, was named national security advisor, a title that did not formally exist but that the president helped cement in the public consciousness by using it with the press for the first time. [110] Johnson's instructions to Rostow were direct. The president told him: "I want you to do everything that Bundy did, but two additional things. One, I want you to generate some ideas, new ideas for policy. . . . [Second,] I want you to build that staff so we'll be proud of them."[111]

Johnson wanted to have pride in his NSC, but he spent so little time with its members that at one point an advisor took pains to introduce the president to the "bright young men" on the NSC roster.[112] They were bright, and thanks to the decisions of Truman, Eisenhower, and Kennedy, the mostly young team was there to serve the presidential position in Vietnam and other national security matters. Still if the president did not use or empower the staff, they could, bright or not, only do so much.

Even with limited influence, the NSC staff, as Forrestal had proven, was a good place to use it. His plans for counterinsurgency and the Diem coup had helped propel the United States far deeper into the Vietnam War and further transformed the American way of war. But the staffer had to resort to misdirection and even mischief to get each choice adopted, and by the time he and others on the NSC started to have some doubts about the rush to war, they did not have the power or partners to slow down the decisions. Whether a strong NSC could have stopped the escalation is one of many unanswerable questions about Vietnam.

Still, even Forrestal's limited influence and the position of the NSC staff would have shocked those like his father who had hoped to bring some regular order to Washington's national security decision-making. Though many post–World War II leaders sought to put an end to presidential juggling, they had created a staff that gave ambitious presidents the support to order a coup and then gradually escalate a war from the White House. The ironies would only continue as the war the younger Forrestal helped deepen provided the still bureaucratically young NSC, under increasingly powerful national security advisors, the opportunity to grow more influential in the years to come.

CHAPTER TWO

The "Center of the Foreign Policy Universe in America"

"We Will Not Make the Same Old Mistakes"

A little more than five years after Forrestal left government, another NSC staffer followed suit. In May 1970, the *New York Times* broke the news of the resignations of Morton Halperin, who was serving as an outside consultant to President Richard Nixon's NSC, and four other staffers.[1] They quit over Nixon's decision to invade Cambodia in a fitful attempt to finally end the Vietnam War, a divisive and deadly inheritance from the Johnson administration.

Yet the *Times* and other outlets focused less on what the staff resignations meant for the war than on what they said about the "very exciting new procedure" to manage foreign policy Nixon had promised when he won the presidency.[2] Nixon, who had served as vice president under Eisenhower, saw danger and disorder in what he called Kennedy's and then Johnson's "catch-as-catch-can talk-fests," and he blamed their informality for the battlefield stalemate in Vietnam.

The failures in Southeast Asia and Washington were proof to Nixon of what he believed was a "massive organizational problem" in government, and the president-elect tasked his pick for national security advisor, Henry Kissinger, with fixing it.[3] Despite the Harvard professor's World War II military intelligence service and his time as a consultant to the Eisenhower and Kennedy NSCs, the forty-five-year-old Kissinger had more experience writing about government than serving in it. Working with a boss he did not know well, inheriting a divisive war in Vietnam and the wider Cold War, and having to manage the NSC, Kissinger turned to an old colleague for advice.

The thirty-year-old Halperin, who had taught alongside Kissinger at Harvard, nearly matched the soon-to-be national security advisor's considerable ambition. As a kid in Brooklyn, Halperin read the *New York Times* daily and dreamed of shaping the world he saw in its pages.[4] When his plan to be an American diplomat was denied, first by the State Department's age restriction and then by a failed entrance exam, Halperin established an academic career before joining the Pentagon and working on a war that made headlines every day in the *Times* and elsewhere, few of them good.[5]

During the campaign, Nixon had promised to "end the war and win the peace" but admitted he had no "magic formula" on Vietnam.[6] Most in the US military and government, including Halperin, agreed. As the war divided the nation, it had exhausted those at the Defense and State Departments, in the embassy and military headquarters in Saigon, and at the Paris peace talks working to find a negotiated settlement that everyone, including Nixon, knew was the only way out of Vietnam. Many ideas, like counterinsurgency, had been tried—and proven insufficient—while other proposals, including massive ground invasion of the North, had been rejected.

Ending the war is one reason why Halperin jumped at the chance to help Kissinger build a new way of managing national security. In the administration's first weeks, the national security advisor gathered the staff and told them: "We will not make the same old mistakes. We will make our own."[7] Nixon, Kissinger, and the staff made plenty of mistakes in the years ahead, but they also changed how Washington worked. By supporting increasingly influential national security advisors like Kissinger, the NSC staff saw their institutional power grow as well.

The "Coup D'état at the Hotel Pierre"

A strong national security advisor and staff were important because Nixon, who wanted to be seen as a serious statesman, explained in the days after winning the election that he planned to "run foreign policy from the White House."[8] In figuring out how to do so, the president-elect thought the Eisenhower system was too rigid and the Kennedy-Johnson model too loose.

He tasked his soon-to-be national security advisor with finding a process that was just right.

But before Kissinger could fully dedicate himself to the project, the tenured Harvard professor had one more class to teach in Cambridge, Massachusetts.[9] Kissinger had used the fifty-member course, "Government 259: National Security Policy," to invite policymakers up from Washington for off-the-record talks where he would play devil's advocate. His guest for this last class was his former colleague Halperin, who was in his final days working at the Johnson Pentagon. Polishing his own star and gaining favor with a reporter, Halperin decided to tip off the *New York Times* that it was Kissinger's last class, and the newspaper duly sent a photographer and reporter to write up the session for the next day's edition.[10]

Halperin, with a low center of gravity and a high self-regard, knew Cambridge well. After earning his doctorate at Yale, Halperin had, after being advised to establish an academic career before serving in government, joined the faculty at Harvard, taught alongside Kissinger and others, and turned down a few entreaties to join the Kennedy and Johnson administrations. Eventually, Halperin did go into government and rose up the ranks at the Pentagon, which he planned to leave in weeks to join the Brookings Institution, a Washington think tank.

In the story that ran the next day, the paper of record missed the real news in the classroom: in a long conversation after class, Kissinger not only asked Halperin to join the NSC but to come to Manhattan, where the Nixon transition offices were located in the Hotel Pierre, to begin work at once. An ambitious and canny Halperin still wanted to continue in government, and he accepted the job from the equally, if not more, ambitious and canny Kissinger. Halperin convinced the Pentagon to lend him to the transition, but the Defense Department would not pay for a hotel, which left Halperin commuting from his parents' home in Brooklyn.[11]

One day at the Hotel Pierre, Kissinger asked Halperin to write a paper on how the NSC could better incorporate systems analysis, a relatively new practice of evaluating various road maps and options to reach an end goal. But Halperin did not have much of an opinion and had heard Nixon was asking for a new policy process design, so the eager soon-to-be-staffer told Kissinger, "I can only answer that in the context of suggesting how the whole NSC staff might be structured."[12] Halperin worked on the draft for the system with a number of campaign staff, former Eisenhower officials, and Foreign Service Officer Lawrence Eagleburger, who had been detailed to the transition by the State Department.[13]

After receiving the first draft, Kissinger conspiratorially gave Halperin's paper to Eagleburger and asked him to rework the plan without telling its author. Upon seeing the national security advisor listed as chair of critical meetings and empowered to ask the bureaucracy for options, Eagleburger asked, "Whatever happened to the Secretary of State?"[14] Without telling Kissinger and instead laughing off his conspiratorial tendencies, Eagleburger and Halperin ended up working together to finish the memorandum.

Their plan came to be known as the "coup d'état at the Hotel Pierre." The new system proved contentious from the start by making the national security advisor, and not the secretary of state, chair of most important meetings and principal advisor to the president.[15] Nixon informed Secretary of State designee William Rogers, Eisenhower's last attorney general, and the soon-to-be Secretary of Defense Melvin Laird, a former congressman, of his decision at a late-December meeting in Key Biscayne, Florida, and the two voiced their displeasure in the days that followed.[16] After Kissinger told the president-elect, "The State Department has now begun to object to the NSC procedures which you approved in Florida," Nixon simply approved the plan again.[17]

More than dethroning the State Department and positioning Kissinger at the center for the national security process, Nixon also agreed to a new organization for the NSC. As designed by Halperin, the staff would support an empowered national security advisor by "synthesizing and sharply defining the options, and occasionally by providing an independent staff study."[18] Compared to Forrestal and other Kennedy and Johnson staffers, the Kissinger NSC was going to have the power to review and either approve or reject the bureaucracy's ideas; and if the options were still bad, the staff could develop new ones for the president and then, as the national security advisor told one staffer, "tell him what to do."[19]

Such a role put a premium on competent NSC staffers. Halperin, a registered Republican but a supporter of Nixon's opponent in the presidential election, was reflective of the deeply intelligent and strong-willed team Kissinger recruited regardless of their political backgrounds. The national security advisor was able to hire so much talent because many of the staffers suspected, as one explained, that the NSC would be the "center of the foreign policy universe in America" and seized the opportunity to serve.[20] The high-octane team would not have a deputy, however, even though Halperin wanted the job, because Kissinger, who preferred the reins in his hands alone, said naming a second-in-command could not be done right away.[21]

The "First Whiff of Trouble"

In these first decisions and hires, one longtime Washington observer smelled the "first whiff of trouble" and predicted that the system and the "cast of characters" would cause Nixon "endless difficulties if he is not very careful."[22] The disagreements even before Nixon took the oath of office, and his decision to overrule frustrated National Security Council principals, established tension and distrust at the outset of an administration that was inheriting an evolving Cold War as well as regional challenges like the hot war in Southeast Asia.

Vietnam had roiled not just Washington but American life itself. Despite the deployment of hundreds of thousands of American troops to Southeast Asia, the insurgency quickly regained the initiative. The Tet Offensive of late January 1968, in which more than 80,000 insurgents and North Vietnamese fighters attacked South Vietnamese cities and reached the US Embassy in Saigon, had demonstrated to much of the American public just how badly the war was going and convinced many it had been a mistake.[23] Still the US military was eager to turn the tide and escalate the fight, but Johnson, who had decided not to run for reelection, instead replaced his commander in Vietnam, declared a partial and then a full bombing halt, and committed to peace talks in Paris.

Like many in the United States and its government, Halperin, who was serving in the Pentagon at the time of Tet, believed it was past time for the United States to leave Vietnam. That was an about-face for a foreign policy strategist whose first book had declared the value of limited wars, like the one the United States found itself in Vietnam. The then assistant professor of government at Harvard, along with 117 other scholars and policymakers, had even signed an advertisement in the New York Times in December 1965 calling for all Americans to support Johnson's war and "help the people of South Vietnam resist subversion, hit-and-run terror, and foreign military intervention."[24]

By 1968, Halperin, with a view at the Pentagon very different from the one in Cambridge, had concluded there was simply no way to win. At the Pentagon, he saw how the South Vietnamese military had—despite US support, training, and sacrifice—struggled, and even hesitated, to fight for its own country. Even more, the secretary of defense had asked Halperin to develop a classified history of the war that later became known as *The Pentagon Papers.* The multiyear study demonstrated to Halperin that the US government, and the Eisenhower, Kennedy, and Johnson administrations, were well aware of the war's impossible dynamics but nevertheless chose to intervene and then deepen America's role in Vietnam.

For Halperin, getting the United States out of the war had become a personal imperative, one he believed Nixon shared. Although much was made during the 1968 campaign of candidate Nixon's secretive plan to end the Vietnam War, by the time the transition was in full swing at the Hotel Pierre, Halperin recalled, "There may have been a plan in the president's head" but "there was nothing written down."[25] To get something on paper before gaining access to the government's manpower and machinery, the Nixon team hired the RAND Corporation, a nonprofit think tank established by defense analysts in the late 1940s where Kissinger had served as a consultant, to help the administration hit the ground running when they took office.

The RAND analysts drafted a Vietnam options paper for the soon-to-be national security advisor and others on the Nixon team to consider. A first draft included a unilateral withdrawal option, but that was rejected after it was presented to Kissinger, Halperin, and others in December in New York. Kissinger also reportedly said at the meeting: "How can you conduct diplomacy without a threat of escalation? Without that there is no basis for negotiations."[26] This interjection was not one of reflexive hawkishness but a reminder of the strategic assumptions—and Kissinger's willingness to question them—that had been hanging over America's choices from the beginning of the war.

Throughout America's involvement in Vietnam, there had been a ceiling to how much force was used. Eisenhower and Kennedy had always been hesitant to put too many Americans on the ground. The holdovers from the Kennedy administration had then convinced Johnson of the need for a gradual increase in reprisals and then force, hoping, in vain, that North Vietnam would credit the United States for holding back and recognize there were still ways it could escalate further. Another limit had been born in Johnson's worries about taking the fight to the point where the Soviet Union or China would be compelled to join the war on the side of North Vietnam. This restraint left some in government, particularly in the military, suspicious that more could have and should have been done to inflict punishment on North Vietnam and the insurgency in the South.

The soon-to-be national security advisor Kissinger appreciated both sides of this argument and the dilemma it posed. Kissinger also understood, despite not having served much in government, the bureaucratic tendency toward inertia at times of disagreement and uncertainty and the need to break the stasis to garner fresh ideas. Months before Nixon named him national security advisor, Kissinger had argued in a lecture in Los Angeles that an effective president must, in his first four months, "give enough of a shake to the bureaucracy to indicate that he wants a new direction and he must be brutal enough to demonstrate that he means it."[27]

"No Consensus as to Facts"

RAND's final paper, which included an escalation option, shook the government when distributed on Inauguration Day and discussed at a National Security Council meeting on January 25, 1969. To end the war, the recently sworn-in president told his team, "We will need about six months of strong military action, combined with a good public stance which reflects our efforts to seek peace."[28] Since before taking office, Nixon had been looking for ways to take strong military action, including bombing Vietnam's neighbor Cambodia, but there were few proposals ready at that first meeting.[29]

Another Halperin project demonstrated why. Based on his own experience with the *Pentagon Papers*, the new NSC staffer knew that among the agencies, whether in the various parts of the Defense Department or elsewhere, there were significant disagreements about what if anything could be done in Vietnam. To help draw actionable intelligence and ideas out of the government, and to underscore to the new team how few in government thought the war was going to work, Halperin and a RAND analyst proposed that a survey be sent to many of the agencies with a role in Vietnam.[30]

The concept appealed to Kissinger, who had heard that Kennedy's defense secretary Robert McNamara overwhelmed the Pentagon in 1961 with a ninety-six-part questionnaire.[31] The draft of Nixon's Vietnam survey, with twenty-eight main questions and dozens of sub-questions, was nearly that long when it was distributed on the day after the inauguration.[32] National Security Study Memorandum (NSSM) 1's length and complexity were fine by Kissinger, who according to one aide, thought it would tie "up the bureaucracy" and buy "time for the new president."[33]

NSSM 1 also tied up Halperin, who was charged with summarizing the five hundred pages of responses, even if, as Kissinger said, the findings revealed "no consensus as to facts, much less to policy."[34] Illuminating the divisions was one of Halperin's purposes in the first place, and the question of escalation proved the point. Although the uniformed military, in Vietnam and Washington, believed that a "vigorous bombing and interdiction campaign could choke off enough supplies to Hanoi to make her stop fighting," civilian officials in both the CIA and the Pentagon's policy offices did not think such a strategy was viable.[35]

Regardless of the strategic disagreement, Kissinger asked Army General Earle Wheeler, the chairman of the Joint Chiefs of Staff, "What could be done in South Vietnam which could convey to the North that there is a new firm hand at the helm[?]"[36] The Joint Chiefs recommended a short attack by B-52s on the headquarters of the insurgency in neighboring Cambodia. Nixon ordered the attack carried out covertly in Southeast Asia and secretly in Washington, but when Rogers, worried about public opinion, and Laird, believing the mission was badly timed, heard about the plan, they both argued against it.[37] Nixon rescinded the order, leaving Kissinger, according to one colleague's journal from the time, "very disappointed."[38]

It was not only the canceled bombing campaign that was frustrating the national security advisor. In the administration's first months, Nixon and Kissinger's choices were far more constrained than they would have liked. As the survey had demonstrated, there was little consensus in government for big moves like an escalation; and their new ideas, like persuading the Soviet Union to help cow North Vietnam, were not faring much better.[39] Although Kissinger was working without the State Department's knowledge to establish a back channel to Moscow through the Soviet ambassador to the United States, it was not yet proving to be the boon—or "key to peace"—Nixon believed, and had suggested publicly, it could be.[40]

More than unworkable ideas, Nixon and Kissinger were facing significant popular frustration with the war.[41] Nixon, who had ridden disappointment over the war to the White House, told one associate he did not want to become ostracized from the public the way his predecessor had.[42] The president was not the only one worried. Laird, the other politician on the National Security Council, believed Nixon's reelection was contingent upon withdrawing from Vietnam and that the United States needed to get "the hell out of there."[43]

"If in Doubt"

On the staff, Halperin agreed. The national security advisor, and others in the White House, knew of Halperin's desire to end the war: Kissinger had recruited the staffer with the promise they would do so together.[44] But Halperin's views were becoming a liability for the national security advisor, whose own influence and high-profile position depended on his access to a prickly president. Among Nixon and other hardline and hawkish Republicans in the White House, who wanted to end the war by winning it, Halperin was assumed—wrongly—to be both a dove (he had written a book on the virtues of limited war) and a Democrat (the staffer was a registered Republican).

When the administration began, Halperin had showed up at the White House expecting to work out of a West Wing office near the national security advisor's suite; but instead the staffer was pointed across the driveway to the third floor of the Executive Office Building. The distance was not far enough for some. The Chairman of the Joint Chiefs of Staff Wheeler, who had grown tired of Halperin's doubts about the war when they both had been in the Johnson Pentagon, as well as hardline US senator Barry Goldwater of Arizona, complained to Kissinger about the NSC staffer.[45]

At one point, Kissinger admitted to a friend he could not "afford to keep" Halperin, because it might make the national security advisor look like a "softy."[46] Rather than fire Halperin, whose intellect and knowledge of government were still formidable and useful, or confront war opponents like him, Nixon and Kissinger resorted to deeper secrecy. The president and his national security advisor both shared conspiratorial and paranoid tendencies. With fierce external and internal opposition to the war, the two also came to believe the country could only secretly take the harder military actions they deemed necessary to bring about a negotiated settlement in Vietnam.

Of course, Nixon and Kissinger still needed help, especially from a staffer who knew how to get a bombing run organized and most importantly how to keep one secret. Al Haig, a forty-four-year-old army colonel detailed to the NSC and working out of the Executive Office Building, proved the man for the job. A native of a suburb near Philadelphia, Pennsylvania, Haig had gone to West Point and then to war. He deployed to Korea, served at the Pentagon, and then fought in Vietnam where he was wounded and awarded the Distinguished Service Cross.[47] Kissinger named him his military aide during the transition at the Hotel Pierre, and then assigned Haig to the NSC to coordinate intelligence reports from the Executive Office Building.

With Halperin seen as a liability, Kissinger began to rely more and more on Haig, who had the military bearing and the political leanings, including a vote for Nixon in 1968, valued in the conservative White House.[48] The staffer also built a relationship with his superiors by pulling late hours and delivering on hard assignments like his work arranging the plans for the canceled Cambodia bombing. In the first few months of the administration, Haig leveraged his time with Kissinger, the president's attention, and growing frustrations with Halperin to try to empower the NSC and himself.

At one point, when Kissinger, angered by some tardy staff materials, blew up about the NSC, Haig proposed a reorganization.[49] The staffer wanted to revise Halperin's system by clarifying responsibilities, establishing regional teams, and empowering Kissinger's personal suite of offices, which at that point included Special Assistant Eagleburger, who had worked in the transition and been detailed to the staff by the State Department.[50] With the national security advisor's approval, Haig moved to one of the cubbyholes near Kissinger's office in the West Wing and began to act like a deputy national security advisor, though he was not officially given the title.[51]

An empowered Haig, who believed the war could be won if brought "home to Hanoi," helped the president and his national security advisor search for ways to hit hard in Vietnam.[52] Still, at the time, with so few new ideas and so much opposition in government, they tended to always default to hitting Vietnam's neighbor hard—as Nixon later wrote, "If in doubt we bomb Cambodia"—since strikes there elicited so little resistance in the Situation Room or in Southeast Asia.[53] In March, in response to an insurgent attack in Saigon, the president secretly ordered Operation Breakfast, part of what was later known as the year-long Menu Operations that would eventually drop almost 3 million tons of bombs on Cambodia.[54]

A "Moroccan Whorehouse"

The Operation Breakfast bombing revealed how far Halperin had fallen out of favor and how secrecy was proving more important than the process he and Kissinger had designed. The NSC staffer was initially kept in the dark about Breakfast, but he was sitting in Kissinger's White House office talking to the national security advisor when Haig burst in with a report on the bombing. By the time he realized Halperin was sitting there, Haig had already divulged that airstrikes had caused secondary explosions, a sign the bombing had hit ammunition depots.[55] With Breakfast out of the bag, Kissinger shared some of the details, but immediately swore Halperin, who was both frustrated and amused, to secrecy.[56]

Despite Halperin's design and Haig's reorganization, the NSC and the national security advisor were struggling in the spring of 1969. The staff was, according to one member, "like a Moroccan whorehouse, with people queuing up outside [Kissinger's] door for hours."[57] The bottleneck was partly the result of mismanagement: according to Haig, Kissinger might have been the "dominant intellectual on the staff," but he was "less at home as an administrator."[58] Paper stacked up and people lined up because Kissinger had a hard time managing it all while advising and conspiring with the president on the phone and in person.

Of course, the centrality of the national security advisor was also part of Halperin and Kissinger's design from the beginning. Instead of the secretary of state, the national security advisor was the intellectual engine of America's foreign policy: all ideas that did not come from the president went through Kissinger, who chaired all the meetings and jealously protected his time with Nixon. When the national security advisor stalled, the system did as well.

Likewise, the staff's potential influence was dependent on their proximity to and acceptance by Kissinger. The national security advisor liked being around high-powered intellects; it was one reason why Kissinger kept Halperin around despite complaints from conservatives. Yet rather than empower the staff to act on their own, he used them to write first drafts, develop his own thinking, and plunder actionable intelligence and ideas from around town for his own purposes.

The national security advisor's personal assistants, Haig and Eagleburger, tried to keep up and keep the NSC working. These staffers, according to a later assistant, could help Kissinger "explore, analyze, [and] refine" his thinking but no one could necessarily change it.[59] The assistants also tried to fill the administrative gap by reading Kissinger's mail, distributing feedback on written products, briefing him whenever a free moment developed, and listening to the national security advisor's phone calls to prepare transcripts. As a result, their offices were where, according to one aide, "everything important happened and all interesting papers were kept in safes."[60]

The incredible pressure of the assistants' job and Kissinger's disorganized and demanding style soon took a toll. After only a few months on the staff, Eagleburger, who was thirty-eight when he joined the NSC, was having a hard time keeping pace with the workhorse national security advisor. The aide was so overstressed he brought an extra set of clothes to work to wear after he sweated through the day's first outfit.[61] In June, Eagleburger passed out from exhaustion and anxiety on the couch outside of Kissinger's office and was taken to the hospital. When the national security advisor arrived on the scene a moment later, Kissinger screamed, "But I need him!"[62]

Although few collapsed, most on the NSC staff were deeply frustrated. According to minutes from one meeting, there was a "uniform feeling" among NSC staff that they needed "more face-to-face contact" with the national security advisor.[63] Even the system's designer Halperin complained that "many of his memoranda" were "never answered."[64] After the staff all had the chance to vent, they were encouraged to "keep close and intimate contact with what is occurring in the departments and agencies and to flag difficult problems" for Kissinger.[65]

The NSC staffers were also annoyed they rarely met with Nixon. Though Kissinger had suggested that they would be able to tell the president what to do, few on the staff ever spoke with the elusive and awkward Nixon. To smooth things over, the national security advisor soon arranged a fig leaf of a meeting between the president and the staff, where Nixon told the group to ignore the bureaucrats, particularly the "impossible fags" at the State Department, and "handle the rest of the world."[66] Tellingly, Nixon then turned to Kissinger and said, "And you and I will end the war."[67]

That mission, however, was about to face another test. In March, the president had explained to his National Security Council principals the United States needed to de-Americanize the war in South Vietnam, which remained dependent on US military, political, and economic support. Laird said, "What we need is a term 'Vietnamizing' to put the emphasis on the right issue." Nixon, who feared the political pressure to bring troops home would soon limit options, agreed, and added, "We should agree to total withdrawal of US forces but include very strong conditions which we know may not be met."[68]

In short order, "Vietnamization" became code for withdrawing troops, and Kissinger, who worried the drawdowns weakened the American hand at the peace negotiations in Paris, tried to slow it down.[69] Even with Haig and other NSC staffers' help, however, Kissinger, with so little government experience and no feel for the Pentagon bureaucracy, had a very hard time controlling the plan for and pace of Vietnamization.[70] In some ways, the national security advisor met his bureaucratic match with Laird, who wanted out of Vietnam, and began a tug-of-war over the size and speed of troop withdrawals that the secretary of defense was better positioned to win.[71]

"Because It's Nixon"

In early May 1969, the *New York Times* broke the news of the secret Breakfast airstrikes in Cambodia. The story, written by William Beecher, said the bombings were meant to "signal [to] Hanoi that the Nixon administration, while pressing for peace in Paris, is willing to take some military risks avoided by the previous Administration."[72] According to the sources for the article, the decision was made earlier in the year to "demonstrate [to Hanoi] that the Nixon administration is different and 'tougher'" than its predecessor.[73]

When Kissinger, accompanying the president on a trip to Key Biscayne, Florida, read the story by the hotel pool, the national security advisor screamed, "Outrageous!" Infuriated by the disclosure, he later told Nixon: "We must do something! We must crush these people!"[74] At first, Kissinger accused one of his bureaucratic rivals of the leak. He called Laird and said, "You son of a bitch, I know you leaked that story, and you're going to have to explain it to the president." The defense secretary just hung up on him.[75]

The president, in a meeting with his national security advisor, had another culprit in mind. Nixon told Kissinger to "take a hard and objective look" at the NSC and at Halperin in particular.[76] Worrying about the implications of the president's accusation on his own standing, the national security advisor asked Halperin, who was also on the trip, to take a walk on the beach to discuss the leak. Arguing he had only found out accidentally about the Breakfast bombing and had only limited information at that, Halperin denied leaking it. In response, Kissinger proposed cutting off the staffer's access to the most sensitive of material to prove that the next leak, should one arise, did not come from him.[77]

But that was not Kissinger's only plan. The national security advisor told one White House aide of a "detailed plan for tapping all suspects."[78] In the hours after the story broke, Kissinger placed several calls to FBI Director J. Edgar Hoover, who had his own suspicions of Halperin.[79] Hoover immediately ordered a wiretap on the staffer's home phone. The next day, Haig carried a Kissinger request to FBI headquarters for two other NSC staffers to be bugged and for summaries of calls to be shared with the White House through Haig, who kept the materials in a safe.

In addition to their concerns about the staff, Nixon and Kissinger's plan for Vietnam was adrift. As the summer began, events and their own policy drifted out of control. Even with the bombings in Cambodia and entreaties to the Soviet Union, North Vietnam was not showing any signs of giving in. Nixon's public commitment to begin withdrawing American troops as part of Vietnamization—25,000 were set to start returning home later that summer—had also altered the negotiating calculus in Paris and contributed to the national security advisor's and the president's feeling that events were drifting beyond their control.

To regain some command, Nixon and Kissinger decided, in the former's words, to develop an "elaborate orchestration" of diplomatic and military pressure to try to break North Vietnam.[80] Although they did not tell many in Washington or on the NSC, the president sent two messages, one later released publicly and the second kept private, to North Vietnamese leader Ho Chi

Minh.[81] In the private message, Nixon warned that unless there was a break-through in negotiations by November 1, the one-year anniversary of Johnson's bombing halt, the United States would pursue "measures of great consequence and force."[82]

The "November Ultimatum," as it became known, reflected the intro-verted but not un-self-aware Nixon's appreciation for his own reputation as a hawk on defense and hardliner on Communism. During the 1968 campaign, he had told an advisor about what became known as the "Madman theory," by saying, "They'll believe any threat of force that Nixon makes because it's Nixon."[83] Although some doubt whether Nixon ever used the term or believed in the Madman Theory, it is clear both the president and Kissinger saw value in threats and hoped the ultimatum might change the dynamic before Vietnam-ization's troop withdrawals had an effect on the battlefield or in the Paris talks.

"Salted Peanuts"

To take control of negotiations, Kissinger needed diplomatic help and hired Anthony Lake, an idealistic thirty-year-old Foreign Service officer. Lake, who grew up in New England and studied history at Harvard, had joined the State Department after being inspired by Kennedy's call to service in his 1961 inau-gural address.[84] The new diplomat's first assignment was to Vietnam, where, among other embassy and consular jobs, he worked as an aide to the US ambas-sador before taking a sabbatical to pursue his master's degree at Princeton.

Although Halperin had tried to recruit Lake to join his NSC team earlier, and Lake himself had requested another assignment abroad, the State Depart-ment sent him to replace Eagleburger on the NSC.[85] Even if it had not been his first choice, Lake, rail thin and with an air that was both intense and pious, knew the value of a White House assignment both for his career and his oppo-sition to the war. Lake took the job because Kissinger had promised—and the young diplomat, like Halperin before him, had believed—they would end the Vietnam War at the negotiating table.

In late July 1969, Kissinger and his new staffer flew in secret to Paris. The negotiations, which included the South Vietnamese, had been launched the year before in the Johnson administration and proceeded fitfully since then, subject to frequent breakdowns over everything from the size and the shape of the meeting table to North Vietnam's demand for regime change in the South. On this trip, Kissinger, hoping for progress, opted for direct, secret negotiations with the North Vietnamese representatives.[86]

In Paris with Lake, Kissinger reiterated the November Ultimatum and said that if by the first of that month no major progress had been made toward a solution, "We will be compelled—with great reluctance—to take measures of the greatest consequences."[87] In response, according to the national security advisor, the North Vietnamese negotiator fell back on an old demand: America's unilateral withdrawal and a change of government in South Vietnam.[88] Instead, Kissinger was willing to offer "mutual withdrawals."[89]

To back up the commitment, Lake had to draw up a timetable for the plan, but because of Kissinger's insistence on secrecy, the new staffer had to figure one out on his own. So, Lake called the Pentagon to ask for the number of US troops in Vietnam and then asked the CIA for the data on North Vietnamese personnel. Lake later explained, "Basically, I then divided the numbers by twelve and drew up a month-by-month chart of a one-year mutual withdrawal schedule." On the flight home, however, the new staffer realized he had divided wrong. When he told Kissinger, the national security advisor just laughed at the mistake.[90]

The correct timetable would not have mattered much anyway. In late August, Ho Chi Minh replied to Nixon's letter with what the president called a "cold rebuff."[91] North Vietnam's unwillingness to give in to the bombings in Cambodia and the November Ultimatum left a dilemma for the increasingly impatient Nixon and Kissinger.[92] In August, Lake predicted their feeling of powerlessness was only going to grow worse as troop withdrawals slowly drained any leverage that Nixon and Kissinger had. The staffer explained time was working against their plan for the "problem with Vietnamization was that it was like salted peanuts: once the public got a taste for it, there was no stopping it."[93]

Worsening matters for Kissinger, the NSC was also losing a founding team member. In August, Halperin, who had grown frustrated with being cut out of the loop and started to look for jobs in the weeks after Kissinger confronted him over the *New York Times* leak, decided to leave the NSC for the position at the Brookings Institution he had declined the year before. After the staffer gave notice, Kissinger called Halperin at home, either forgetting or not caring about the wiretap on the line. The national security advisor, who had come to rely more on Haig and Lake, still encouraged Halperin to stay on, but the staffer, who did not know about the bugging although there were rumors among the NSC that phones were being tapped, was fed up.[94]

Before leaving the Executive Office Building, Halperin tried to fix the two things he cared most about: the interagency system he had designed and the war he despised. In one memorandum on "danger signals" in the NSC, Halperin said the process was not being allowed to work because the most important issues, including Vietnam, were "dealt with largely outside" the formal process and instead in private sessions between Nixon and Kissinger, where they conspired without the rest of government.[95] With a colleague, Halperin also wrote Kissinger an option memorandum on the war, ruling out an escalation and arguing the United States needed to choose a path before "time runs out" or "we may be forced to choose later under more difficult conditions."[96]

The "September Group"

Although Halperin agreed to continue on as a consultant after leaving the Executive Office Building in September 1969, his departure along with others from the staff made public the NSC's management problems. A *Washington Post* story, "Kissinger Staff Resignations Show Flaw in Nixon Method," was largely accurate: the national security advisor was "both much in demand . . . and not much of a manager," the president was "rarely" seen, and the NSC, despite staffer expectations, was "where the action wasn't."[97] Instead, the staff had to input their ideas and drafts to Kissinger, who was free to augment—and advise the president—however the national security advisor saw fit.

That did not mean the NSC was not doing any good work in the first year. In one member's recollection, the staff and the Halperin-designed system had, particularly on less controversial issues than Vietnam, helped breathe "fresh intellectual life into the departments."[98] After one NSC staffer chose to review the United States' use of chemical and biological weapons, the military and the State Department agreed to a prohibition on biological weapons and limitation on chemical agents. Eventually, Kissinger, who admitted to one member of the staff. "I can't read this paper, let alone understand the issues," still recommended the plan, and Nixon agreed to the ban. The decision was a boon to arms control as well as a demonstration to some on the staff "how the inter-agency process, in a model way, could work."[99]

The model's successes, however, were too rare and on matters too small for many in Washington, including Nixon and his White House team, who began to question Kissinger's management of not just the NSC but foreign policy more broadly.[100] To repair his reputation, the national security advisor focused on Vietnam.[101] Kissinger wrote Nixon in mid-September about how the with-drawal of American forces from Vietnam meant that time was running against the US strategy, but he believed, and Nixon underlined in the memorandum, that American "success or failure in hurting the enemy remains very impor-tant."[102] The next day, Kissinger sent Nixon another paper with options for the way forward, including accelerated negotiations, a faster-paced Vietnamiza-tion, and an escalation.[103]

Neither memorandum was a Kissinger original. Both began as far more pessimistic papers written by Lake and Halperin respectively that had been repurposed and made more optimistic by Kissinger. Building on his "salted-peanuts" analogy, Lake had originally argued the "present course" would even-tually lead to an abandonment of American goals "over a longer period of time and at greater pain and cost."[104] Meanwhile, Halperin had ruled out the escala-tion in the original memo that Kissinger later cribbed.[105]

At a September 12 meeting, the National Security Council principals and the Joint Chiefs shared the NSC staffers' pessimism.[106] Still, Nixon persisted in asking about an escalation, perhaps on "new terms, with all targets open," while Kissinger pointedly asked of the North Vietnamese, "There is nothing that can hurt them?"[107] Reflecting an evolution from the winter's survey, the American commander in Vietnam replied, "They can carry on," while the chairman of the Joint Chiefs said directly, "There would be no fatal blow through seeking a no-holds-barred solution in a couple of weeks."[108] A CIA assessment from earlier in the summer had concluded much the same.[109]

Nixon and Kissinger were unwilling, however, to accept the military's judgment and the intelligence community's assessment for two main rea-sons.[110] Though members of the staff, including Lake, thought there was a chance some "shock" might shake North Vietnam into concessions, the presi-dent and national security advisor genuinely believed, as Nixon wrote, that the "only hope for negotiation" was to "convince Hanoi we are ready to stay with it."[111] The two had also staked tremendous national and personal prestige on the November Ultimatum, including with the Soviet Union, whose representatives Kissinger had warned that time was almost up.[112]

Antiwar protests were one reason why time was short, and growing shorter: massive marches were planned for Washington in October and November.[113] By promising to end the draft during the campaign and starting to withdraw US troops under Vietnamization, the president had tried to buy patience from the American public. But daily protests outside the White House gates were proof the plan had not yet worked. The demonstrations were often personal for those on the NSC: one staffer, who worried about the potential for domestic turmoil should the president opt to escalate, walked out of the Executive Office Building only to find his wife and children holding candles and marching against the war and the White House.[114]

To regain the initiative, Kissinger decided to take planning for options even further outside the policy process. After reviewing what he considered stale Defense Department contingency plans, Kissinger decided the bureaucracy was incapable of solving the problem and turned to the NSC, in particular to a "September Group" that included Lake, Haig, and other staffers, for "fresh advice," "fresh perspective," and a "fresh initiative."[115] According to one member's recollection, Kissinger told them, "I can't believe that a fourth-rate power like North Vietnam doesn't have a breaking point."[116] He assigned them to design a "savage, punishing" blow that could break the opposition.[117]

The plan, cowritten by Lake, became known by several names, but the one that stuck was "Duck Hook."[118] The staff gave Kissinger what he wanted: a series of steps, including in an early version the use of nuclear weapons to destroy a North Vietnamese railway, aimed to deliver the "maximum political, military and psychological shock," while reducing North Vietnam's "overall war-making capacity and economic capacity."[119] The comprehensive and detailed strategy, which included draft speeches and timelines, was delivered to Nixon in early October. The planning was mostly kept from the secretaries of state and defense until word of it leaked.[120]

Even among those privy to Duck Hook, opinion was divided on the plan. According to one contemporaneous account, Kissinger felt the United States "must escalate" or the president is "lost."[121] Lake, who like Halperin wanted to end the war, believed that a threat and even a shock might prove useful in negotiations with North Vietnam, but that carrying out the attacks was just going to exacerbate the public pressure to withdraw. As one NSC staffer wrote to Kissinger at the time, the plan could "lead to uncontrollable domestic violence" and throw the United States into "internal physical turmoil."[122]

Before an October 11 meeting to discuss Duck Hook, Kissinger encouraged Nixon to make it clear to the Joint Chiefs that action had to be taken to enforce the ultimatum.[123] But at the session with Laird and the chairman of the Joint Chiefs of Staff, Wheeler told the president there was no "sound military plan" on the table. Regardless, Nixon asked, "What can we do in two weeks?" to deliver "maximum shock impact, with limited civilian casualties."[124] The president said, "The only ingredient missing is support of public opinion," but the truth was that he did not have the military on board, a workable plan, or the support of Rogers and Laird, who both opposed the concept once they had heard of it.[125]

"Bleeding Hearts"

Both Nixon and Kissinger were serious about Duck Hook and the ultimatum, and for years they would regret not taking harder action in 1969.[126] But the fundamental—and strategically unsound—dynamics of the American approach, which Halperin and Lake had identified, had not been altered: they were still trying to negotiate in Paris while reducing military pressure through Vietnamization. In a late October memorandum, Lake and another staffer proposed that since the bluff was going to be called and there was no shock in the offing, the United States should make a "take-it-or-leave-it" offer to get out of the war.[127]

But even though Kissinger knew the dynamic at hand, the national security advisor and Nixon thought they had time: in early October, Nixon had said that summer 1970 "wouldn't be too late to go hard."[128] So as additional troop withdrawals were announced and the stalemate continued in Vietnam with heavy losses (nearly 12,000 Americans were killed in 1969 alone), Nixon and Kissinger continued to work, mostly alone or secretly with a few trusted NSC staffers, to gain leverage for the negotiations.[129] They tried covert programs, pressured the Soviet Union, and began the secret diplomacy that led to the opening to China, but time still continued to tick away, and the war went on without end.

In winter 1970, North Vietnam invaded Cambodia in response to a pro-US coup there. Though Laird and Rogers were more cautious and worried about expanding the war, Nixon, in a fit, decided to hit hard and ordered an attack. On May 1, 1970, American forces entered Cambodia, following an earlier invasion by South Vietnamese personnel. The escalation, and the manner in which the decision had been made, were too much for several on the NSC.

When Lake and a few other staffers walked into the national security advisor's office late one Friday evening before the attacks were finalized, Kissinger said, "Ah, here are my bleeding hearts."[130] Though the staffers rarely got time with the president, Lake later explained that the national security advisor, to "his great credit," encouraged members of the NSC to argue with him.[131] The assembled staff, who were not representative of all their colleagues (Haig later called them Kissinger's "mutinous young protégés"), proceeded to make their case against the war and its expansion.[132]

The national security advisor had a rejoinder for each of the staff's arguments. When Lake pointed out that US troops, which had not yet been committed, would inevitably be dragged into the fight, Kissinger replied, "No, we'll be able to stay in control."[133] After the staffer said the United States would end up "bogged down in a wider war," Kissinger scolded him: "Well, Tony, I knew what you were going to say." To Kissinger, Lake and the staff were being inconsistent or worse hypocritical. After all, Lake and some of the others had helped write the much tougher Duck Hook plan, but many of these same NSC staff members had cautioned against the program less over moral concerns than strategic ones.[134]

The dynamic spoke to the continued limits on NSC staff influence even in the Nixon administration and under a dominant national security advisor. If the staff members could not convince Kissinger, their ideas had no chance of becoming policy. The national security advisor's control of access to the president and commitment to secrecy made staff influence even more difficult because so few really knew everything that was going on, which made it difficult for staffers to advocate forcefully and easy for Kissinger to dismiss those with only partial awareness. And because the secretaries of defense and state were often cut out of the loop, the staff could not outflank Kissinger by developing support among cabinet officials.

For Lake and for Halperin, who was still a consultant to the NSC, the Cambodia invasion made clear it was simply time to move on. Halperin wanted to be free to criticize Nixon's decisions, which he did not feel able to do when still tied in some way to the president's staff.[135] More than powerlessness and policy differences, Lake and one colleague wrote a draft of their letter of resignation in which they complained of the "atmosphere of suspicion, manipulation and malice" in the administration. However, their final submission spoke only of an "increasing alienation" from Nixon's policies.[136]

As the war widened to Cambodia and then spread to Laos, Nixon and Kissinger—with those still on the NSC staff—finally got their escalation. After North Vietnam's so-called "Easter Offensive" in 1972, the United States launched Operation Linebacker, the first continuous bombing since November 1968, and later, after Nixon's reelection, what became known as the "Christmas bombings." The resulting Paris Peace Accords—which included a US withdrawal and established political negotiations between South and North Vietnam—were signed in late January 1973. The deal was done but the war's ultimate costs were staggering.

In addition to the lives lost in Southeast Asia and trust shattered throughout the United States, Nixon and Kissinger's escalation in Vietnam also transformed the prevailing American way of war. Far from Eisenhower's hands-off approach to the fight in Vietnam, Kennedy's counterinsurgency, or the more gradual escalations of the Johnson years, the United States had finally hit hard and done so relentlessly. Out of frustration and a furious effort to build leverage, Nixon's decisions were also about sending a message in the broader Cold War. Yet the ultimate impact of the escalation, and what was required, like ending the draft, to keep the United States engaged in Vietnam for years, exhausted the American military, which endured internal misconduct, smaller budgets, and public scorn, for years to come.

"Moral Responsibility"

In October 1973, Kissinger, whom Nixon had named secretary of state while preserving his White House role as national security advisor, was awarded a share of the Nobel Peace Prize for the agreement that, according to the jury, "brought a wave of joy and hope for peace over the entire world."[137] The dual-hatted national security advisor and secretary of state called the award "one of the proudest moments" in his life, but in assessing the NSC staff he recruited and the "exciting new procedure" he and Halperin designed, another judgment must be considered.[138]

When Halperin found out about the wiretap on his home's phone, which began in May 1969 and continued for another twenty-one months despite Halperin's departure from the staff and resignation as consultant, he sued his former friend, colleague, and boss. For Halperin it was as much a personal betrayal as an assault on the Constitution he and Kissinger had sworn to protect when they joined government. After one court awarded damages, Kissinger appealed for years until, in 1992, he finally relented and apologized in exchange for Halperin dropping the lawsuit. In a letter to his former staffer, Kissinger accepted "moral responsibility" for the invasion of privacy.[139]

Despite the bugging, neither Kissinger nor the NSC were implicated in the wrongdoing, including the Watergate burglary and subsequent cover-up, that eventually brought down the Nixon presidency. Yet it is important to remember that the Halperin wiretap was the first the Nixon administration ordered, it was not the last on the NSC (Lake's phone was tapped as well), and all the bugging, in the end and in Haig's own words, "yielded no clue as to who the leaker or leakers might be."[140] The spying was one of many missteps the national security advisor and his team made, mistakes Kissinger had predicted at the start of the administration for which he eventually, reluctantly accepted responsibility.

These were not simple errors. They were driven by the same mistrust that drove Kissinger in those early years to strengthen his role, and it continued to drive him in the years ahead. After Lake and Halperin resigned in 1970, Kissinger gathered the NSC staff for a meeting to discuss the way forward. Undeterred, Kissinger said, they must commit instead to "cranking up the NSC system." He urged the staff to continue to "stay conceptually ahead of the bureaucracy" and "ask the questions that no one else is asking."[141]

Amid the wiretaps, the Watergate controversy, and Nixon's eventual resignation, the NSC did just that: they cranked up the system, continuing to serve and feed Kissinger information. Those who stayed or joined the NSC did so out of greater comfort with Nixon's policy choices and the challenge of a hard-driving boss like Kissinger. For some staffers, like Haig, who not only became deputy national security advisor but eventually White House chief of staff, it was both. Although structural changes were made and new coordination committees were created, the NSC were influential as long as they were empowering the national security advisor and Nixon to run foreign policy alone.

Through it all, Kissinger became a public celebrity, a strategist with Hollywood starlets on his arm who made the "national security advisor" a household title in America. Thanks to its connection to him, the Nixon NSC became, in Washington circles, the "center of the foreign policy universe in America" even if individual staffers were anything but empowered.[142] Despite the legend and its growing size (almost fifty staffers were working on policy by 1971), the staff lacked institutional influence.[143] They were only adjacent to the true center of foreign policy: the president and his national security advisor. The example of Duck Hook demonstrates the staff's limited power: if the plan had been sounder, the NSC staff would not have been able to stop Kissinger from recommending it, or Nixon from ordering it. The NSC was really only as powerful as Nixon and, in turn, Kissinger allowed them to be.

Even so, the lasting impact of the Halperin-designed NSC came not from Nixon or Kissinger or in ending the Vietnam War, but from the administrations to follow. The coup at the Hotel Pierre was never fully reversed. Instead, despite complaints about Nixon and Kissinger's foreign policy and real questions in the Watergate era about government misdeeds, the next presidents and their high-powered national security advisors affirmed the NSC's position in the system and began to empower the staff members themselves.

"We Can't Give the President Garbage"

The legacy of the Kissinger NSC would outlast Nixon's resignation, Gerald Ford's brief presidency, and Brent Scowcroft's even shorter tenure as national security advisor. The laconic Scowcroft, a native of Utah, Columbia PhD, and air force brigadier general, first replaced Haig as deputy and then Kissinger as Ford's national security advisor in November 1973. The NSC, led by the low-key Scowcroft, first in uniform and then as a civilian after resigning his military commission, was trimmed some, but its practices and procedures were not changed dramatically.

As Kissinger's influence continued at the Executive Office Building, Jimmy Carter, the governor of Georgia, called for an end to the one-time national security advisor's "Lone Ranger" approach to foreign policy in the 1976 presidential campaign.[144] Carter, who won that election, was not the only critic of the Kissinger model. In the wake of Watergate and Vietnam, dozens of scholars, including Halperin, were developing ideas for how best to understand and reform national security decision-making, as the Cold War evolved again to less of a confrontation than a negotiated standoff.

The Carter transition took these ideas to heart, and even considered abolishing the National Security Council itself and reducing the size and influence of the NSC staff.[145] But ultimately and ironically, by the end of the administration, the Carter NSC would prove to be far more similar to Kissinger's than anyone would have guessed at its start. The soon-to-be president, who would himself prove to be if not a lone ranger then a micromanager, picked a dominant personality as national security advisor. Carter wanted an advisor who was a "top conference staff person," and he got that and more when he chose Zbigniew Brzezinski, a Columbia University professor, campaign advisor, and Kissinger rival.[146]

Brzezinski also had an eye for talent, which he used to build an NSC that, while less secretive and hierarchical than Kissinger's, was still dependent on the national security advisor for its influence. For years, Brzezinski had kept a notebook with the names of impressive, young foreign policy professionals who caught his attention; and when appointed, the national security advisor-designee pulled it out and began hiring.[147] One name on the list was Madeleine Albright, a Columbia PhD who like Brzezinski had immigrated to the United States from Eastern Europe. Albright, who was forty when she joined the staff, was an idealistic voice in the post-Vietnam foreign policy debate and on the Carter NSC's legislative team.

But Brzezinski also inherited a great deal of talent from the Ford staff. Bob Gates, a pragmatic CIA Soviet analyst with a Georgetown PhD, served as the national security advisor's intelligence aide. Robert Kimmitt, an army detailee, Vietnam War veteran, and Georgetown Law graduate, worked in the NSC legal team and on arms-sale policy. And Gary Sick, a US Navy commander with a Columbia doctorate, who was on loan to the Ford NSC from the sea service, continued under Brzezinski as the director for Near Eastern Affairs.

As a result, between political appointees and government detailees, the Carter NSC had, according to one press account, an "accent on youth and Ph.D.'s."[148] The staff aimed to provide quality control by reviewing and occasionally replacing agency drafts because, as one staffer explained, "We can't give the president garbage."[149] Because of the staff's scholarly bent, Brzezinski also wanted them to serve as a "think tank" for Carter, and the national security advisor reviewed daily reports from each staffer and gave them access to the president or, at least, his thinking.[150]

Even as the Washington press corps—not to mention members of the State Department, Pentagon, the military, and Congress—kept an eye out for a Kissinger-esque NSC, the staff grew more powerful, and more valuable to Brzezinski and the president, as Carter's administration grew dysfunctional. The National Security Council was rife with personal and philosophical differences, especially over the Cold War, among Brzezinski, Secretary of Defense Harold Brown, and Secretary of State Cyrus Vance. Their disagreements trickled down, leaving the NSC staff to contend with the acrimony in the interagency process even as they were responding to a rapidly changing world.

The Middle East for one was a hotbed of Cold War intrigue and new developments, partly the result of Great Britain's decision to withdraw its military from the region. Amid a regional security vacuum in the 1970s, Israel went to war with its neighbors, the Soviet Union invaded Afghanistan, and crises in the global oil market pinched America's economy. Iran alone demonstrated how much the region and America's relationships there were changing. The United States, hoping the country would serve as a "pillar" and stabilize the region, began the decade supporting the Iranian regime with arms deals, only to see the US-friendly regime collapse amid domestic unrest in 1979.

NSC staff member Sick, who worked as a one-man Iran desk on the NSC for three years, tried to help Brzezinski and Carter keep up with all of these developments and attempt to wrangle a coherent policy out of a divided government. As Iranian anger at the United States simmered after the revolution and Carter's decision to allow the overthrown Iranian shah Mohammed Reza Pahlavi to enter the United States, the work never seemed to stop. It only grew more intense when, in November 1979, a crowd of students finally overran security at the US Embassy in Tehran and took more than fifty Americans hostage.

As the Carter administration expressed outrage, quietly negotiated, imposed sanctions, and eventually broke diplomatic relations with the provisional Iranian government, the US military also developed plans for a military blockade of Iran as well as a complex raid to free the hostages. The proposed rescue plan required at least six Marine helicopters to travel in one night to rendezvous at a small Iranian airstrip known as "Desert One." Once refueled, the helicopters would then wait until the next night to proceed to the embassy, secure the hostages, and escape Iran in darkness.

In April 1980, with the hostages still not free and the American presidential election gaining steam, Carter, who was partial to a diplomatic solution, began to consider the raid despite the known opposition of Secretary of State Vance. On April 8, Sick argued in a memorandum to the national security advisor, with the subject "Getting the Hostages Free," that Carter should approve the mission.[151] The NSC staffer explained to Brzezinski that time was of the essence: not only would waiting until later in the summer mean shorter nights and thus a three-day operation instead of two, the raid could also quickly end the crisis. Sick's memo, which Brzezinski submitted to Carter under his name with few additional sentences, argued the planned rescue operation was "quick and almost totally under our control."[152]

On April 11, Carter met with most of the National Security Council— Vance, however, was not told of the meeting and resigned after being left out— and approved the raid. Two weeks later, eight helicopters departed an aircraft carrier en route to Iran. Unfortunately, only five were still operational at Desert One after two had to turn back and one broke down once on the ground. The mission was scrapped, but as the evacuation began, a helicopter collided with a refueling aircraft and exploded, killing eight service members. In the aftermath, blame fell on Carter, who continued to negotiate the hostages' release until they were freed on January 20, 1981, his last day as president.

Although some might have suspected in the post-Watergate era that anything associated with Nixon and Kissinger would have been forbidden or at least reformed in Washington, the Carter staff, including Sick's advocacy for the Desert One raid, demonstrated that the NSC, when paired with an influential national security advisor, could be a powerful player in Washington. Like his predecessor in the Nixon administration, Brzezinski believed the purpose of the NSC staff was "helping the president make policy decisions."[153] As Sick and other members of the Carter NSC did so, they demonstrated how the staff, Carter's and future presidents', could grow more powerful still in a dysfunctional government and dynamic world.

CHAPTER THREE

"Reckless Cowboys, off on Their Own on a Wild Ride"

"More with Less"

In September 1983, as US Marines were taking fire in Beirut, several NSC staffers in Washington drafted a cable detailing President Ronald Reagan's latest decision on the US military's deployment in Lebanon. The staff had been pushing the president, who had deployed American personnel to try to bring peace to the country's long civil war, to change the rules of engagement and allow the Marines to join the fight instead of serving as a buffer between the warring parties.

After Reagan balked on the advice of his more cautious secretary of defense and the chairman of the Joint Chiefs of Staff, the staffers did not hide their disappointment. In a note to one of their NSC colleagues in Beirut, they wrote, "We tried hard, but this was the best we could do."[1] Philip Dur, a US Navy commander detailed to the NSC, and Howard Teicher, a young Middle East expert on the staff, were two of the dissatisfied staffers. For weeks, they had been traveling to the frontlines of the civil war even as they battled with colleagues in Washington, where policy discussions were complicated by interpersonal discord and philosophical disagreements about the use of force.

Dur and Teicher wanted to do "more with less" in Lebanon, as the latter recalled.[2] They sought to expand the mission of the Marines in Beirut not just to help the Lebanese Armed Forces in their fight against domestic and regional opponents, but also to demonstrate that the United States was more than willing to use its military after the disasters in Vietnam and Desert One. But because of stern objections from Defense Secretary Caspar "Cap" Weinberger and Chairman of the Joint Chiefs of Staff General John "Jack" Vessey at the Pentagon, the NSC had to try to do all of it with less—with fewer troops, limited artillery, and tighter rules of engagement.

During his time at the Executive Office Building, Dur was caught in the middle of this disagreement. He was just a high school student, standing in the cold at Kennedy's presidential inauguration, when Dur asked himself what he could do for his country. When he got to college, he decided to join the navy, and upon graduation, he went to sea—off the coast of Vietnam, around the Mediterranean, and in the North Atlantic—before receiving a job offer from the NSC. After Commander Dur told a navy mentor that he already had orders to attend a prestigious training program, the senior officer replied, "Well, we can fix that."[3]

The thirty-eight-year-old Dur, with the broad face and shoulders that looked just right in dress blues, was ordered by the navy to the NSC, where the service continued to pay his salary. As is custom, however, the staffer did not wear his uniform on the staff, and Reagan repeatedly asked him why not.[4] After all, the president sought to revitalize the American military in the wake of the Vietnam War—in part, to ensure that those who served felt proud to wear the uniform. Even when Dur was in a business suit, some military leaders who disagreed with his more strident advocacy on Lebanon took to reminding the loaned, or in government parlance "detailed," staffer that his career would be in their hands again when he returned to the fleet.

Dur bore the pressure while pushing for what he believed an inscrutable president wanted. Reagan, who disliked details and confrontation in equal measure, liked to talk tough to young staffers like Dur, and in the pages of his diary at night, but the president often let the National Security Council principals fight relentlessly, caution him, and even ignore his opinions. At the same time, Reagan, who promised a return to more orderly government after the dysfunctional Nixon and the Carter administrations, did little—and did not empower his national security advisors to provide much-needed discipline—as personal differences paralyzed his National Security Council.

Amid this breakdown on the National Security Council, doing more with less was often the best the Reagan NSC could do, and frequently more than they should have ever tried. Despite intelligence warnings and Pentagon resistance, Dur, Teicher, and others on the NSC pushed American troops deeper into Lebanon's civil war. Unfortunately, more than a month after they sent their cable, the Marines in Beirut paid the ultimate price when terrorists detonated a bomb in their airport barracks. Even after the catastrophe, an undeterred and undermanaged NSC staff kept pushing and finally went rogue: as the Iran-Contra affair later demonstrated, doing more than was advisable became the rule on the Reagan NSC and soon led some staffers to break the law.

The "Tectonic Plates Were All Shifting"

Of course, Reagan had promised something very different from a rogue NSC on the campaign trail in 1980. In the light of Carter's dysfunctional National Security Council, then-candidate Reagan promised orderly cabinet govern-ment. More than matching the political moment, such an approach fit Reagan's style. The actor-turned-governor-turned-president preferred, according to one close observer, to have "the boys," as Reagan called the older, and even elderly, men who were his advisors, settle any disagreements and then give him a con-sensus recommendation to approve.[5]

Reagan, who took office at sixty-nine, relied on "boys" who had been around Washington and war for decades. Secretary of State Al Haig, age fifty-six, a retired general, a former NSC staffer, and Richard Nixon's last chief of staff, was replaced after more than a year in office by George Shultz, sixty years old when Reagan took office, a marine who fought in World War II, an economist and business executive, and a former Nixon cabinet member. The Pentagon leadership was no younger: Weinberger, age sixty-three, was a World War II veteran and a close friend and aide of Reagan's from California, while Chairman Vessey, age fifty-eight, had deployed in World War II, Korea, and Vietnam.

When they joined the Reagan NSC staff, no one would confuse Dur, thirty-eight, and Teicher, twenty-six, with Reagan's gray-haired boys. Dur looked torn right from the bridge of the destroyer he had been commanding just months before his NSC assignment began, and Teicher, with the dark beard of the age and the intensity of a man in a hurry, had been working in government on

Lebanon issues and the Middle East at the end of the 1970s. The two staffers were both passionate about the region, and about confronting its challenges, when others had been far more focused on Vietnam and the wider Cold War.

Dur, the son of an American diplomat, took to sea life as a young navy officer instead of doing the intelligence work he thought would be his focus. Assigned to the USS *Little Rock*, a guided missile cruiser in the navy's sixth fleet with responsibility for the Mediterranean, he made a port call in Lebanon in the mid-1960s. Walking the Corniche, Beirut's seaside promenade, he became intrigued by the former French protectorate's history and tenuous political and governing balance between its communal and sectarian groups, which included Phalangist Christians, Shia and Sunni Muslims, Druze, and Palestinians, some of whom had arrived as refugees with leaders of the Palestinian Liberation Organization (PLO) after the 1967 Arab-Israeli War.

The United States long had an interest in maintaining stability among these factions. Less than a decade before Dur walked Beirut's streets, President Dwight Eisenhower had briefly deployed American troops to successfully calm a restive Lebanon. Afterwards, the State Department and Defense Department began arming and training Lebanese Armed Forces, which was seen as an important bulwark against both domestic and regional instability. It was also one of the many bilateral arrangements that characterized the patchwork nature of the US relationships in the Middle East and kept young policymakers in Washington busy.

Among them was Howard Teicher, who was assigned to work Lebanon on his first day at the State Department. Teicher, who had grown up in St. Louis, Missouri, first became committed to public service and working on Middle East issues during childhood trips to Israel. Upon graduating from Boston University in 1976, he demonstrated how large Henry Kissinger and his NSC staff loomed in the country. Teicher told a friend he was going to graduate school at the Johns Hopkins University's School of Advanced International Studies in Washington in order to ultimately work on the NSC and bring peace to the Middle East. When the friend laughed, Teicher just said, "That's my dream."[6]

While at Johns Hopkins, Teicher interned at the State Department's Bureau of Politico-Military Affairs, where he worked on Lebanon, among other issues. At the end of his unpaid internship, Teicher was told that if he passed the clerk's typing exam, he would be hired, at $4.20 per hour, for a full-time paid position. Teicher passed and went on, at a young age, to help guide US relationships around a changing Middle East.

The 1970s were a busy time for those interested in the region, where, in Teicher's estimation, the "tectonic plates were all shifting."[7] Lebanon was ground zero for the convulsions. Communal groups, including Christian Phalangists associated with the central government, Druze, and Shia factions, began to fight a civil war over government representation in 1975. Meanwhile, outside actors like Israel, frustrated by attacks launched by Palestinians living in Lebanon, and Syria, which had historically maintained some influence there, picked sides and intervened to support their proxies and seek advantage. Of course, nothing stayed local for long in the Middle East, especially during the Cold War: the United States provided some support to the Lebanese government, and Iran, Syria's ally the Soviet Union, and other parties all intervened in the civil war to serve their own interests.

This dynamic moment in the Middle East was an opportunity for young, ambitious policy professionals like Teicher and the navy's Dur, who first worked together at the Pentagon in the late 1970s where they had tried to shape the United States' defense relationships and posture in the changing Middle East and counteract the Soviets' Cold War designs in the region.[8] Despite America's post-Vietnam reticence to use military force, Dur and Teicher were driven by a desire not to improve the lives of the Lebanese or combat the germs of terrorism growing rapidly in the shadows of the civil war but instead to score geopolitical points in the Cold War competition.

"Don't Come to This NSC"

Unfortunately for the younger Dur and Teicher, most senior American officials held more traditional views of the Middle East. Reagan's "boys" were more tempered by experience, in particular the frustrations over Vietnam; more bound to the status quo; and less concerned by the communal vagaries of Lebanon. Many in the older generation would have agreed with Reagan, who said of the country's civil war before taking office: "I can't see why they're fighting. After all, they're all Lebanese."[9]

Reagan and his senior team were not interested in getting deeply involved in Lebanon's fight. Their hesitancy was an example of how, in Teicher's words, "old expectations" continued to hold sway in Washington.[10] As the Lebanese crisis worsened, Reagan assigned another of the old guard, the sixty-one-year-old Philip Habib, a career Foreign Service officer who had been one of Kissinger's Vietnam negotiators in Paris, to be Middle East envoy.

The Lebanese-American Habib did not have the traditional background of a member of the foreign policy establishment: he had been a forest ranger when he first applied for a job at the State Department. But trouble-spot by trouble-spot, the diplomat worked his way onto the short list of people whom presidents call for tough assignments. As Habib tried to find a sustainable solution to the complicated crisis in Lebanon for Reagan, he and the rest of the president's team struggled in part because of the president's ad hoc process for making national security decisions in Washington.

Before the election, Reagan's principal foreign policy advisor on the campaign, Richard Allen, a forty-one-year-old former Nixon NSC staff member, promised to limit the authority of the national security advisor to avoid some of the contretemps of the Kissinger and Zbigniew Brzezinski years. Even after Reagan named Allen to the position, the new advisor took steps to downgrade his office and give greater authority to National Security Council principals. Despite Allen's surrender, Haig, who had seen on the Nixon NSC how marginalized the State Department could get, wanted the deal put on paper. He crafted a draft interagency blueprint meant to protect the State Department from another coup and from losing any more influence. Haig's power play and lobbying for his memorandum on the day of Reagan's inaugural parade, however, backfired, setting off the alarms of turf-conscious White House staffers who ignored his proposed plan.[11]

Without a process to run or a strong national security advisor to support, the Reagan staff was downsized to only thirty-five policy members and and, as one member later said, "emasculated."[12] Such an NSC was fine by Allen, who wanted the staff to be an "honest broker," collating options and opinions, and warned potential hires, "If you're looking for the high-voltage action and the big visibility and all the other perks, don't come to this NSC."[13] As a result, one staffer later wrote, the staff were "isolated, out on a limb, yet eager for some opportunity to prove themselves."[14]

The ineffectual arrangement left the National Security Council principals at a loss in moments of crisis, like during the March 1981 assassination attempt on Reagan, which wrought confusion in the White House Situation Room and left too many questions—about what was happening and who was in charge—unanswered. In the wake of that episode, Allen recruited then–navy rear admiral John Poindexter to the NSC as a military assistant and tasked him with finally better organizing the staff and system.[15]

When the forty-four-year-old Poindexter arrived at the Executive Office Building, he was shocked at how haphazard the NSC's operations were compared to the navy.[16] He upgraded the entire operation technologically, including in the Situation Room. Eventually, Poindexter introduced video-teleconferencing and email to the NSC, which allowed the staff first to better communicate internally and then with the colleagues around government. Even after the improvements were finalized, Poindexter remained at the staff, taking on a larger role in policy, including on counterterrorism and Lebanon.

Despite the technological improvements, personality conflicts—between Haig and the White House advisors suspicious of his political motives—upended policy development since no one, not Reagan, the national security advisor, or the staff, could get anyone on the same page. The result was a contentious atmosphere where screaming matches were not uncommon in the White House Situation Room and more and more Americans disapproving of Reagan's handling of foreign policy.[17] After less than a year in office, Allen resigned due to alleged improprieties during the transition.

"Contenders"

In January 1982, Reagan named William "The Judge" Clark to be the new national security advisor. Clark was a former justice on the California Supreme Court and a longtime friend of Reagan, who had come east with the president and become known in Washington for a disastrous confirmation hearing to be deputy secretary of state in which he admitted his inexperience on national security. As Joe Biden, US senator from Delaware, said of Clark after the session, "He doesn't know the first thing about foreign affairs."[18]

Regardless, Reagan trusted him, and with the new national security advisor's arrival, one NSC staffer recalled, "Everything changed."[19] Clark made Robert "Bud" McFarlane, a former marine, his deputy. When

McFarlane, who had been an aide to Kissinger and then Brent Scowcroft at the NSC, returned to the staff, he told his assistant, "We were back where we had started. Back home again."[20] The new deputy did not go home alone; he brought Teicher, who had been staffing McFarlane at Foggy Bottom, as well as a long-delayed plan for a formal national security process. Reagan signed the plan, in National Security Decision Directive 2, or "NSDD 2," almost a year after being sworn in.[21]

The NSC took to the new boss, with good reason: he made the staff, in one member's recollection, "contenders."[22] Clark gave them more structure and titles commensurate with their interagency peers, which required promoting several to "special assistant to the president" level.[23] Even more, the new national security advisor, because of his own discomfort with the national security issues and comfort with Reagan, gave staffers far greater access to the president.[24] Those with the "hot issue" typically joined Clark at his in-person briefing with Reagan at 9:30 a.m., which allowed the staffers, as one recalled, to "hear the president . . . on what he thought about policy and what he wanted his options to be."[25]

The deepening crisis in Lebanon provided an opportunity to exert some of their new influence. After Palestinian assassins tried to kill the Israeli ambassador to the United Kingdom in June 1982, Israel launched a massive invasion of Lebanon, the size and speed of which caught some on the Reagan NSC flat-footed, to try to evict the PLO's leadership and wipe out Syrian aircraft in and above the country.[26] Although Haig's forcefulness had long been a concern for Reagan's White House, the last straw was his perceived timidity in the face of the Israeli invasion. Reagan fired his secretary of state, replaced Haig with Shultz, and counted on Habib to avert a regional war in the Middle East.

The diplomatic troubleshooter managed to arrange a ceasefire and convince Lebanon to agree to the deployment of a Multinational Force (MNF), which included American Marines as well as French and Italian troops, to help peacefully resolve the civil war's latest flare-up and ensure the evacuation of Palestinian leaders from Lebanon. Despite dire warnings from Weinberger about the risks of the mission, the MNF was by all measures a success. In a little more than two weeks, American, French, and Italian personnel had helped facilitate the removal of the PLO.

But even as the US Marines sailed home under a banner that read "Mission

Accomplished—Farewell," all was still not right in Beirut or in Washington.[27] Although many hoped the dismissal of Haig would lead to greater comity on Reagan's national security team, Shultz and Weinberger, who had a long and complicated personal history, began to quarrel. And the disagreements over Lebanon soon led to bureaucratic gamesmanship: the defense secretary had pushed the MNF to redeploy before Reagan had himself issued the order.

"Behave like a Great Power"

The Marines' mission to Lebanon had been a welcome decision to Teicher and his boss on the NSC, Geoffrey Kemp, the senior director of Near East and South Asia affairs. The British-born, Oxford-educated Kemp, who joined the Reagan White House in its the first days, became an American citizen in order to work in the 1970s Pentagon and had earned his NSC position as a Reagan campaign advisor while teaching at the Fletcher School of Law and Diplomacy at Tufts University.

Both Teicher and Kemp shared a belief that the United States needed, in the words of the latter, to "behave like a great power" and try to shape conditions in the Middle East.[28] In their interpretation, such a country would use its military to fashion the dynamic region in its own interests, and Lebanon provided an opportunity to do so. On the other side of the administration's debate were Weinberger and many in the military leadership, who had resisted deploying the Marines and pushed for their swift exit. They believed some degree of restraint made more sense in the post-Vietnam era and in particular on Lebanon where dozens of actors were jostling for influence and the United States did not have deep military relationships with any of them.

As this debate smoldered in August 1982, Dur arrived at the Executive Office Building. The navy commander offered Kemp and Teicher a teammate with military expertise, and the Lebanese civil war gave Dur, the new NSC director on the political-military affairs team, a chance to get in on the action. After all, Reagan, though known as a hawk for his belligerent Cold War rhetoric, did not launch many significant military interventions in his first two years in office, leaving the NSC staffers who worked on defense issues with little real action to manage. Lebanon gave the new staffer a portfolio and a hot issue for face time with the president.[29]

Lebanon was certainly heating up, and events soon made the more cautious in the military, who questioned Beirut's stability, look prudent. In mid-September, a Syrian-connected assassin killed Bashir Gemayel, Lebanon's newly elected (and Israel-supported) president, before he took office. In retaliation, some of Gemayel's Phalangist supporters massacred hundreds of Palestinian refugees at camps near Beirut. In the aftermath of the bloodshed, against the objections of Weinberger and Vessey, Reagan ordered American Marines back to Lebanon in what became known as MNF II, which eventually included French, Italian, and British troops.

To Reagan and his NSC, who had all been deeply upset by the camp killings, the Marines were going to provide "support and stability while the Lebanese Government seeks to reunite its people," to facilitate the removal of all foreign troops, including Israel's, from Lebanon, and provide an opportunity to make some peace in the contentious region.[30] With Israel overstretched and Syria weakened by its losses in Lebanon, Reagan had wanted to seize the "moment," and he encouraged Shultz and Habib to attempt to diplomatically push for a breakthrough on Middle East peace in what became known as the Reagan initiative.[31]

But the Marines' actual mission was far less clear. The Lebanese and US governments could only agree the American personnel would serve as a "presence" amid the conflicting groups in Beirut.[32] The mission gave everyone in Washington something to complain about: for those who, like Dur and Teicher, wanted the Marines to do more to force a withdrawal and keep the peace, a "presence" was too limited, while an unnerved Pentagon did not believe it was a mission the Defense Department had trained for.[33]

On the ground, American commanders of the 1,200-member Marine amphibious unit, which occupied positions at the Beirut airport, were left to figure out how to maintain only a "presence" in a war while also ensuring the security of their own lightly armed troops. To help, the Marines were issued peacetime rules of engagement, printed on a "White Card," to carry with them. As opposed to a more permissive "Blue Card," the White Card told the Marines not to "chamber a round unless instructed" or unless action was required in "immediate self-defense."[34]

For the remainder of the fall of 1982 and all of winter 1983, as Habib's shuttle diplomacy failed to end the crisis in Lebanon or bring peace to the wider Middle East, Washington debated what could and should be done with the Marines operating under peacetime rules at the Beirut airport amid deepening violence. Though personal differences led to screaming matches, and bureaucratic jealousies confounded policy development, a fundamental generational disagreement over the use of force in the post-Vietnam era stymied a decision on Lebanon.

"The Vietnam Syndrome"

For his part, Reagan had leveraged disappointment over the Vietnam War and frustration over a more chastened postwar US foreign policy under Ford and Carter to win the White House. During a campaign speech to the Veterans of Foreign Wars convention in August 1980, he said, "For too long, we have lived with the 'Vietnam syndrome.'"[35] The candidate defended the war, and those who fought and perished in it, and argued America's mission in Southeast Asia had been a "noble cause" that only ended prematurely because the American public had been convinced otherwise.

Though Reagan blamed Carter for allowing this Vietnam syndrome to limit American foreign policy, it was a far more prevalent affliction. Following the leak of *The Pentagon Papers*, Nixon's escalation of the Vietnam War, and the revelations about covert warfare that came out of the Watergate era and hearings into US intelligence activities, Americans had grown far more dovish. By 1981, Gallup found that half of respondents, the highest percentage they had polled in a decade, believed war itself was an "outdated way of settling differences between nations."[36]

Not surprisingly, American policymakers and government officials had grown less hawkish as well. Aside from limited operations like the disastrous Desert One, neither Ford nor Carter launched any significant military interventions, and aside from the MNFs, Reagan was following a similar, less interventionist path. Each president was restrained by an appreciation for public hesitancy as well as concern over opinion in Congress, which had been empowered by the 1973 War Powers Act that required congressional consent for extended military deployments.

Perhaps even more important, the US military was tentative about another fight. Most of the military brass had served in combat, and many, like Vessey, had been officers in Vietnam. They had seen what happens in battle and what it is like for the military to be overstretched and damaged by bad decisions in Washington, and by risky missions like the one in Southeast Asia. In the 1970s, the military had also learned what can happen when the public turns against a war and its warriors: service members turned bitter amid discontent and the military grew brittle as it was hollowed out by shrinking defense budgets.

Although Reagan sought to end the Vietnam syndrome, he still thought the United States should learn lessons from the war. In his Veterans of Foreign Wars speech, Reagan had also said, criticizing Lyndon Johnson's decisions, that the United States should "never again ask young men to fight and possibly die in a war our government is afraid to let them win."[37] With US Marines in Lebanon, both the NSC staff and the Pentagon could find arguments to like in then-candidate Reagan's remarks: for Dur and Teicher, and much of the NSC staff, the Marines' deployment to Beirut represented an opportunity to demonstrate American resolve that was too good to waste, while Weinberger and the Pentagon saw Lebanon, particularly the "presence" mission there, as too big a risk to take.

While this disagreement played out in Washington into 1983 and each day of the mission passed without progress, the NSC, from its view on the third floor of the Executive Office Building, saw Reagan's and their opportunity slipping away. As setbacks occurred in Lebanon and in the diplomacy to end the crisis there, the NSC staffers complained about delay, drift, and deadlines missed, and they called again and again for a "bold move to assert American influence," only to find their arguments ignored by the State Department and, most consequentially, overruled by Weinberger.[38]

"Hawks for the Sake of Being Hawks"

The NSC was pushing to do more in Lebanon not because, as Teicher explained, they were "hawks for the sake of being hawks."[39] He believed, in the years after the US failure in Vietnam, that the United States needed to "un-emasculate," especially militarily.[40] In the MNF, the United States had all it needed—troops on the ground, multinational support and personnel, and a diplomatic initiative—to exert influence in the Middle East.[41] More than the regional impact, the deployment, in the eyes of the NSC, sent an important signal to the world—and to the Soviet Union in particular.[42]

The NSC also believed they were doing what the president wanted. As the MNF mission went on, Dur spent more time with the president. One day, Clark had taken the NSC staffer to meet with Reagan alone in the Oval Office. After another update on the situation in Lebanon, the president turned and looked out the window and reflected on Eisenhower's willingness to dispatch American troops to the country in the 1950s. The commander in chief then said, wistfully, to no one in particular, "Ike didn't have to worry about being impeached under the War Powers Resolution."[43]

At the Pentagon, Weinberger and the military had other worries.[44] Like Vietnam before it, the fight in Lebanon was someone else's civil war. Many senior leaders at the Defense Department did not believe the US military had close enough relationships on the ground to trust any of the parties, and many at the Pentagon feared eventually getting dragged into the conflict on one side or another. As Colin Powell, a Vietnam veteran and then–army major general serving as an aide to Weinberger at the Pentagon, later said, the United States was "sticking its hand into a thousand-year-old hornet's nest with the expectation that our mere presence might pacify the hornets."[45]

The Defense Department saw more than Marines at risk in that hive. The mission was a risk to what the Reagan Defense Department thought was its principal mission: to revitalize the military. Even before the president took office, the Pentagon had been trying to improve how it recruited, trained, and equipped what had become an all-volunteer force with Nixon's decision to end the draft. On Reagan's orders and with Congress's funding, Weinberger had also launched a massive push to increase the size of the American military, spending more in four years than over similar durations during the Vietnam and Korean wars.[46] This buildup was "too valuable," in the words of one Pentagon official, to be sacrificed for such a risky mission with such inconsequential stakes for the United States.[47]

In the Reagan administration, these sorts of policy disagreements often grew personal, and Lebanon was no different. As they worried about drift and a feeling of "déjà vu" among the delays and debates, the NSC pushed on both the military and Habib to be bolder in their thinking and actions. When nothing changed, the staffers questioned the motives and even the courage of their counterparts: some called Weinberger the "Secretary of Procurement and Pacifism."[48] Another staffer said, "Weinberger and Vessey were charter members of the Vietnam never again club." He continued, "It was not just Lebanon; they opposed every military operation during that time."[49]

The ill feelings were mutual. The NSC was also making its share of adversaries around Washington. The defense secretary believed the NSC staff was so eager "to get us into a fight somewhere—anywhere" that he was reminded of the "old joke 'Let's you and him fight this out.'"[50] It was not only the Pentagon that was frustrated; at one point, Habib told Teicher, "Butt out, I don't need the NSC staff telling me when and how to get things done in Lebanon."[51]

"The Hub of Activity"

On April 18, 1983, a truck bomb detonated at the US Embassy in Beirut, killing sixty-three people, seventeen of whom were Americans, including the CIA director of the Office of Near East and South Asia Analysis, Bob Ames. One reporter, covering the devastation, later concluded the bombing was America's introduction to the "local rules of engagement."[52] Although the attack shocked those at the White House, the American intelligence community was astonished that the introduction had taken so long. Looking ahead, they predicted "more attacks on the U.S. presence—especially" the Marines.[53]

Even more, in the aftermath of the bombing and additional diplomatic frustrations, one intelligence analysis foresaw a "Downward Spiral in Lebanon."[54] As Habib's diplomacy ran into a dead end and violence increased between various communal and sectarian factions and growing interventions from outside actors like a revitalized Syria, the CIA concluded the United States had "reached the end of the road" in Lebanon. And yet, at the Executive Office Building, Teicher, Dur, and the rest of the NSC, along with their supervisors Clark and McFarlane, still saw an opportunity to assert American leadership and argued for a change of course.

At the end of July 1983, Reagan empowered the NSC to give it a try. The president appointed McFarlane to replace Habib as envoy. As a former aide who had accompanied Kissinger on some of his secret diplomacy, McFarlane felt his moment to make history had arrived. Even more, the deputy national security advisor had been deeply frustrated by the pace and pitch of Habib's diplomacy. At one point in the winter, McFarlane had scrawled angry comments all over a copy of one of the envoy's updates on the lack of progress in the Middle East. The deputy national security advisor wrote, "All this is absolutely bunk!"[55] Like others on the staff, he wanted the United States to use its diplomatic and military might to force countries like Lebanon, Syria, and Israel to compromise.

An envoy would typically report to Shultz and the State Department, but McFarlane convinced Clark and Reagan to allow him to keep his role on the NSC because a direct line, which was arranged, to the White House might prove useful in negotiations. More than access, the new envoy chose Dur, Teicher, and their colleague Kemp to serve on his traveling team, though the staffers alternated trips because each was still needed at the White House. The high-profile role put the NSC staff in the region doing the work of diplomats and military strategists, and made it look to many in Washington that the NSC had taken the reins of Reagan's foreign policy. One newspaper headline from the time read, "For NSC Staff, It's Heady to be the Hub of Activity."[56]

Far from the hub at the Executive Office Building and high above that August's growing violence in Lebanon, which included sniper fire at the Marines, Dur and Teicher were brainstorming for new ideas at the US ambassador's residence in the hills above Beirut. When they came up with what they thought was their best idea, Dur and Teicher wrote it on a piece of paper, rolled it in a scroll, and raided the ambassador's pantry closet in search of a silver platter and dome to add the dramatic flourish they thought the proposal deserved. Once it was properly covered in silver, they delivered their idea to McFarlane—to deploy the USS *New Jersey*, an Iowa-class battleship then patrolling Latin America, to the waters off Lebanon.[57]

Dur and Teicher wanted to bring the *New Jersey*, which had been built to fight in World War II and pulled out of mothballs to help meet Reagan's promise for a larger navy, to Lebanon's shores to protect the Marines and add muscle to McFarlane's diplomacy. But, as Dur explained, if they could also convince Reagan to change the Marines' rules of engagement to allow a more robust role in fighting the militias supported by Syria and Iran, the *New Jersey* would already be positioned to provide much-needed and, in his words, "decisive" firepower to send a message in Lebanon.[58]

"Yes, Sir"

To get Reagan to make that decision, the two staffers and their NSC colleagues also began to write a draft presidential directive or NSDD. As with previous proposals to deepen the American intervention in Lebanon, Dur and Teicher, and their draft order, were met with stiff resistance in Washington. Shultz and the State Department preferred only to allow the Marines to practice more aggressive self-defense.[59] Weinberger simply wanted to "dissolve the MNF" and leave Lebanon.[60] Meanwhile, though the navy and Marines were more open to forceful action, the Joint Chiefs and their staff criticized everything from the NSC's writing style to its strategy. The brass challenged the feasibility of the mission itself, asking, "Can we use our military power to help a friendly but weak government?"[61]

More than the substance of the policy, the Pentagon began taking issue with Dur's growing assertiveness. The NSC staffer believed he was doing what Reagan wanted, and the president's diary from the time suggests a growing restlessness for results as well as concern for the Marines' safety. After Reagan read one cable outlining a "Worst Case Strategy for Lebanon," which suggested that incremental escalation and aggressive defense were not enough to prevent a worsening crisis, Reagan wrote on his personal copy, "I consider this very important. R.R."[62]

As Dur fought with the Pentagon to get Reagan the necessary orders and capabilities to try to change course in Lebanon, high-ranking defense officials warned the staffer, on more than one occasion, that he was going too far. At one meeting, after Dur proposed a bold idea—deploying the 82nd Airborne division to southern Lebanon—Weinberger questioned how a junior staffer could have the temerity to make such a suggestion.[63] As the pressure on Dur continued to build, he asked Poindexter, who was also a navy officer on loan to the NSC, for advice on how to manage the "heat" from the Pentagon. Poindexter told him, "You don't work for them; you work for the president." Dur replied, "Yes, sir."[64]

On September 10, 1983, Reagan, in a meeting with National Security Council principals, balked at the NSC's plan to assume responsibility for defense of Beirut and the Lebanese armed forces.[65] When Shultz and Weinberger opposed the staff's proposal, the president instead opted for a "measured response to the current crisis" and made no major changes in the mission's objectives or rules of engagement. Even Dur and Teicher's *New Jersey* deployment was a hard sell: Reagan worried that removing it from Central America would have a "bad morale effect on our friends" there.[66]

After the session, Reagan issued NSDD 103, which directed US forces to take a posture of "aggressive self-defense against hostile or provocative acts."[67] Even though Dur and others on the NSC had helped write the directive, none of them believed it was aggressive enough, especially since the violence was escalating in Lebanon when Israel began to withdraw its troops from the high ground near Beirut and local forces and outside actors fought to grab it for themselves. The frustrated NSC staff members cabled a copy of Reagan's order to McFarlane, who was with their fellow staffer Kemp in Beirut, telling him it was the best they could get done in Washington.[68]

"Precise Enough"

No one was ready to give up yet, however, not Dur and Teicher at the Executive Office Building where they had the support of Clark, nor McFarlane and Kemp at the ambassador's residence in Beirut. After the NSDD cable arrived from Washington, a Lebanese commander asked the McFarlane delegation to arrange US military support for his troops near the mountaintop of Suq-al-Gharb, more than 20 kilometers east of Beirut, from attacks by what some on the American team suspected were Syrian-supported militias. American forces had long denied these requests, and Reagan's latest directive would not have allowed for this kind of direct support.[69]

Amid shelling of the ambassador's residence near Beirut, McFarlane thought "it was the moment of truth for our entire Lebanese strategy."[70] With NSC staffer Kemp's "wordsmithing," the envoy sent an impassioned plea to the White House to try to shock Reagan into approving measures beyond what he had issued just the day before.[71] The cable was meant to tell Reagan, according to Kemp, that it was time to "fish or cut bait."[72]

But to some in the military, what became known as the "sky-is-falling cable" felt desperate and overcooked.[73] They thought McFarlane's Chicken Little routine was overly dramatic and a manipulative attempt to get a decision he wanted. Even Dur, who shared McFarlane and Kemp's sense of urgency and had been one of those trying hard to convince Reagan of it just the day before, thought the alarmist message overstated the gravity of the situation on the ground.[74]

Judgments of tone aside, the cable worked: the White House called a crisis session for Sunday, September 11, 1983, and after an intense round of meetings, the president approved a rare addendum to his earlier decision.[75] The new order, drafted by Dur, was meant to expand the MNF's mission and rules of engagement to allow not just aggressive self-defense, but also the use of force to protect the Lebanese Armed Forces as well as terrain outside Beirut.[76] As such, "appropriate U.S. military assistance in defense" of Suq-al-Gharb was authorized and "naval gun fire support and, if deemed necessary, tactical air strikes" were allowed.[77]

In drafting the order, Dur had tried to write language he later called "precise enough" to force the military to change the Marines' rules of engagement.[78] When the NSC cabled the revised decision to McFarlane in Beirut, they appeared sufficiently satisfied with the final product that no editorial comments were included on the cover sheet. Reagan also appeared content; the president wrote in his diary that he had "ordered the use of naval gunfire."[79] Accordingly, the White House and the media both treated the decision as an expansion of the Marines' mission.[80]

Despite Dur's writing and Reagan's order, the Pentagon was less clear on what if anything had changed. On September 12, according to one Pentagon report, the Defense Department formally authorized naval gunfire and tactical airstrikes to protect Lebanese Armed Forces because it was "essential to the safety" of American personnel.[81] By contrast, the Defense Department's European Command, responsible for Lebanon, told the Marines that, as far as they were concerned, "nothing in this message shall be construed as changing the mission" or the rules of engagement.[82]

In short, the White Card remained operative. The two communications left the Marines, who were increasingly targeted, to judge for themselves when to request fire support. On September 19, amid desperate Lebanese Armed Forces' requests for help and prodding and targeting guidance from McFarlane, who was still in Beirut, the US Navy destroyers in the Mediterranean fired into the hills of Beirut against those attacking the Lebanese Armed Forces.[83]

As the American forces, which had taken fire since the summer but held their own, now joined directly in the fight, Weinberger, with Clark's urging, wrote Reagan that "every effort" had to be made to protect the MNF personnel in Beirut, where they were "outgunned."[84] The defense secretary requested and Reagan finally approved that the *New Jersey* be dispatched to the theater for support. And as Dur and Teicher had envisioned, McFarlane used its imminent arrival to pressure Lebanese forces and other militias to agree on September 26 to a cease-fire and reconciliation talks.[85]

"We'll Go Direct to President"

In the weeks after the diplomatic breakthrough, changes were afoot in Washington and Beirut. A frustrated Clark, who struggled to manage the discord in the National Security Council, left the White House, and Reagan appointed McFarlane national security advisor and Poindexter the deputy. With two of their own ascendant, the NSC staff felt emboldened. Yet when Teicher returned to Lebanon after the cease-fire, he noticed the Marines were no longer considered a neutral force: instead US forces were being treated as just another militia.[86]

In the middle of the night on October 23, 1983, the White House Situation Room called Dur's home and told the staffer to report to work immediately. A yellow Mercedes truck weighed down with explosives and gas canisters had detonated in the US Marines' Beirut airport barracks. In all, 241 Americans were killed and more than 100 were injured in the attack mounted by an Iranian-aligned jihadist group, and a separate strike killed dozens of French service members.

The *Washington Post* headline read: "The Beirut Massacre."[87] The assault was the single deadliest attack on US Marines since World War II's Battle of Iwo Jima, where coincidentally the USS *New Jersey* had also supported the fight.[88] Even after the April embassy bombing, the Reagan team was shocked at the attack, including Teicher, who had just left Beirut after having a beer and a friendly debate with some of the Marines at the barracks the night before the bombing.[89] Still, many at the White House, and even Shultz at State, wanted to fight on: on hearing the news, Reagan said, "Those sons of bitches. Let's find a way to go after them."[90]

The bombing, however, was not the only crisis up for discussion in the Situation Room, where different members of the NSC were just as busy responding to other events elsewhere around the world and in the Cold War. The month before, the United States had been put on alert when a Soviet fighter jet mistook a Korean Airlines plane, inadvertently flying in Russian airspace near the Sea of Japan, for a US spy plane and shot it down, killing over two hundred people on board. In October, Reagan had also ordered American troops into the Caribbean nation Grenada, where a coup had resulted in violent protests that some feared were a threat to Americans there. Within a few days, US personnel gained control of the island before transferring authority back to the government there.

Despite the busyness of the moment and investigations into the Beirut bombing, the NSC believed the attack was proof that America's adversaries would exploit any weakness, and they thought a quick MNF withdrawal would further damage American credibility. Their influence can be seen in Reagan's remarks to the nation after the bombing, in which he asked, "If we were to leave Lebanon now, what message would that send to those who foment instability and terrorism?"[91] As the president considered his policy on Lebanon in a landscape dramatically altered after the bombing, the NSC pushed for the same ideas and fought the same resistance as before the attack—indeed much of the discussion was based on papers written days prior.[92]

With Teicher en route home from the Middle East, the NSC's Dur and Kemp wanted Reagan to act "once more in a bold way" and finally change the rules of engagement to allow for direct support to the Lebanese Armed Forces.[93] But rather than share their draft language with Weinberger, Shultz, or other senior officials on the National Security Council, Poindexter ordered, "We'll go direct to President."[94] The National Security Council principals were only informed that, "in light" of an October 18 discussion—five days before the bombing—and so-called "subsequent developments," the president had approved a directive to change the rules of engagement.[95]

Reagan's decision—and the staff's end run—further frayed relations in Washington. Though Shultz at the State Department was more supportive of the choice, for those at the Defense Department, as one official recalled, it appeared the NSC was putting "their finger on the scale" to get what they wanted regardless of events on the ground or the opinion of the military leadership at the Pentagon.[96] Even after the decision was made, the Joint Chiefs of

Staff wrote that they could "not recommend promulgating a change" to the rules of engagement "at this time," and Weinberger concurred.[97] Their continued hesitance frustrated the White House and forced the NSC to work to reaffirm the decision in the weeks ahead.

The breakdown in trust grew so severe that Dur and the others on the NSC believed that Pentagon leaders, particularly Weinberger, were taking deliberate steps to ensure that Reagan's decisions were not implemented.[98] Indeed, McFarlane himself said the defense secretary's resistance "constituted insubordination."[99] As if it were possible for tensions to worsen, McFarlane and others at the White House later believed the Pentagon ignored a direct order from Reagan, with the support of Shultz and the NSC, to launch air strikes against Iranian-supported facilities in retaliation for the October bombing. The confusion and mistrust of those days still make it impossible to determine just what was ordered and who called it off.[100]

"Last Gasp"

On December 14, Reagan wrote in his diary, "The *New Jersey* finally did it!" The president added, "All of Beirut thought there was an earthquake," but he noted, there were "no reports on results yet."[101] Dur—who was in Beirut at the time on a diplomatic mission with Reagan's new envoy, Donald Rumsfeld, a former congressman and secretary of defense—knew that because the United States had no spotters on the ground to direct the fire, the results would not be what they could have been.[102] All the eleven rounds from the *New Jersey* did, according to one Pentagon official, was "bounce the rubble around a little bit."[103]

The ineffectual fire proved the NSC staff had taken their fight and their Lebanon plans as far as they could go. The Defense Department and Joint Chiefs had continued to push for the remaining Americans to be removed from Lebanon as soon as possible, and Reagan was not willing, despite the encouragement of some on the staff, to force the Pentagon to acquiesce. As Lebanon's government and military broke further apart and Washington rang in the 1984 election year, White House political advisors also began to worry about the mission's impact on Reagan's reelection prospects.

On February 7, 1984, Reagan announced that US forces would redeploy to ships off the coast of Lebanon.[104] A few weeks later, they departed Beirut during a massive, final bombardment from the *New Jersey*.[105] There could be few more frustrating ends for Dur and Teicher, who had fought for the United States to use its military in Lebanon to send a signal to the Middle East and the rest of the world. The *New Jersey* shots, which Dur called a "last gasp," reflected how short the mission had fallen of the NSC's ambitions.[106]

Looking back, one NSC staffer wrote that after the airport attack it was "not a question of would the MNF leave, but when."[107] To Dur and Teicher, however, it was not that simple. The navy detailee, who recalled that the most "depressing sight" of his military career was seeing Marines hidden in underground bunkers during his December visit to Beirut, believed the initiative had been lost in Lebanon and in Washington because no one had been willing to call the Pentagon's "bluff" and push back on bureaucratic resistance.[108] Teicher agreed, but he tended to blame the failure on Reagan, who was not, in his staffer's estimation, doing what it took to ensure that his orders and intent were realized.[109]

Of course, neither Dur, Teicher, nor others on the NSC were blamed publicly for the bombing or the failure of the president's Lebanon policy even though their ideas had contributed to the tragedy. The US failure in Lebanon, for two staffers who had been so keen on the United States making a bold move to assert itself in the Middle East, resulted in suggestions that, after Vietnam, the US military was not prepared for or capable of the types of bold moves the staff recommended.

Far from ending the Vietnam syndrome, Beirut gave another reason for Americans, in government and out, uniformed and civilian, to be wary of military intervention. A little more than a year after the airport bombing, Reagan's defense secretary, long concerned by the MNF's mission and the NSC's insistence on expanding it, gave a speech in which he defined what became known as the "Weinberger doctrine." In November 1984, the Pentagon chief sought to establish strict requirements—such as clear objectives, sufficient public support, and necessary resources—for when the United States used military force abroad. The speech frustrated Dur, who favored leveraging the military in so-called "coercive diplomacy," which uses the threat of force to extract concessions, and in the continuing Cold War competition for proxies, resources, and influence.[110]

But to many in the military, Weinberger's rules were a useful guide for the use of force abroad and, in turn, a limit on the types of missions the Reagan NSC had pushed the United States into in Lebanon.[111] Such a test was welcome to Powell, who was sitting in the audience for the speech and had been the one to call the defense secretary and inform him of the October bombing. The military aide explained that the "shattered bodies of Marines at the Beirut airport were never far from my mind in arguing for caution" in the years ahead.[112]

The Reagan administration's experience with Beirut also helped transform the US chain of command. Dur had encouraged Reagan to "discipline" the rogue Defense Department for hesitating to implement the president's orders.[113] But looking at Beirut, Vietnam, and other decisions, Congress thought it was important to empower the military to give advice to the White House. The landmark 1986 Goldwater-Nichols Act, among other reforms, authorized the chairman of the Joint Chiefs to attend National Security Council sessions in order to help strengthen the military's voice in debates like those that occurred in September 1983 when the NSC was pushing the nation deeper into Lebanon.

Rather than reshape the Middle East in America's interests, the misadventure in Lebanon instead drew the United States deeper into conflict with the Middle East's extremists. Reagan's intervention did not end Lebanon's civil war or the nation's sectarian tensions, which simmered for years. Worse, it brought the United States into greater contact with the terrorist groups growing stronger in the country. Within months of the MNF's departure, groups and individuals affiliated with Hezbollah, a Lebanese political and militant organization with links to Iran, again attacked the US Embassy compound in Beirut and continued to take Americans, including the new CIA station chief, hostage.

"Risk Doing Something"

Just as Reagan's foreign policy challenges in the Middle East or broader Cold War did not end the day the Marines redeployed from Beirut, the personal and philosophical disagreements that had frustrated Dur and Teicher continued to plague Reagan's policymaking team. McFarlane, without Clark's close relationship with Reagan and without the procedural powers of his predecessors like Kissinger, Scowcroft, and Brzezinski, struggled as Weinberger and Shultz fought bitterly.

In the middle of persistent division, drift, and indecision, the NSC tended to overcompensate. Although the intervention in Lebanon had been a source of frustration in Washington and tragedy in Beirut, it had, paradoxically, taught many on the NSC that sometimes they needed to "risk doing something," as one Reagan White House insider said at the time.[114] With so much going on in the world, Teicher and the rest of the NSC—Dur departed after Reagan's 1984 reelection—filled the vacuum left in Washington when bickering cabinet officials at National Security Council meetings prevented the president from making or realizing decisions.

For the technologically advanced NSC, doing something, as Dur and Teicher had with McFarlane in Beirut, included pushing for policy changes and performing operations that were usually the responsibility of the military, diplomatic corps, and intelligence community. That meant the NSC was not only conceiving and convincing the president of moves in Washington, it was also trying—despite limited expertise and oversight—to implement them abroad. As one member of the NSC explained, this sort of behavior began with McFarlane, Teicher, Dur, and Kemp serving not just as staffers, but also peace negotiators, military planners, and artillery targeters in Beirut in the fall of 1983.[115]

Such operations on the staff would be difficult to manage in a well-run organization, and the Reagan NSC was anything but. In many ways, the process never recovered from its early ad hoc approach. One government study of the Reagan system described its decision-making process as entirely "too informal" and "flawed."[116] National Security Council meetings were rare, advanced notice and agendas were rarer, and formal records of decisions were rarely complete. The result was uncertainty and room for improvisation and even mischief.

Beyond just the process, NSC management was haphazard. By the end of 1985 when Poindexter replaced McFarlane, Reagan, who was not a detail-oriented manager himself, had had four national security advisors in less than five years. The different styles and different rules of each boss made discipline harder to maintain. The staff, which had grown to almost sixty policy staffers in 1985—twice its size at the administration's start—sometimes had deeper institutional knowledge of the president and his policies than the national security advisors.[117]

Making matters riskier, the Reagan NSC, as one member also explained, was always "conducive to secret activities." [118] The system's long-running informality made details hard to nail down. In addition, staffers could argue that intricacies should be kept from a president unfocused on the details, just as they could justify keeping options from those in the agencies whose bosses were fighting or disagreeing with policy proposals. More than simple classification concerns, the Reagan NSC was a need-to-know environment where secrets were too common, and the staff often decided who needed to know and who did not.

"Reckless Cowboys, off on Their Own on a Wild Ride"

Few came to embody this NSC more than Oliver North. The marine lieutenant colonel was the son of an army officer, a graduate of the US Naval Academy in Annapolis, and a Vietnam veteran. First detailed to the NSC in 1981 at the age of thirty-eight, North stuck around longer than the average two-year assignment and rose to be the deputy director of the politico-military office working on terrorism issues. At one point, he shared both an office and a secretary with Dur.

North was aggressive and opinionated even for the Reagan NSC: one colleague described him as "hyperthyroid" and a "loose cannon." [119] In 1985, he was assigned to lead below-the-radar outreach to elements in Iran to secure the release of hostages taken in Beirut, whom Reagan was deeply worried about, and to counter Soviet influence in the country. Working through Israel and with Reagan's consent and against the recommendation of both Weinberger and Shultz (a rare concurrence), North, along with McFarlane, who had departed the White House but continued as a consultant, agreed to sell Iran weapons to free American hostages held in Lebanon.

In May 1986, North and a team, which included Teicher and McFarlane, traveled to Iran with a cake baked in the shape of a key to signify the opening of a new relationship. [120] While the trip and the pastry came to nothing, and only a couple of hostages were released during the whole scheme, North had secretly taken an additional step. He began diverting the funds from the arms sales to fund Nicaraguan Contras, who were fighting the socialist Sandinista government in Nicaragua. Though funding the Contras, which was expressly forbidden by Congress, was not part of Reagan's approval of the plot, support for their fight had been a keen interest of his White House and NSC.

When news of what became known as the Iran-Contra affair finally broke in late 1986, the scandal was serious and sexy enough—secret missions, illegal money transfers, and deals with mysterious actors—to engulf Washington and those on the Reagan team. Teicher's life, for one, "became a living hell" when he was publicly implicated in the affair.[121] Eventually, the NSC staffer, who claims to have been completely unaware of the plan's full scope, was cleared of wrongdoing and departed the NSC and government altogether in 1987 with a bitter taste for Washington score-settling.

More than any one staffer, the scandal and resulting cover-up threatened the entire Reagan presidency. After first denying his administration had made a deal for hostages, the president created a special review board—which became known as the Tower Commission after its leader John Tower, a former US senator from Texas—and took responsibility for the operations in an Oval Office address in March 1987.[122] Although Reagan and his vice president avoided legal culpability, several officials, including Weinberger, were indicted, mostly for false statements, and were later pardoned, while North and Poindexter were convicted for their efforts to cover up the affair, though their convictions were later reversed.

McFarlane, who had aspired to climb to the heights of his former NSC boss Kissinger, was left distraught by the scandal. Eventually, Reagan's former national security advisor attempted to kill himself with an overdose of Valium. Although he lived and later pled guilty before eventually being pardoned, McFarlane felt he had failed his president and the country.[123] The former NSC staffer, who called the NSC "home" upon his return, had also helped undermine the institution that had meant so much to him.[124]

Although most had long seen the NSC as aides to powerful national security advisors, Iran-Contra introduced the staff to the nation as players in their own right and, in the words of one journalist, "reckless cowboys, off on their own on a wild ride."[125] While blame was placed on individual staffers, many in Washington came to believe the institution itself was part of the problem. The Tower Commission, including Tower, former secretary of state Ed Muskie, and former Ford National Security Advisor Brent Scowcroft, got an office at the Executive Office Building and began to look into how and why, as Weinberger's aide Powell later wrote, the "NSC had gone off the rails."[126]

"Certain Functions Which Need to Be Performed"

Scowcroft recruited Stephen Hadley, a lawyer and former NSC staffer, to look into the Reagan NSC and become one of the main writers of the investigation's 550-page report. The Commission pored through NSC files from both the Reagan administration and previous presidencies. More than simply exposing wrongdoing, according to Hadley, Scowcroft was "keenly focused" on saving the staff, the interagency system, and the role of the national security advisor.[127]

Tower and his team attempted to "articulate a model for how [the NSC] should operate," according to Hadley. The Commission suggested staff reforms, including the addition of an independent legal counsel.[128] Yet amid calls for making the NSC and national security advisor answer to Congress, the Commission avoided such a step. More consequentially and ironically, its plain conclusion—"there are certain functions which need to be performed in some way for any president"—ensured that the NSC lived to fight another day.[129]

Even as Hadley wrote the Commission's report, the business of national security continued. After cleaning house, Reagan named former deputy secretary of defense Frank Carlucci national security advisor, and Powell his deputy. It was not the army lieutenant general's first opportunity to join the NSC; he had been interviewed for a job on the Carter staff but resisted for fear it would hurt his career as an infantry officer.[130] Not only would it mean time out of the ranks and in an office in Washington, but as Dur had learned, staffers can also find themselves in conflict with senior military officers who have control over military promotions and assignments.

Regardless of his concerns, Powell felt it was his duty to join the Reagan staff, which meant putting his army uniform in a closet and donning a suit. To get the "rudderless, drifting, demoralized NSC" back on track, Carlucci and Powell, who later became Reagan's last national security advisor, went beyond the Tower Commission's recommendations. They cut the staff's size, eliminated whole directorates, and established new interagency committees and processes.[131]

More than the changes, the NSC's survival of the scandal underscored its institutional importance, independent of the national security advisor, in Washington. Dur, Teicher, and the rest of the Reagan NSC had demonstrated that even with a president committed to cabinet government and with a weak foreign policy process, the staff found a way to have influence, especially amid dysfunction in Washington and disasters abroad. Despite the sins of North and others, the Tower Commission had blessed the NSC staff's fight for ideas, like Dur and Teicher's silver-domed USS *New Jersey* idea, as one of those certain NSC functions the staff must perform for the president.

The challenge was getting the benefits of the NSC without the mischief. Rather than eradicating the staff, putting tighter legal restrictions in place, or making it subject to congressional oversight, the Tower Commission and others in Washington chose to rely on more capable management, by presidents and national security advisors, and common law. Though the restrictions were never written down, the types of operations developed and performed by North and others on the NSC were to be considered verboten in Washington.

Similarly, building on scholarship about the decision-making process and bureaucratic management, Washington began to speak more and more about the need for an "honest broker" or neutral process manager. Although the theoretical concept was developed in the wake of Vietnam and used by Reagan's first national security advisor Richard Allen and others with the tumultuous tenures of national security advisors like Henry Kissinger and Zbigniew Brzezinski in mind, it was also useful for those trying to understand what the NSC staff should—and should not—do. The new norm was that the staff could argue for their own ideas, but they also needed to make sure everyone else's were heard.[132] The scandal helped make honest brokering the standard for the NSC in the years ahead.[133]

When it did, Dur was long gone from the Executive Office Building. When, on his White House departure, Dur wore his navy dress uniform for a photo with Reagan, the president smiled and told his outgoing NSC director, "Finally, you're showing your true colors."[134] Although Dur remained a navy officer throughout his staff tour, he had also been a true NSC warrior, one who continued to answer to some in the military who long questioned his fights at the Executive Office Building. Despite the tragic results of Dur, Teicher, and the rest of the NSC's fight on Lebanon, and despite the Reagan NSC's poor reputation, future NSC members would join an institution defined and, surprisingly, empowered by their behavior.

CHAPTER FOUR

"What No Other Part of the Government Did"

A "Giant Step"

On August 5, 1990, as he strode toward the White House from the presidential helicopter *Marine One*, President George H. W. Bush engaged briefly with reporters asking him about Iraq's recent takeover of Kuwait. At first, Bush spoke in broad terms, but he punctuated his comments with the most direct statement that he had yet made publicly about Iraqi president Saddam Hussein's invasion. Bush said sternly, "This will not stand, this aggression against Kuwait."[1]

The president's message surprised some in Washington, including now-Chairman of the Joint Chiefs of Staff General Colin Powell, who "sat upright" and said, "Wow," at what he considered a "giant step."[2] But Bush's step did not cause a shock to everyone. The last advisor to speak to the president prior to his appearing before the cameras was not wearing a military uniform or confirmed to a cabinet post; it was a young NSC staffer in a borrowed blazer, Richard Haass.

Unlike earlier members of the staff, Haass, a New York native, did not dedicate himself early to a life in service to his country. Instead, fate led him first to a college class on the Bible and then on a school trip to the Middle East. Fascinated, Haass ultimately wrote a doctoral dissertation on US foreign policy in the region, and served as a staffer in Congress, the Pentagon, and President Ronald Reagan's State Department.[3]

After he left government to teach at Harvard the year before the Iran-Contra scandal broke, Haass became an advisor to a presidential campaign and then another after his first candidate lost. Waiting after the election and hoping for a job in the new administration, Haass was about to commit to teach the next semester when he received a last-minute call and a job offer.[4] Lean and hungry and with a shock of hard-to-control hair, Haass joined the NSC at the age of thirty-seven where he worked closely with Bush and his national security advisor Brent Scowcroft, a member of the Tower Commission and the only national security advisor to have served in the role twice, as a new era began.

The Cold War's quiet end was a signal event, and the breakup of the Soviet bloc created waves of change across Europe, the Middle East, and even the United States. In this dynamic era, one thing had not changed, however. In the aftermath of the Reagan NSC's role in the Iran-Contra affair, many had expected that the NSC would be, if not dissolved, then certainly disempowered. Yet ironically and to Haass's and Bush's benefit, Congress and the Tower Commission not only spared the NSC, but its conclusions had actually, in the view of one veteran of the Reagan battles, "offered the NSC Staff an opportunity to increase its authority."[5]

In the scandal's aftermath, Scowcroft tasked Haass and the rest of the NSC with doing "what no other part of the government did."[6] At *Marine One* and throughout the Gulf crisis, which became the Gulf War, Haass took that mandate to heart. While avoiding the controversy of the Reagan team, he and others on the staff demonstrated that the NSC was not going to be neutered in this new era. Rather than resorting to the shadows, NSC staffers like Haass used their seat in the room and the pen in their hands, both provided by Scowcroft, to play a critical role in the process and, in turn, become far more influential than in previous presidencies.

"Honest Broker"

"Who are these people?" was a question many Americans were asking of the Reagan NSC staff at the height of the Iran-Contra scandal.[7] On the faculty at the Harvard Kennedy School of Government in Massachusetts, Haass tried to provide an answer in the school's *Harvard Crimson*. He was a relatively new arrival to campus from Washington, where he had served as an aide first on Capitol Hill and then at the Defense and State Departments, and had gotten to know not just the NSC as an institution but also some of its staffers.

Haass's inspiration for a life in international affairs was also tied in part to the NSC. After Richard Nixon decided to expand the Vietnam War into Cambodia in May 1970, the NSC staff resignations of Halperin and Lake were not the only ramification. A wave of antiwar protests around the country led to tragic violence and the deaths of four students at Kent State University in Ohio, not far from Haass's own Oberlin College. For a time, Kent State students attended class at Oberlin and continued their protests against the war, which freshman Haass chose as a subject for a documentary film he was producing.[8]

Growing up during the Vietnam War and the discontent it produced was formative for Haass, and he became further drawn to international issues when he chanced into a class on religion, which led to the opportunity to participate in an archeological dig in the Middle East.[9] Inspired by the region and its dynamic politics at the time, Haass pursued a doctorate in international relations, wrote a dissertation on U.S. foreign policy in the 1970s Middle East, worked at a London think tank, and then headed to Washington.[10]

Before the NSC's arms-for-hostages deal made headlines, Haass had left government and joined the Kennedy School. In his *Crimson* article, the public policy lecturer wrote of the NSC's dual role: the staff were supposed to "coordinate the design and execution" of national security policy while also providing "independent counsel" to the president.[11] Lest the commander in chief lose what Haass called an "honest broker," the Harvard lecturer put the onus on the staff, and not on Congress, to ensure they met that responsibility without resorting to the kind of shenanigans North and others on the Reagan NSC stood accused of pursuing.[12]

Although he did not say as much in the article, Haass wanted to return to Washington and work for a president. While lecturing at Harvard, he served as a foreign policy advisor for the campaign of US Senator Bob Dole of Kansas, who was running against Bush for the Republican Party's presidential nomination. As Reagan's vice president, Bush, who escaped the Iran-Contra scandal with little blame, was the presumed favorite for the nomination, but Dole had won the Iowa caucus in February 1988 and looked to be on the brink of a major upset.

Ultimately, Bush's win in New Hampshire by almost ten points all but clinched the Republican bid for him. In a different moment, such a loss might have also left Haass with little hope of a plum post in the new administration. But shortly after Dole withdrew, one of the Bush campaign's foreign policy advisors suggested Haass join the nominee's team. He went on to play a small role on the campaign that helped the vice president win the White House in November 1988.[13]

Thanks in part to the memories of the troubles caused by Iran-Contra, the press was more interested than ever in just who was advising the presidential hopefuls—and that included Haass. Even after Election Day, the *Miami Herald* broke a front-page story about a memo he had written recommending a decrease in military support for the Contras in Nicaragua.[14] Haass denied the paper was anywhere near official; it was as much a draft of thoughts as anything else. But one friend of the president-elect joked at the time that with the bad publicity, the aspiring staffer's prospects for being named assistant secretary of state for Latin American affairs had diminished dramatically.[15]

"The Middle East Job"

On November 24, the media soon turned its attention to Scowcroft, Bush's friend and preeminent foreign policy advisor, when the president-elect named him national security advisor. In the aftermath of the Reagan NSC hijinks and the administration's six different national security advisors, selecting a member of the Tower Commission itself and a former national security advisor helped set the right tone. Still, Bush took pains in the press conference to make clear—with three separate mentions that Scowcroft would serve as an "honest broker" of the Washington policy process—that his team would mind the common law.[16]

Scowcroft and Bush worked out their plans for how to manage national security in walks around Camp David before the president-elect's inauguration. To help run the staff, Scowcroft named Bob Gates, a veteran of the CIA as well as the Gerald Ford and Jimmy Carter NSCs, to be deputy national security advisor. The two planned to pare down NSC policy staffers from even the slimmer version of the late Reagan years. Scowcroft picked a "fairly arbitrary" target size of fifty, including administrative personnel, and they began to recruit staffers, which took a little more time than some aspiring public servants would have liked.[17]

Though many assume campaign work automatically leads to administration jobs, Haass's long wait is a reminder that it does not happen overnight. Even if the Latin America position was out of the question, Haass, who was rumored for several jobs only to come up empty, was starting to worry as time grew short. By the end of 1988, Haass needed to tell Harvard whether he planned to teach the next semester. The day before the deadline, Scowcroft telephoned and offered him the "Middle East job" on the NSC.[18]

The offer, which Haass accepted the next day, came as a surprise since he did not have a particularly close relationship with the national security advisor-designee or even much government experience on the Middle East. However, when Haass arrived at the White House in January 1989, he fit Scowcroft's model.[19] The national security advisor procured extra money so he did not have to be constrained to only the bureaucracy's existing talent: he wanted to hire outsiders, like Haass, as political appointees because they were "not burdened by the instincts of government."[20]

The national security advisor made Haass the senior director for Near East and South Asian Affairs because he was also not burdened by well-known positions, or "defined," on its issues, like sensitive Arab-Israeli matters.[21] At least, that is what Scowcroft thought at the time. Although the national security advisor was as close to a Washington wise man as anyone, the national security advisor was wrong about Haass. As reporters hunted for details about the new NSC, they soon found Haass had spent more time writing about—and defining himself on—the Middle East and the intricacies of Israel's borders and negotiations than Scowcroft realized, and a minor controversy erupted over the staffer's earlier writing.[22]

"Nada"

The uproar soon passed, and Haass got to work. Still, with so little money in the budget for staff, Haass, who was also a special assistant to the president, was only allowed two detailed team members to help on the Near East portfolio, which included North Africa, the Persian Gulf, the Levant, and South Asia. He chose to retain Sandra Charles, who had been working Gulf issues on the Reagan NSC; and he convinced David Welch, a Foreign Service officer with experience in the wider Middle East, to serve as the other director.[23] Like members of the NSC since the Truman presidency, their home institutions (the Pentagon for Charles and the State Department for Welch) agreed to continue to pay their salaries while they worked, on loan, on the NSC for limited tenures, a mutually beneficial arrangement that gave the White House added firepower without paying for it and gave the agencies employees who understood the view from the White House.

Despite the Bush NSC's smaller size, a front-page *New York Times* headline read, "Bush Backs Plan to Enhance Role of Security Staff," within weeks of Bush's inauguration.[24] Reports like it evoked memories of NSC staffers on secret missions, and yet Haass contends the "idea of becoming operational in the Iran-Contra sense was a *nada*; it simply wasn't an issue."[25] Scowcroft and Gates kept a close eye on the staff but not a short leash. The national security advisor, who limited his use of email, encouraged staffers like Haass to develop new ideas, come to his office, and then "defend them and argue them."[26]

Advocating for those new ideas could prove a challenge for honest brokers. However, the two-time national security advisor, and his team, defined the art of brokering not only as providing the president the views of all members of the interagency process but also their own.[27] Such a conceptual evolution from the neutral transmitter envisioned by scholars probably made sense for Washington policymakers with strong opinions and the need for a rule-of-thumb approach, but the application and the very ambiguity of the words *honest* and *broker* left room for interpretation and disagreement.

Scowcroft also put the staff in the middle of the decision-making. They were responsible for helping run the two councils Scowcroft established as the heart of policy development and deliberation: the Deputies Committee, which included the policy deputies at various agencies and was led by Gates, and the Principals Committee, consisting of National Security Council cabinet-level officials and chaired by Scowcroft. Because the White House chaired both meetings, Scowcroft ensured that two NSC representatives were always in the room: one to chair (either him or Gates) and one to take notes (often a staffer like Haass).[28]

The Principals Committee, or PC, which formally did not include Bush, was a formidable collection of foreign policy talent and old friends, with experience and trust built up over years together in Washington. In addition to Scowcroft, Secretary of State James A. Baker III was a longtime confidante of Bush's, and he had served as Reagan's chief of staff during the start of the Beirut intervention and then as treasury secretary. Dick Cheney, a former congressman and also a Ford White House chief of staff, proved a formidable Pentagon boss and voice in policy discussions.

And in October 1989, Bush named Colin Powell, Reagan's last national security advisor, chairman of the Joint Chiefs of Staff. Powell was a historic pick (the first African American chairman), a uniquely qualified one (he had both combat experience and high-level policy experience at the Pentagon and White House), and yet still a surprise (the general was the most junior of all the military's four-star officers).[29] Like the rest of the Principals Committee, Powell brought his credentials and his personal memories, including those of running the NSC, to the Situation Room, where Congress's Goldwater-Nichols Act had empowered the military's voice.

"This Is Jell-O"

Although the president's foreign policy team was full, Haass's files were empty. Despite the fact that Bush succeeded a president in his own party and in whose White House he had served, on January 20, 1989, at 12:00 p.m., the Reagan slate—and, more practically, the NSC cabinets and binders—were wiped clean by the National Archives.[30] The new staffer, who would become one of the NSC's go-to writers, was charged by Scowcroft with filling those cabinets with papers, speeches, and memoranda on the new era in the Middle East.

There was a great deal of writing to do. Not only were the changes unleashed in the 1970s still roiling the region (Lebanon's civil war was in its last phase but ongoing nonetheless), but the impact of the Reagan policy had to be considered as well. The now former president had deepened relations with Saudi Arabia, Jordan, and other countries. And in trying to regain the regional initiative in the aftermath of the Marines' redeployment from Beirut, Reagan had chosen to come to the aid of Iraq in its long, bloody, and expensive war against Iran, which ended in a costly stalemate and an uneasy peace in 1988.

In addition, the Berlin Wall fell almost one year to the day after Bush was elected and set off a series of events that changed nearly everything for US foreign policy, which for forty years had been committed to gaining any advantage over or at least containing the Soviet Union. Even as Bush, Baker, Scowcroft, and other American officials spent months trying to set the right tone and trends for the relationship with Russia and the rest of Europe, the Cold War's end had an enormous impact across the world, including in the Middle East. As a result, every national security policy needed to be rethought, redrafted, retested, and reapproved.

Although the Cold War was over, it was also an uncertain victory at home and in government. More than a few Americans and members of Congress were looking for what had been won with the collapse of the Soviet bloc. If winning the Cold War was so important that presidents from Truman onward had persistently pushed the United States to victory, then some Americans wondered if it was now time for some reward or perhaps even a retreat from commitments abroad. One US senator spoke for many when he asked in 1990, "How do we now demobilize?"[31]

Such questions contributed to worries and debates in government offices in Washington and allied capitals around the world, which posed political and practical challenges to the Bush team. Haass had been reminded of this the hard way in his first few months at the NSC. One of the first challenges he had to confront was writing a new US policy toward Afghanistan now that the Soviet Union had withdrawn from the country. The new strategy, which Haass penned, turned out to be the first substantive foreign policy directive of the Bush presidency.[32]

But writing the paper with his interagency colleagues, including those at the CIA, was what Haass called "one of the most frustrating experiences" in his government career. Though he had been to Afghanistan, Haass admitted to not being an expert. Regardless, the staffer found himself in a wrenching government debate with colleagues who disagreed about the future of America's relationship with countries like Afghanistan. Some in government wanted to remain committed to those who had been partners in the decades-long struggle against the Soviet Union, while others like Haass wanted to start to shift toward those who might make better partners in the post–Cold War era. As he faced resistance and completed the tepid final draft, Haass recalled telling Gates, "This is Jell-O, I can't grab it, I know I'm getting the runaround."[33]

"If Iraq Intends Nothing Bad"

Another of Haass's post–Cold War writing projects was a national security directive on the Persian Gulf. Most in Washington—concerned about the radicalization of Iran—shared Reagan officials' inclination to narrow the distance between the United States and Iraq, then led by strongman Saddam Hussein.[34] Iraq appeared, in the words of two analysts, to be a "punch-drunk fighter" after the Iran-Iraq War, too exhausted and too in debt from loans needed to pay for the long, costly war for much ambition or aggression, but it was expected the country could still throw a formidable uppercut.[35] The Iraqi military had more than 900,000 ground troops, many with recent combat experience, as well as modern MiG aircraft, ballistic missiles, and biological and chemical weapons.[36]

Regardless, over the course of 1989, Haass and his team drafted what would become National Security Directive 26. In it, Bush concluded that so-called "normal relations" between the United States and Iraq would serve America's interests and promote stability in the Middle East.[37] The plan, as Scowcroft later said, was to promote deeper commercial ties with Iraq to show Hussein that the United States "bore him no particular ill will."[38] To keep Iraq on a "moderate" path, Haass and his colleagues planned to use economic and political incentives and resort to sanctions if the nation veered to a more aggressive course.[39]

Still, in the months after NSD-26 was signed, Iraq and the mercurial Hussein began to look less like a potential partner and more like a potential problem. Iraq executed a British journalist for supposed espionage, threatened its neighbors, deployed Scud-missile launchers within range of Israel, and got caught trying to illegally import an artillery system.[40] In short order, the world began paying closer attention to the intrigues of what looked more and more like a rogue state and a leader one magazine declared the "Most Dangerous Man in the World."[41]

The Bush administration, members of congress, and the Defense Department's Central Command (CENTCOM), which had responsibility for much of the Middle East and North America, were starting to worry about Hussein as well. To try to reset relations with Iraq, Haass visited the country in late May 1990. Such diplomatic forays were, of course, traditionally done by diplomats, but even in post–Iran-Contra Washington, Haass's visit was considered acceptable in part because it was done openly. Although he did not visit with the Iraqi leader, the NSC staffer met with many members of his cabinet, including Foreign Minister Tariq Aziz. Sitting in the Foreign Ministry, Aziz and Haass drank strong coffee, smoked Cuban cigars, and discussed for several hours the future of the US-Iraq relationship.[42]

The NSC staffer took pains to explain that the United States had tried to build a productive relationship, but Iraq was "making it impossible." Unless Iraq's behavior improved, he continued, "What little there is of this relationship is going to end."[43] When the Iraqi minister accused the United States of already deciding to make Iraq an enemy and suggested the US military presence in the Gulf was aimed at Iraq, Haass tried to reassure him—but also to warn him. The NSC staffer pointedly explained, "If Iraq intends nothing bad, you shouldn't worry about our forces."[44]

As Haass returned to Washington hopeful the message was received, he and the rest of the Bush team were having a hard time figuring out what Iraq intended. When in mid-July 1990 Hussein threatened Kuwait and the United Arab Emirates, American diplomats at the embassy in Baghdad thought Iraq was just "bullying" these states to try to get out of debts incurred during the long war with Iran.[45] Haass and most of the team in Washington agreed. According to him, Iraq appeared to be attempting a modern "form of gunboat diplomacy to put pressure on Kuwaitis" for a quick influx of cash or debt relief.[46]

"Whatever It Was"

But when in late July Iraq positioned 30,000 troops on its side of the Kuwaiti border, the Bush administration began to consider its options should Hussein's rhetoric prove to be more than an empty threat. The days were moving too fast, however. Before one Haass memorandum could even be reviewed, Hussein, in a meeting with the US ambassador to Iraq, appeared to commit to working diplomatically to resolve the disagreement.[47] The embassy summed up the diplomatic meeting with the Iraqi leader: "Iraq Blinks—Provisionally."[48]

In the days that followed, Haass and others in Washington began to doubt Hussein had blinked at all. By the morning of August 1, Iraq had 120,000 troops and 1,000 tanks positioned just north of Kuwait's border.[49] One intelligence officer visited Haass at the White House and convinced him that Iraq was about to go to war. Haass kicked the interagency process into high gear: he alerted Scowcroft and, with Gates on vacation, attended a Deputies Committee meeting at the State Department.

In the five-hour session, Haass and the rest of the deputies tried to interpret murky and conflicting intelligence. In the end, according to the NSC staffer, they concluded, "Whatever it was, we didn't much like it," and recommended that Bush make a last attempt to dissuade Hussein from invading.[50] Haass recalls thinking of it as a long shot, but he returned to the White House to try to sell the plan to Scowcroft.[51] With the national security advisor's agreement, he and Haass then went to visit the president.

They found Bush on the examination table at the White House medical unit. The president was wearing a T-shirt and getting a heat treatment for a shoulder sore from hitting golf balls earlier in the evening.[52] As the three discussed just how a telephone call could be made— "It wasn't as if we had the phone number" for the Iraqi leader, Haass explained later—another message from the State Department informed them, "We've just heard from our people in Kuwait, shooting has started."[53] Bush told Scowcroft and Haass, "I guess we are going to have a war."[54]

The first few days following Iraq's invasion were as confusing as those that preceded it. At a hastily called meeting of the National Security Council on August 2, Bush told reporters, "We're not discussing intervention."[55] But in the disjointed and hesitant conversation that followed in the White House Cabinet Room, where Haass was assigned to sit on the backbench but willing to speak up with facts, clarifications, and ideas, the team discussed just that.

After briefings on the oil markets where prices were skyrocketing and on Iraq's unknown but concerning designs on Saudi Arabia, Powell gave the team an overview of the Defense Department's operational plan for Iraq. The so-called op-plan had not been written overnight. Starting in the late 1970s, some at the Pentagon had begun to think about Iraq as a potential threat.[56]

With the post–Cold War likelihood of war with the Soviet Union now so diminished, the Defense Department's CENTCOM, led by Army General Norman Schwarzkopf, reevaluated their thinking for the Middle East and began not just planning but also practicing how to counter Iraq should action be required. Just a few weeks before the invasion of Kuwait, CENTCOM had circulated draft Op-Plan 1002-90, "Defense of the Arabian Peninsula," which included the strategy for war with Iraq that Powell discussed at the meeting.[57]

"Accepting This New Status Quo"

More than simple discussion of the latest intelligence and plans, the first meeting and the days after revealed a clear division among the team, one in which Bush was hesitant to pick a side. At that point, the president—who had served in World War II, in Congress, as an ambassador, CIA director, and vice president for eight years—was keeping his own counsel to avoid biasing his national security team's debates. Still, Haass recalled seeing in the president's reaction that first night in the medical unit that Hussein had violated Bush's "code in every way."[58]

Among his National Security Council, Scowcroft, Cheney, and Baker, who was traveling during the crisis's first meetings, agreed. They were concerned about the precedent being set and vocal about the need for a strong response, even potentially with military force, from the United States and international community. Haass, who shared their reaction, felt so strongly that he walked out of one early meeting and felt "as unhappy as I've ever been in government" since he believed some of the principals around the table did not grasp the stakes.[59]

One of those principals was Powell, who was hardened by experience and schooled in the Weinberger doctrine. He was showing the doubts of someone who believed Iraq's invasion of Kuwait did not pass the test required to use force.[60] Early on he made clear that a confrontation with Iraq would be "major"—the "NFL, not a scrimmage."[61] When the chairman asked, according to his own recollection, "if it was worth going to war to liberate Kuwait," he immediately noticed a chill in the room and later admitted the query was an overstep.[62]

As Haass worried that everyone on the team was not reacting with appropriate concern, he vented his concerns to Scowcroft, who feared Iraq might just get away with seizing Kuwait.[63] In the first days of the crisis, Haass began writing an argument for why that would establish a dangerous precedent.[64] Once he gave the national security advisor a draft, Scowcroft asked his staffer to refine the case for a memo to the president. Haass wrote that although a potential conflict could prove costly and risky, "so too would . . . accepting this new status quo."[65]

By the time the National Security Council met again on Friday, August 3, the team had found not just agreement that the United States could not tolerate the Iraqis' invasion but also some of the rhythm to a response. Baker and State Department diplomats were working to secure support for United Nations Security Council resolutions, which authorized a strict sanctions regime and prompted a US blockade of Iraqi and Kuwaiti ports, and pushing for what became known as an "Arab Solution," in which moderate Middle East leaders would try to resolve the crisis. Treasury officials were also collaborating with their foreign counterparts to enforce sanctions and the blockade on Iraq and stabilize the oil market, which despite a few spikes grew steadier in the days and weeks ahead.[66]

At a Saturday, August 4, session at Camp David, the Pentagon walked the president through the maturing military plan. It had not been an easy assignment because the options, despite months of work and planning, were far from ideal in early August. The United States had not had the forces in the Middle East to deter Iraq from invading Kuwait in the first place, so preventing further Iraqi aggression, particularly against Saudi Arabia, with the current military posture seemed unlikely. To pull off what Powell called the "difficult but doable" plan to defend Saudi Arabia and potentially evict Iraq from Kuwait, the United States was going to need to send tens of thousands of additional troops to the region.[67]

The only thing more difficult than the plan may have been getting it written. Cheney, who believed the chairman's cautions reflected his and other senior military officers' hesitation about using force in the Gulf, and Powell had clashed during the crisis's first days. Even more than developing military options, the two disagreed over the stakes of a response and the military's role in questioning and even judging them. According to one report, Cheney told Powell: "Colin, you're chairman of the Joint Chiefs. You're not secretary of state. You're not the national security advisor anymore. And you're not secretary of defense. So stick to military matters."[68]

"Just Dictate"

When the Camp David session ended, Haass returned not to his desk in Executive Office Building room 351, but to the White House Situation Room, which by that point in the crisis had become his de facto office. Working there put him closer to the latest information and saved the trip from the Executive Office Building.[69] In the Situation Room that Sunday on another short night of sleep, Haass received a call from Scowcroft, who alerted the staffer that Bush was returning on *Marine One* and would require a briefing before he faced reporters on the White House's South Lawn.

When Haass asked how long he had to get ready, the national security advisor replied, "About half an hour." The NSC staffer recalled that his first reaction was, "Oh shit, I'm not dressed for this," because he was wearing shorts and a T-shirt. He quickly borrowed clothes and a blazer from a colleague. But Haass's bigger problem was that he needed to prepare something new, and hopefully—for the NSC staffer who had wanted to improve on Bush's awkward first comments ruling out intervention after the crisis—more forceful for the president to say.[70]

But Haass was so tired that he could not type fast or coherently enough to meet the tight deadline.[71] Fortunately for him, Condoleezza Rice, who was then NSC senior director of Soviet and East European Affairs, happened to be in the Situation Room too. Rice, a PhD in international studies, former professor at Stanford University, and young up-and-comer in Republican foreign policy circles, was a protégé of Scowcroft. The national security advisor saw her as "tough as nails when the situation required."[72]

When her colleague struggled to type, Rice demonstrated that toughness. Haass recalled that she said, "This is pathetic," and then pulled him out of the chair and ordered, "Just dictate."[73] Together they completed a short and dispiriting brief on the lack of progress in rallying the Middle East behind a plan to reverse Iraq's invasion. After it was ripped out of the printer, Haass was still so exhausted he needed directions to the helicopter landing zone on the South Lawn.

When *Marine One* arrived, Bush waved Haass over. The president asked, "What's going on?" Haass gave him the brief and recommended a "very firm message" to the assembled press.[74] The president did not even finish reading the hastily drafted situation report, which had some details on the failing regional diplomacy.[75] After telling the reporters the situation would not stand, Bush explained: "I've got to go. I have to go to work."[76]

The president had to get to a briefing by Scowcroft in the Oval Office where the national security advisor asked, "Where'd you get that?" referring to the "will not stand" line. Bush replied, "That's mine."[77] All of Washington took notice of Bush's ad-lib: one reporter concluded the president had "all but committed himself to use military force against Iraq."[78] Although neither Baker nor Cheney was taken aback by Bush's comments, Powell, who supposedly "sat up" on hearing the remarks, said he was surprised to hear about a possible "new mission" in that way.[79]

The chairman blamed one person for the manner in which the mission was delivered: Haass, who could be seen standing awkwardly in his borrowed blazer next to Bush during his press gaggle. According to the NSC staffer, Powell made it clear he felt that the NSC staffer "had made policy on the fly" and gotten Bush to "stake out a pretty tough position . . . without having run this through anything like a process."[80] Although Haass had not written the line, the chairman's frustration reflected the tensions around the crisis and the military's hesitation, both of which worsened in the months ahead while the NSC staffer remained on Powell's bad side.[81]

The "Tipfiddle"

Though he relinquished the keyboard to Rice before meeting Bush at *Marine One*, Haass did not give up the pen easily in the first days of the crisis or after the launch of Operation Desert Shield on August 7.[82] He and his team tended to write two types of pieces. The first helped "answer the mail," as Haass called it, for a deeply engaged president.[83] By August 13 alone, Bush had more than thirty-five phone calls with heads of state to discuss the crisis, which meant a lot of mail to be answered by Haass, his NSC directors Sandra Charles and David Welch, and, as Rice's contributions to the *Marine One* briefing suggest, even non–Near East NSC staffers.[84]

More than staffing Bush, Desert Shield was a massive management lift for the NSC. With Scowcroft's blessing, Gates organized and led a small group of deputies from various agencies, which became the engine room of the entire American response to the crisis. Because Gates chaired the group's meetings, he got to bring another NSC staff member, often Haass, to the table. One handwritten list from the August 24 session demonstrated how busy the small group was: that day it considered forty-two items, like "20. Jordan paper," and "32. Convoy," all of a piece with what Haass later called the "tipfiddle," the synchronization of "all the logistical requirements, the diplomatic requirements, the domestic political requirements."[85]

Haass did more than help answer the mail and handle the tipfiddle, however. He also wrote pieces of the "planning sort."[86] Even amid the busy days, Haass, like others at the White House and around Washington, spent time trying to think through Hussein's next steps, as well as Bush's. The writing allowed Haass to try to answer the hard questions that he considered part of his responsibility as an NSC staffer. Typically, he would then meet with Scowcroft and Gates, often on Saturday mornings, and work together through questions like "We're in this mess, how are you going to get us out of it?"[87]

To Haass, they were trying to "stay one step ahead of events" in a mess that none of them had seen coming; but the uncertainty inherent in the new era often left more questions than answers.[88] At one point after Iraq's invasion of Kuwait, Bush and Scowcroft were in the middle of a four-hour fishing trip off the Maine coast when, with nothing biting, the two began to talk about the end of the Cold War. They were genuinely intrigued, according to Scowcroft, about "What's this new world going to be like?"[89]

As the old friends bobbed in the sea aboard the president's boat *Fidelity*, there was much to consider. After the Berlin Wall's fall, the two cold warriors, who had both served in uniform and then worked in government for much of the long confrontation with the Soviet Union, also saw an opportunity. Given their early success in collaborating with Russia to bring a peaceful end to the Cold War in Europe, Scowcroft believed they had a chance to create a "world order" that "would be able to deal with cases of aggression in a way that it had never been known before."[90]

At that point, Bush and Scowcroft did not have many concrete ideas, in Haass's writing or anywhere else, for what that world order could look like, but two things were clear aboard that boat. Despite calls at home for the United States to pull back from abroad, the two believed the United States, including its military, would need to be central to any new global order. At the same time, Hussein's invasion threatened more than Kuwaitis: it also put at risk the promise of the post–Cold War era, in which at least Bush and Scowcroft hoped the world could learn from history and avoid its mistakes.

Unfortunately, that was about all that was clear in those days, and uncertainty made the American team cautious. At that point, the sanctions were just starting to hit Iraq's economy and the United States only had 30,000 troops in Saudi Arabia, though Powell's op-plan required 200,000 to 250,000 Americans in place to ensure deterrence.[91] Iraq's history, including Hussein's willingness to use biological and chemical weapons and support terrorist entities, also gave the team worry, especially about the foreign nationals, including hundreds of Americans, being held hostage by the Iraqi government.[92]

An August incident, when an Iraqi oil tanker made a run at the naval blockade established after the invasion, drove home the risks to everyone on the team. According to Gates, he, Scowcroft, and Cheney all believed they needed to sink the tanker; but Baker, calling from his ranch in Wyoming, urged Bush to give the Soviet Union the opportunity to try to resolve the matter diplomatically. The president sided with his secretary of state, and the Soviets helped settle the matter.[93] To Bush's team, the tanker incident, though relatively minor in the scope of the crisis, was indicative of the era's promise even as it served as a warning of what can happen when what comes next is unclear.

The "Reluctant Generals"

Since early in the crisis, Haass had been writing and talking with Scowcroft, Gates, and colleagues around government, to try to figure out, "What next in the Gulf?"[94] Even if the status quo—Iraq in control of some or all of Kuwait—was unacceptable to Haass, the status quo ante was not much better. Haass wrote that a future with Hussein "in power" and with "Iraq's industrial and war-making capability intact" would not be beneficial to American interests.[95] The United States had already tried that with NSD-26, only to see the country invade its neighbor.

Changing either status quo, however, would likely require war and, as Powell was at pains to remind the team, it would be a "major" fight.[96] Bush was not afraid to use the military: he had dispatched troops to Panama the year before and to Saudi Arabia in the early days of Iraq's invasion. But the president and the rest of the team knew a war was a counterintuitive way to launch what would ideally be a peaceful new world order. Still, Haass believed a war, however undesirable and dangerous, might be worth the risk if it could help establish a post–Cold War precedent for taking action, including under UN auspices, to prevent territory from being seized by military force.[97]

Yet even a war that might be a good idea was a hard sell for a nation still battling the Vietnam syndrome and doubts about America's post–Cold War relationship with the world. Although the American public, according to polling, approved of the troop deployment to Saudi Arabia, it was split on doing anything more: about half the country thought Iraq's invasion and occupation of Kuwait was worth going to war over, while the other half did not.[98] Congress reflected the public's discomfort with a post-Vietnam war, especially one over less than clear-cut interests, with some prominent members wondering "why we have to rush this thing" and others opposing military action altogether.[99]

As had been clear since the earliest days of August, Powell and the Joint Chiefs were worried, too. Part of their reluctance about the potential war was pragmatic. The United States was not scheduled, under the current plan, to have the forces in the region necessary for deterrence until early December.[100] Anything more than deterring Iraq would require far more personnel and additional equipment, as well as a viable military strategy, which—despite efforts by Schwarzkopf and his team at CENTCOM and in the Pentagon—was still a long way from being ready.

The brass also worried about Iraq's military strength. The US military, due to technological innovations, strategic decisions in the 1970s, and Reagan's defense buildup, had largely recovered from Vietnam and was showing signs of remarkable breakthroughs in its capabilities. But Iraq, which at that point had the sixth-largest military in the world, was a far more seasoned fighter.[101] Even if years of war with Iran had left Iraq broke, many at the Pentagon assumed its military had learned a great deal in the conflict, especially about land and attrition combat.

But even more, Powell continued to doubt Kuwait was worth a war. The congressional reforms to the chain of command in the wake of Vietnam, Desert One, and Lebanon had put Powell in the Situation Room, where he was, in his own words, the "ghost of Vietnam, the ghost of Beirut." Once at the table, the chairman was committed to voicing his opinion, and if, as he said later, that made him the "skunk at the picnic," the chairman was willing to make a stink whether it frustrated Cheney, Haass, or anyone else.[102]

Of course, the legacy of Vietnam also shaped the other side of the civil-military divide. According to Baker, Bush was "aware of the experience of Vietnam consistently." The president also took important lessons from the war, including the widely held suspicion that President Lyndon Johnson had micro-managed the gradual escalation of the war to poor results.[103] Cheney explained in an interview that after the disappointment of Vietnam, and the feeling that Washington had kept a ceiling on the military's intervention until it was too late, many in the military wanted to know if the political leaders were "going to do it right this time."[104]

Bush took pains to demonstrate he was listening, including during a visit to the Joint Chiefs' Pentagon meeting room, known as the "tank," to ensure that the brass felt their voice had been heard.[105] Scowcroft, Gates, and Haass had also not yet resorted to any end runs or secrecy like those of the Nixon and Reagan administrations that might have left the Joint Chiefs out of military decisions. But that did not mean the White House was not frustrated: as Powell continued to raise doubts, some on the Bush team took to calling the chairman and the Joint Chiefs of Staff the "reluctant generals."[106]

"How Do We Bring This to a Head?"

Although Haass believed it was "important to show that you're reluctant to go to war when you go to war," the NSC staffer was growing worried about the ticking clock.[107] He had predicted in August that at some point, enough time would have passed that "simply allowing more time to pass will not serve our interests."[108] By the end of September, as Iraq looted Kuwait, American troops sweated in the desert in Saudi Arabia, and Bush and Baker worked hard to keep the global coalition together, the NSC staffer worried the crisis had reached that critical point.

The tanker event had reminded everyone that drift, or the feeling that events were beyond their control or soon could be, was a source of stress in Washington and a potential source of mistakes. At the end of September, Haass felt, in his view from the backbench of the Situation Room and the third floor of the Executive Office Building, a sense of drift, that all the "arrows were pointing" in the wrong direction due to Iraq's intransigence, the US military's hesitance, and the unpredictability of events.[109]

In early October, Haass met with Robert Kimmitt, an undersecretary of state and a former member of the Ford, Carter, and then Reagan NSCs, at the State Department to discuss "How do we bring this to a head?"[110] The answer turned out to be an idea that Haass had been writing about since the crisis's first couple of weeks: an ultimatum, which the NSC staffer later called a commitment to "liberating Kuwait by force unless Iraq withdrew fully by a date certain."[111] Following his conversation with Kimmitt, the staffer, who began writing an options paper, suggested to Gates that the deputies consider "under what circumstances" an ultimatum could work.[112]

Issuing an ultimatum, however, required the military personnel—and a plan—to enforce it, and in early October, no workable strategy existed. On October 10, Cheney and Powell were briefed on Schwarzkopf's four-phased military plan to retake Kuwait if so ordered. Although most were comfortable with its first phase, the air campaign, the ground invasion was roundly criticized. In it, the United States and international forces were to be sent straight into the mass of Iraqi forces rather than around their western flank, since the latter maneuver required many more troops.[113]

After the session, Powell told a disappointed Cheney, "We've still got time," but the chairman was called to the White House the next day to present the plan.[114] Afterward, an unimpressed Scowcroft said the "unenthusiastic" presentation had been "delivered by people who didn't want to do the job."[115] The "generous part" of Haass, who heard the session had gone badly from the national security advisor, knew the military had not had a lot of time to be creative, but the staffer's "dark and suspicious side" questioned whether the reluctant brass may have developed a strategy Bush was likely to reject.[116]

To get a better proposal, Scowcroft said to Cheney, "If, this is what we're going to get, then we'll just have to find a different way to do the military planning."[117] Yet, despite the amount of work and writing being done by Haass and others on the NSC in those busy days, the White House hesitated to draft an operational strategy themselves. Even though Scowcroft had served in the air force and Gates and Haass had been in the national security business for years, none believed they had the details to write a complete plan, which the military would have to own and implement if war became the only alternative.[118]

Even if the White House did not write a strategy, Cheney thought some in-house competition might be beneficial. He told Powell to have the Joint Chiefs draft its own plan even as Schwarzkopf's group continued their work in Saudi Arabia. The defense secretary also organized a discussion within his team at the Pentagon to convey to the brass that, in his words, "one way or another, we are going to be prepared to do this."[119] Eventually, all the plans—Cheney's, Powell's, and Schwarzkopf's—included a western approach to envelop Iraqi troops in Kuwait.[120]

As the military planning evolved, Haass was surprised that some on the team, including the military, continued to "fall in love with sanctions."[121] They had some evidence on their side: according to a mid-October intelligence analysis, the constraints were "taking a toll" in Iraq, where food prices were up, raw materials and spare parts were harder to find, factories were shutting down, and little oil was being pumped.[122] But even with the pain, as those less enamored with sanctions pointed out, the intelligence community saw "little anti-regime activity" that might have altered Hussein's calculations on Kuwait.[123]

"Your Maximum Leader"

On October 24, 1990, Bush met with Baker, who worried about the use of force, and Cheney, who was more comfortable with it, and the president explained that he was leaning toward action to remove Iraq from Kuwait.[124] The two cabinet secretaries agreed with the decision, but Bush knew from the bad briefing two weeks earlier that Powell, who was traveling during this meeting, still required convincing. As the president said later, they had a "long way to go before the military was 'gung ho.'"[125]

Powell and the Joint Chiefs were not done pushing against what they felt was a rush—and an NSC staff push—to war.[126] On the same day of Bush's meeting with Baker and Cheney, the Vice Chairman of the Joint Chiefs of Staff David Jeremiah wrote an aggressive response to Haass's now much more refined paper and the ultimatum it included among other options.[127] At the top of his memorandum, Jeremiah handwrote: "Richard: I recognize your maximum leader has trouble with this option"—here, a line pointed to the one proposal to let sanctions run their course—"but there is daily, increasing evidence that [this] is becoming more effective."[128]

Even though "supreme leader" was meant as a joke about Scowcroft, the vice chairman's continued support for sanctions and pointed feedback for Haass, which would not have been sent without Powell's knowledge, demonstrates that the Joint Chiefs' love affair with sanctions and concern about the march to war continued far later than most histories of the Gulf War suggest.[129]

Jeremiah wanted Haass's ultimatum, which he thought had the "highest risk," to be "identified up front for what it most likely will be: a decision to go to war."[130] The argument and memo itself were proof, as Gates said years later, that "right up until the end of October," the brass did not "agree with where Bush wanted to go."[131]

Arguably, it is better when the military leadership is not gung ho, as Bush had said, about going to war. Haass, who was occasionally targeted by the Joint Chiefs for his outspokenness and impatience, believes it is a "good thing" that military leaders in recent history have "been more reluctant than not," even if it frustrated civilian leaders.[132] The challenge for the White House was that Powell, who later admitted proudly that he was "guilty" of being a "reluctant general," had been told at least three times—twice by Bush and once by Scowcroft—that the president did not see enough time for sanctions to work and was beginning to see benefits in military action.[133]

To finally get the so-called "reluctant generals" on board, the White House decided it was time for a "nut-cutting" session, as Gates called it.[134] Bush met on October 30 with what was called the Gang of Eight, which was a smaller, more informal group that included the president, vice president, White House chief of staff, national security advisor, the secretaries of state and defense, the chairman of the Joint Chiefs of Staff, and the CIA director. Bush preferred the gang over the larger, leakier National Security Council.[135] NSC staffers were generally not included in these sessions though Scowcroft and Gates were both there, but Haass's revised memorandum, which included some of Jeremiah's edits, served as the briefing paper and talking points for the president and national security advisor.[136]

At the start of the session, Scowcroft asked, "Are we at a break point in the situation in the Gulf?"[137] After a debate about what to call the ultimatum and the date for the deadline, Powell said, "The forces won't be in place before 15 January."[138] When Scowcroft asked, "What size of force are we talking about?" the chairman replied, according to his memoirs, "If the president opts for this offensive, we'll need a hell of a lot more." "How much more?" Scowcroft asked. "Nearly double," replied the chairman, to which the national security advisor said simply, "Whew."[139]

Scowcroft was not alone in being staggered by the new estimate, even though Iraq had added troops to Kuwait since US troop deployments had been set in August.[140] Whether Powell was trying to game the decision or dissuade Bush is up for debate; regardless, according to Gates, "Bush pushed his chair back, stood up, looked at Cheney, and said, 'You've got it, let me know if you need more,' and walked out of the room."[141] Formal approval was given the next day in the Oval Office for the ultimatum, but the news was to be held until Saudi Arabia agreed to the deployment of more troops.

"A Somewhat 'Messy' End"

Despite a last-minute diplomatic overture, at 10:30 a.m. on January 15, 1991, Bush met with the Gang of Eight in the Oval Office.[142] The president signed another directive, "Responding to Iraqi Aggression in the Gulf," in which the president authorized "military actions designed to bring about Iraq's withdrawal from Kuwait."[143] At 1:30 a.m. (Saudi time) on January 17, 1991, the war commenced with a Tomahawk missile launched from the USS *Bunker Hill*, and it ended 42 days after it started—and 211 days after Haass and Scowcroft found the president on a White House exam table—with Iraq out of Kuwait and its military degraded but Hussein still in power.[144]

Between the October 30 decision on the ultimatum and the end of the war, Haass and the rest of his NSC team remained busy as they tried to guess just what Hussein would do before the deadline. Haass also traveled with Baker to do the diplomacy required to pass UN Security Council Resolution 678, which included the ultimatum and a January 15 deadline, and with Bush to visit troops in Saudi Arabia. With the rest of the small group, Haass worked the "to-do" lists and the tipfiddle—including a "Use of Force Checklist"—for the massive economic, diplomatic, and military effort, eventually known as Desert Storm, that included dozens of countries.[145]

The staffer had also continued to write. Even as the NSC was busy supporting a president deeply involved in the implementation of diplomatic and military matters, Haass was also thinking through what the war would mean for the United States and the region. As the Iraqi military collapsed, he wrote a memorandum to Bush with the subject, "Ending the Gulf War."[146] On his copy, Bush, writing in his traditional thick, marker-style pen, wrote "yes" next to a specific suggestion: "We would be wise to withdraw most of our ground and air forces."[147]

Haass recalled, however, that Bush's "enthusiasm for this memo was limited." After all, it made plain the war would "come to a somewhat 'messy' end."[148] The president had wanted a cleaner conclusion, one that looked more like a traditional victory; and the NSC staffer wrote the memo to prepare the president for reality. The postwar Middle East, with Hussein still in power, was, as Haass recalled, "not going to be nirvana."[149] Regardless, the staffer told Bush, "We can declare the war to be over and won when three criteria are met": if Kuwait were freed, its government restored, and no Iraqi units remained perched to invade again.[150] Again, Bush highlighted the section with his pen.

While some called the Gulf War a classic, others judged the conflict an "incomplete success," especially as doubts about Hussein and the decision to leave him in control lingered. Haass himself was comfortable with its end, however messy.[151] To the staffer, Hussein's survival was the "one fly in the ointment": the war made the world and the region more secure by cutting Iraq's military "vastly . . . down to size" so that it was not "in a position to threaten anybody for some time to come."[152] As Bush and Scowcroft had brainstormed on their fishing trip, the war had also sent important post–Cold War messages around the world and established precedents about the UN's involvement as well as America's willingness to take military action.

After the frustrations of Vietnam and Beirut, the military's performance in the Gulf War was startling, even if it came against a poorer-than-expected showing by the Iraqi military. The Pentagon's technology, strategy, and prosecution in combat were the result of incredible progress made in rebuilding the nation's military after Vietnam and reforming the way of waging war, including the Goldwater-Nichols revisions to the chain of command. Twenty-four hours a day on CNN and other broadcast channels, the US military demonstrated the type of new operational advances that inspired awe at home, respect abroad, and concern among America's few post–Cold War adversaries.

Regardless, Bush was wrong when he said in the weeks after combat ended, "We've kicked the Vietnam syndrome once and for all."[153] Even with lobbying by the president, Congress remained cautious up until the last moment and only authorized force on close votes. The concerns on Capitol Hill reflected the public's. Americans, who were hesitant about a potential war early on in the crisis, grew more comfortable—80 percent approved of it the night it began— only to cool on it again just a year later.[154]

The military brass was also just as cautious after the Gulf War as it had been before. Powell remained chairman, and a reluctant general, not just through Bush's presidency but into the next administration. He later wrote, "War is a deadly game; and I do not believe in spending the lives of Americans lightly."[155] More than setting a high bar for what the nation should go to war over, Powell, with his push for a massive force in the Gulf War, set a new standard for how the nation would go to war with what became known as the "Powell Doctrine," which recommended the use of overwhelming force once a war was deemed necessary.

The "Order of the Boot"

Although Haass later joked that his time standing next to Bush during his press remarks on the South Lawn was his "Andy Warhol 15 minutes of fame," the president himself praised the NSC staffer, who had a "key role . . . every step of the way."[156] In turn, Haass spreads the praise around to the commander in chief, the "collegial" team working at the NSC and in the cabinet, and especially to Scowcroft and Gates, with whom he shares credit for authorship of many critical documents.[157]

After the war, Haass continued on at the White House until the last day of the Bush administration. Through all four years, Haass's opinion of the NSC did not change from what he had written in the Harvard *Crimson* during Iran-Contra.[158] While at the Executive Office Building, in the Situation Room, and even on *Marine One*, the staffer felt it had been his "responsibility to say and write things, even if no one else did."[159] Haass had done so from the war's first hours all the way to its end even if it frustrated some of his colleagues.

Not everyone was a fan of Haass's opinions and writing. Among the operators, charged with executing the global project of establishing what had become known as Operation Desert Shield and then fighting in Desert Storm, the drafting and redrafting of papers could feel a distraction or drain on time that could be better spent on following through on massive global diplomatic, economic, and military operation. Haass's and the NSC's paper chase could feel inconsequential to the time at hand, and the ownership of ideas like the ultimatum, which was as one member of the Deputies Committee explained "something in the air" at the time, is harder to nail down.[160]

What is clear, however, is that as opposed to its NSC predecessors, the Bush staff was formally empowered to be in the room and write the options and ideas for nearly all the president's conversations and decisions about the war. Haass played an active role in perhaps the most important forum—the Gates-led small group of department deputies—that managed American response to Iraq's invasion. Even in Principals Committee and National Security Council meetings, it was his memos and talking points sitting before the president and others, and the staffer was encouraged to interject from the backbench when necessary.

The staff could be trusted with this sort of access because it had such respected managers and Bush's cabinet-level leaders trusted each other, but also because the post–Iran-Contra common law rules kept Haass and the NSC in check. He left the war planning to the Pentagon, limited operational work to the occasional diplomatic foray, and ran his ideas—for the ultimatum and more—through the process. In part because Scowcroft insisted on such an open approach and the staff took one, opponents of Haass's ideas, on the Joint Chiefs of Staff and elsewhere, took their complaints through the same process.

If imitation is the highest form of flattery, the greatest compliment to and legacy of the Bush NSC—including Scowcroft's management and Haass's writings—is that it would serve as the standard for every NSC that followed. In some ways, the Scowcroft approach was easy to replicate—establish a Principals Committee and Deputies Committee and give the staff the pen and access to ask hard questions. But the model of honest brokering, with its allowance for opinion and advocacy as done by Haass, would prove harder to copy in administrations with less trust among principals and less experienced presidents, national security advisors, and staffers.

Despite his writing for Bush, Haass was not appealing enough to be kept on to fight for the next president. After Bush's loss to Arkansas governor Bill Clinton in the November 1992 presidential election, the Clinton transition interviewed and asked several members of the Bush NSC to stay on and serve in the new administration. But shortly before the inauguration, Scowcroft received word that Haass was one of those the new team had "insisted be out" before Clinton took the oath of office. On the "order of the boot" as he recalls, Haass left government in January 1993.[161]

CHAPTER FIVE

A "Policy Person First and Foremost"

The "Test Case from Hell"

In July 1995, President Bill Clinton was upset. The war in Bosnia, which by then had killed hundreds of thousands of people and created over a million refugees, had also led to criticism of the president—by the public, his counterparts abroad, Congress, parts of his own government, and even himself.[1] An aggravated Clinton vented to aides and looked everywhere for ideas. At one point, he turned to a young navy sailor who was in the Oval Office to set up a telephone line, and asked, "What do you think we should do on Bosnia?" The aide replied, "I don't know, Mr. President."[2]

Two NSC staffers were working on an idea for what the president could do. Alexander "Sandy" Vershbow, a career Foreign Service officer, and Air Force Colonel Nelson Drew had served together at the US mission to NATO in Brussels in the early 1990s, as Yugoslavia dissolved amid strife between its main ethnic groups: Bosniaks or Bosnian Muslims, Croats, and Serbs. By summer 1995, Vershbow and Drew had both arrived at the Executive Office Building and been tasked by Clinton National Security Advisor Tony Lake, himself a former member of the NSC staff, to try to help end the bloodshed in Bosnia.

When candidate Clinton campaigned against President Bush just a year after the Gulf War's messy end, the then-governor of Arkansas worked hard to burnish his credibility on foreign policy issues. To many, the youthful Clinton represented the generational hopes of the post–Cold War era, and the candidate promised a "new covenant," one that would ensure the United States was "ready and willing to use force when necessary."[3] As president, however, Clinton struggled—with discomfort with the military leadership, indecision, and a desire to focus on domestic policy—to meet that lofty promise and to counter the many crises of the new world.[4]

By summer 1995, the war in Bosnia had already become, in one NSC staffer's words, a "test case from hell."[5] It was a test of the world order promised by Bush and the covenant coined by Clinton. A test of post–Cold War European and NATO leaders' thinking about how to preserve unity and security on a continent still haunted by memories of past wars. A test of the United States as a superpower without peer. A test of humanity fifty years after the Holocaust. And it was a test for the young president and his team, one they were failing as Clinton desperately asked the navy aide for ideas.

As the bloodshed in Bosnia continued in summer 1995, threatening to create a humanitarian catastrophe as well as a wider war in Europe, a discouraged Lake turned to Vershbow, who as senior director for Europe was the staff's point person on Bosnia. National Security Advisor Lake, who had resigned in protest from the Kissinger NSC in part because of its intrigues, believed he and the rest of Clinton's National Security Council principals were not "getting it done."[6] So Lake, in Vershbow's words, "unshackled" the NSC staff and encouraged them to think big about how to realize a peaceful "endgame" in Bosnia.[7]

Just six weeks later, Clinton agreed to the NSC staff's plan and launched a renewed diplomatic and military push directed by US Ambassador Richard Holbrooke, which resulted in the historic Dayton Accords, ending the war in Bosnia and establishing a fragile peace in the region. Although the NSC staff played little role at Dayton, it was Vershbow and Drew's plan that helped the United States get there. Along the way, the two showed how a forceful NSC staff, working mostly within the interagency process, could continue to help meet the tests of the post–Cold War world.

"Without the Barbarians"

Vershbow and Drew were thinking about Yugoslavia long before the beginning of Clinton's presidency. At the time of the inauguration in Washington, they were thousands of miles away in Brussels at NATO headquarters. Amid dramatic change in a once-divided Europe, Vershbow was serving as the deputy chief of the US diplomatic mission to the alliance, while Drew was a plans officer in a small Defense Department unit assigned to the mission.

As the Cold War ended, it was a time of much hope, but also many questions. Drew later wrote of one poem often repeated at the time in the hallways of the NATO headquarters. Greek poet Constantine Cavafy had asked, "Why this sudden bewilderment? . . . Because night has fallen, and the Barbarians have not come! . . . What's going to happen to us without the Barbarians?"[8] Without the Soviet threat, many wondered what the future would hold for NATO, whether the Cold War would be replaced by a prolonged peace, and how long the United States would stay engaged in Europe to find out.

While the barbarians of the past were gone, Vershbow, Drew, and others at NATO headquarters did not have to look far for brutality. With long-time leader Josip Broz Tito's death in 1980 and Communism's weakening grasp, Yugoslavia's long-simmering ethnic and nationalist tensions, prodded by leaders like Serbian Slobodan Milosevic, had erupted among its Serb, Croat, Muslim, Slovenian, Albanian, and Macedonian populations. After the fall of the Berlin Wall, an increasingly torn Yugoslavia—really a collection of six nations: Bosnia-Herzegovina, Croatia, Serbia, Macedonia, Slovenia, and Montenegro—began to break apart.[9]

An October 1990 American intelligence estimate was blunt about what was happening: Yugoslavia "will cease to function as a federal state within one year, and will probably dissolve within two." The assessment accurately predicted that, with the threat of violent spillover, the Yugoslav civil war would "rapidly become a 'European' problem."[10] But Europe, still emerging from the Cold War and with loyalties spread among the various Yugoslav republics, was not yet equipped to handle tough problems like the Balkans. Regardless, a war-weary Bush foreign policy team decided to let Europe try, believing, as Secretary of State James Baker said of the United States in 1991, "We don't have a dog in that fight."[11]

In Brussels, both Vershbow and Drew saw that the Balkans crisis was a more complicated problem, among many on the postwar continent. Although they had both come from different places, dedicated their lives to national service in a much different world, and taken very different paths to Brussels,

Vershbow and Drew were of similar minds on the Balkans. They shared an appreciation for the difficulty of ending the violence in Bosnia, as well as a belief that the United States needed to be a leader in the sorts of post–Cold War challenges the Balkans represented.

"A Bit of a Tea Party"

Growing up in the Cold War, Vershbow had dedicated himself to a career in it. He had grown passionate about the Soviet Union during a high school visit and dedicated his time at Yale and then during his master's at Columbia to learning about America's foreign policy toward the USSR. When most of his graduate school classmates were considering fields like journalism and investment banking, Vershbow, intrigued with dedicating his life to diplomacy, took and passed the State Department's entrance exam.[12]

The new Foreign Service officer, whose diplomatic nature betrayed his new profession, joined the State Department in 1977, where he happened to share an office with future Reagan NSC staffer Howard Teicher. From that first assignment onward, Vershbow had a series of well-timed Cold War career assignments—he served in Moscow during the crackdown on the Solidarity movement in Poland and as the State Department's director of Soviet affairs as the USSR's disintegration began. The assignment to NATO, beginning just after the dissolution of the Soviet Union, looked to be as fortunately timed.[13]

When Vershbow arrived in Brussels in 1991, Drew was already there, having joined the American mission at NATO the year before but as a military officer, wearing the air force uniform. Drew was born in Europe to an army officer in Wurzburg, Germany, in February 1948, three years after World War II ended.[14] He joined Air Force Reserve Officers' Training Corps or ROTC, which trains college students to be military officers and pays for part of tuition in exchange for a few years of service, midway through his time at the University of North Carolina at Chapel Hill. However, because Drew's eyesight was not good enough to be a pilot, he instead became an intelligence officer after graduation.

Further twists of fate landed Drew at Ramstein Air Base in Germany during the Iranian revolution, where intelligence analysts were studying the Middle East. Because Drew did not speak Farsi, he was asked by an intelligence supervisor to look into what would happen in the Balkans when Tito eventually died. The by-then air force captain ran with the challenge, becoming, according to one fitness report, the "recognized theater expert on Yugoslavia."[15] After Drew left Germany, he continued to study and write about Yugoslavia as the air force took him around the United States for his doctorate at the University of Virginia and a professorship at the Air Force Academy in Colorado before sending the airman back to Europe.

The former cold warriors Drew and Vershbow were together at NATO as the violence in the Balkans deepened and reports of atrocities and detention camps depressed those who remembered the horrors of World War II. Even then, at the end of 1991, one analyst accurately predicted, "So far, we've had a bit of a tea party compared to what's coming."[16] The following year, as Bosnia tried to declare independence and its military fractured along ethnic lines, the United Nations agreed to deploy a European protection force of 12,000, known as UNPROFOR, to provide humanitarian support. But when Bosnian Serb forces went on the offensive, the UNPROFOR personnel were caught unprepared in a deepening war.

"Firepower"

Vershbow and Drew were also abroad as the 1992 US presidential election began in earnest. In the face of the horror in the Balkans, the Bush administration had announced sanctions against Belgrade to try to pressure Serb forces to stand down, and the United Nations had placed an embargo on arms shipments to Yugoslavia to try and stem the violence. When neither stopped the bloodshed, Clinton and his campaign—which included Lake, one of Kissinger's bleeding hearts—pounced and called for tighter sanctions and the establishment of a no-fly zone in Bosnia so airpower could not be used in the killing.[17]

On his election victory, Clinton rewarded Lake with the national security advisor position and tasked him and his deputy, Samuel Berger, an attorney who had worked under Lake at the Carter State Department, with empowering the White House to control policy and the process. On paper, it did: as drawn in the early interagency memoranda, the Clinton process resembled Bush's, with Principals and Deputies Committees at the center. But in practice, a couple of early choices made the White House, and the NSC, too weak to control the process, let alone find solutions to difficult problems like Bosnia.

For one, the laconic Lake, who had served at the foot of Kissinger, opted instead to follow Scowcroft's example; but the new national security advisor chose the wrong tenure. Instead of following Scowcroft's more hands-on management of Haass and the rest of the Bush interagency, Lake relied on his impression of Scowcroft's behind-the-scenes approach in the Ford administration.[18] As each day passed, it became clearer that the 1970s approach would not suffice in the 1990s: it left the Clinton team with no "captain," as one member later explained.[19]

The president was in no position to do the job himself. Clinton was inexperienced, but even more, he chose to make it clear not just publicly but also internally that he and his administration would "focus like a laser beam" on the stagnating economy.[20] On his own, Lake struggled to wrangle policy choices on Bosnia and other issues out of the opinionated National Security Council principals. Eventually, even a former national security advisor, Colin Powell, whose term as chairman of the Joint Chiefs—and worries about White House overreach—continued, told Lake to be more forceful.[21]

In addition to Powell, the Clinton team included Secretary of State Warren Christopher, a prudent attorney and Carter's deputy secretary of state; US Ambassador to the United Nations Madeleine Albright, an NSC veteran and passionate voice for interventionist foreign policy; and Secretary of Defense Les Aspin, a former congressman. Each of them brought strong opinions, memories of the Carter administration's breakdowns, and ghosts of World War II, Vietnam, and Beirut to long, inconclusive debates in the Situation Room, about the Balkans and much more.

The NSC staff could have helped bring clarity to these conversations and build consensus, but the early Clinton staff was hamstrung by a campaign commitment. Candidate Clinton had promised to reduce the White House staff by 25 percent, which turned out to have been based on a mistake: he had been told that Bush and Scowcroft had dramatically increased the NSC's size.[22] When the transition team, as Berger later said, found out the Bush NSC staff was actually "quite spare," the president-elect chose to stick to the commitment and the NSC staff was cut to about sixty people considered policy staff.[23]

Philosophically, Lake, who worried about political influence on the NSC, preferred a smaller NSC made up of "career officials chosen primarily for their expertise" instead of their party affiliation.[24] After members of the Bush NSC were interviewed, Lake and Berger decided to keep on board ten members of the existing staff.[25] Budget-strapped, they also pushed hard for additional detailees from the agencies while adding a few campaign advisors for—in Berger's words—"firepower."[26]

The result was an NSC with a mix of career officials and political appointees; Republicans, Democrats, and independents; and both old and new blood. Mort Halperin, who finally quit the Nixon NSC with Lake after being frustrated by Kissinger's management and the failure to end the Vietnam War, returned to the Executive Office Building at the age of fifty-six to work on democracy and human rights. On the other end of her career, Susan Rice, age twenty-nine, joined the NSC in 1993. It was one of the Stanford graduate and Oxford PhD's first job in national security, and Lake and Berger assigned her to the peacekeeping team and then to the Africa group as senior director.

The national security advisor handed the Bosnia portfolio to a campaign hand. Jenonne Walker, a former CIA and State Department analyst, and think tank fellow, became the senior director for European affairs. Walker, who had known Lake for more than a decade, had helped reinforce the campaign's criticism of the Bush Balkans policy: she told the *New York Times* that "Eastern Europe is a major historical challenge from which we are AWOL."[27] As senior director, Walker was responsible for getting the country, and the young president, to report for duty everywhere from "Portugal to the former Soviet border," including in Central Europe, Eastern Europe, and the Balkans.[28]

The "Safety of 'Middle Options'"

While Vershbow and Drew continued to work at NATO to try to bring an end to the crisis in Bosnia, Clinton, Lake, and Walker took office in Washington and the helm on the Balkans. Like Kissinger and Halperin at the Hotel Pierre before Nixon's inauguration, Walker had developed an option memorandum during the transition to help get the ball rolling early. But once in office, no decision on the options could be made with a distracted president and deep divisions among the national security principals.

Still, Lake, at one of the administration's first meetings, tried to push on them all to realize an "endgame" in Bosnia.[29] To Lake, an "endgame" meant something. It had been the title of a chapter of his book, *Somoza Falling*, which he had written four years before about the frustrated and frustrating bureaucratic response to a 1978 crisis in Nicaragua during which Lake had served in the Carter State Department. He concluded that when career officials and political appointees clash, there is a "natural tendency toward compromise . . . [and] the safety of 'middle options.'"[30]

The safety of the middle was what Lake heard around the Situation Room and interagency policy process in the first months of the Clinton administration. In addition to simple bureaucratic inertia, there were several limits on the new president's options. The Bush team had already tried disowning the Balkans, only to see the situation worsen, for which they were criticized on the campaign trail. The CIA had also told Clinton's team that lifting the arms embargo, or "lift" as the proposition became known, would make only a modest military difference, and within a few months, Clinton publicly ruled out sending American ground troops.[31]

More international options, like the one pushed by the United Nations and former US secretary of state Cyrus Vance and former United Kingdom foreign secretary David Owen, were not much better. Clinton believed the United States had "bigger fish to fry" with its European allies, so the team was hesitant to push too hard on Britain, France, Germany, and other countries.[32] Though many, including Walker, believed Europe could do more heavy lifting on Bosnia, there were continuing concerns in Washington about asking too much of these countries at a time when Clinton wanted Europeans, both as a whole and as individual nations, to take on more of the burden of global leadership in the post–Cold War world.

By April 1993, with Bosnian Muslims increasingly overmatched by Serb forces, the Clinton team considered two of its remaining options. The first became known as "lift and strike": arming Muslim forces with imported weapons and using US and NATO airstrikes to degrade Bosnian Serb positions. The second was establishing a cease-fire, monitored by additional peacekeepers, to allow for humanitarian assistance and negotiations.[33] According to one former NSC member's account, Lake, Christopher, Albright, and even Powell preferred the first option, while the defense secretary Aspin preferred the second.[34]

Nightmares

Breaking the disagreement fell to Clinton, who at one point had reportedly said: "On this foreign policy thing, I know I can get it. I just need some time to think about this."[35] As the president struggled to get it, Lake explained that the president could not "simply ask for opinions," especially in meetings with the military. That, however, was Clinton's style: as Berger said, "The president wanted to know my views, but he wanted to know everybody's views."[36] As meetings became bull sessions without resolution, Lake explained to Clinton, "You've got to go in there, listen to them and then tell."[37]

After a five-hour meeting with the National Security Council on May 1, 1993, Clinton told his team he was for "lift and strike." However, shortly after dispatching Secretary of State Christopher to get European allies on board with the plan, Clinton, who had just read—and misinterpreted—Robert Kaplan's history *Balkan Ghosts*, questioned what could be done to save a region so historically prone to violence. When the president voiced his doubts to some at the Pentagon, one official concluded the president was "not on board" with the very plan he had sent his secretary of state to sell.[38] Neither, it turned out, were the Europeans, who believed that lift and strike was a nonstarter—as one British diplomat said, "especially lift"—with their UNPROFOR personnel in harm's way.[39]

Although a NATO no-fly zone was arranged in April 1993 by Vershbow, then acting as US ambassador to NATO, and others in Brussels, little other progress was made on Bosnia in the administration's early months. With Clinton's vacillation, Lake's inability to push harder for resolution, and a weaker NSC, Walker recalled, the team spent "all these hours on Bosnia with enormous difficulty making any decisions."[40] The result was continued fighting in the Balkans, growing frustration at the White House, concerns on Capitol Hill, and disappointment around government about the promise of Clinton's administration and the new post–Cold War era.

This was the Washington Vershbow found on his early return from NATO in June 1993. He had been brought back from Brussels to become principal deputy to the assistant secretary of state for European and Canadian affairs and a member of Walker's Bosnia interagency working group. While he knew NATO and everyone else had failed so far to change the situation on the ground in Bosnia, Vershbow still believed a stronger military response with American leadership could stem the violence.[41]

Though Vershbow's new portfolio included European trouble spots like the Balkans, it was the despair in the department's Foggy Bottom headquarters that was his initial focus: one of his first tasks in the job was to convince State personnel, some of whom had been focused on the Balkans for years, to stop resigning in protest. One departing State official, whose resignation letter leaked to the press, wrote that Clinton's policies were "misguided, vacillating and dangerous," putting at risk those in the Balkans as well as "vital U.S. interests."[42]

Vershbow asked those considering a departure to give the president and him a chance.[43] Though some stayed to keep trying to change the policy, Vershbow's was a hard sell. Many of those considering resignation had been monitoring the reports of mounting horrors in the Balkans—rape, torture, and ethnic cleansing—but not empowered to do anything to stop them. One resigning State staffer said, "It's a very tragic commentary that at the end of the 20th century, we are not able to respond to genocide." Another told Vershbow he had to leave because the atrocities and US inaction gave him nightmares.[44]

The "Whiff of Gunpowder"

In July 1993 the Serbs began an assault on the Bosnian capital of Sarajevo that played out on televisions around the world. The president was so upset, he asked to review potential military options, including a deployment of US ground forces to keep the peace, and Walker and Lake worked with their colleagues across government to develop a plan for review. But when told by the Joint Chiefs, still led by Chairman Powell, that relieving Sarajevo would require tens of thousands of troops, the Clinton team had lingering concerns about the use of force.[45]

As the deliberations demonstrated, even after the Gulf War, the Vietnam syndrome and ghost of Beirut still had plenty of power. The chairman reflected the instincts of many at the time. At one point, Powell told an NSC staff member, "I'm doing everything I can to keep the United States out of getting involved in the Balkans."[46] Years later, Powell explained why: "When ancient ethnic hatreds reignited in the former Yugoslavia in 1991 and well-meaning

Americans thought we should 'do something' in Bosnia, the shattered bodies of Marines at the Beirut airport were never far from my mind in arguing for caution."[47]

This caution frustrated those who thought that Powell's own success, along with the rest of the Bush administration's, against Iraq might finally curtail Americans' reluctance on war. Vershbow saw the Gulf War as the "final effort to get out of the Vietnam syndrome and the defeatist approach to the use of force." Even more, Vershbow for one believed the conflict with Iraq had demonstrated the real value of "diplomacy backed by force." Haass's ultimatum, the technologically advanced war plan, and the military's execution offered a tantalizing model for so-called coercive diplomacy, especially for those trying to end crises in the still young post–Cold War world.[48]

Yet the Gulf War strengthened hesitant voices as well. The reluctance of Powell and others in the brass, which had vexed the more hawkish voices on the Bush NSC and elsewhere in government, was one reason why the plan and manpower were in place to make Desert Storm such a success. Many at the Pentagon believed the war had established a threshold for acceptable risk and considerable requirements for troops and firepower. Such high standards were important in the Clinton administration, because, as one senior Defense Department appointee explained, many in the military believed some at the White House and State subscribed to the "whiff of gunpowder theory": the idea that the nation's enemies were "weak and bullies," who would "capitulate at the first whiff of gunpowder."[49]

In the face of reluctant generals, Clinton struggled to push back. For one thing, he had protested the Vietnam War and avoided the draft, which were political liabilities on the campaign trail and then in the president's civil-military relationship. Candidate Clinton had also promised to end the military's ban on gay service members, a change that discomfited many, including Powell, and was ultimately rejected. The president was even wary of Powell's public profile, which made him a formidable presence at National Security Council meetings and, Clinton worried, a potential political opponent.[50]

But Clinton's political concerns included whether the American people cared enough about Bosnia to support sending American troops. After his election, in a meeting with one member of Congress, Clinton said, "I just went through the whole campaign and no one talked about foreign policy at all, except for a few members of the press."[51] As opinion polls reminded his team, military interventions—like the one in Somalia, where American troops were supporting the United Nations as it provided humanitarian relief, and a potential mission in the Balkans—were a hard sell for a public still questioning America's post–Cold War global engagement.[52]

Instead of sending troops in summer 1993, the president agreed to push American allies for airstrikes to break the siege and to try to force the Serbs to negotiate. To get the Europeans to agree, however, the United States had to accept a constraint on the strikes—namely a complicated "dual-key" that required any mission to be authorized in a decision shared not just by NATO commanders but also UN civilian leadership. The arrangement gave the United Nations, also trying to establish its role and power in the post–Cold War world, a veto on what should have been NATO's military decision to make.

A "Cancer on Clinton's Entire Foreign Policy"

A year later, an exhausted Clinton team was nowhere closer to an endgame in the Balkans. In addition to the dual-key, a few factors had made finding one much more difficult. Deploying US troops had come to be seen as even riskier following the disastrous "Black Hawk Down" raid in Somalia that had left eighteen Americans dead in October 1993 and saw the bodies of American service members dragged through the streets of Mogadishu. Moreover, the Vance-Owen multilateral diplomatic solution for the Balkans had fallen apart, in part because the Clinton team chose to expend its diplomatic capital on different endeavors, particularly the president's ambition to expand NATO.

Meanwhile, in Washington, the president, who had considered firing his whole team in his first year like a "slaughterhouse right in one whack," had made significant changes to his national security team.[53] At the Defense Department, Aspin had been fired in the aftermath of the tragedy in Mogadishu. His deputy Bill Perry, a longtime Pentagon wonk and investment banker, become secretary. At the end of Powell's term, Clinton replaced him as chairman with Army General John Shalikashvili, who was more sympathetic to—though far from enthusiastic about—humanitarian interventions.

At the State Department, Christopher named the forceful Holbrooke assistant secretary of state for Europe. Holbrooke, who had served as a young diplomat in Vietnam with Lake, cut a wide swathe in Democratic foreign policy circles, charming admirers and developing enemies along the way.[54] Though it could have been a banishment, he had made a success of his appointment as ambassador to Germany. When he returned to Washington, Holbrooke, who worried about both the geopolitical and humanitarian implications of the Balkans, had a broad mandate for post–Cold War Europe.

Despite rumors that Clinton's national security advisor was also on his way out—even US allies joined in the palace intrigue, with one French official trying to forecast "who will end up with the losing card"—Lake stayed on and brought changes to the NSC.[55] Walker, who remembers dedicating 90 percent of her time to Bosnia, was frustrated because Lake was unable to "press Clinton into decisions"; and reports suggest the feeling was mutual. Lake had not hidden his desire to replace his senior director, and she was soon named ambassador to the Czech Republic.[56]

In June 1994, with Walker's departure, Lake brought to the Executive Office Building the forty-one-year-old Vershbow, who was up-to-speed on the Bosnia decisions and debates as State's representative to the NSC working group.[57] The bespectacled and soft-spoken Foreign Service officer, according to one aide, also brought "a lot of intellectual weight" to the NSC.[58] Vershbow was also able to be loaned by the State Department: the new senior director's salary remained on his home agency's books instead of those of the cash-strapped White House, which only had so much budget for direct hires.[59] But the real reason was that the national security advisor saw in the NSC staffer a shared belief in using force to back up diplomacy in Bosnia.

As such, Vershbow's pen was busy at the NSC: he was one of the primary notetakers for the running discussion about Bosnia and Lake's "main man for most of the memos to the president" on the Balkans.[60] In one memorandum, the new senior director quickly diagnosed the challenges on Bosnia as he saw them from his new third-floor office, number 368, in the Executive Office Building. Vershbow wrote, the "administration's weak, muddle-through strategy in Bosnia was becoming a cancer on Clinton's entire foreign policy—spreading and eating away at its credibility."[61]

Vershbow knew a solution was not going to be easy. As he recalled, "nobody really knew how to solve these kinds of conflicts effectively with a mixture of territorial conflicts, ethnic tensions, with humanitarian dimensions, with human rights violations of the kind we had not seen in Europe in decades."[62] Still, despite the muddle-through debates and strategy to that point, the new NSC staffer believed that the United States was the only country capable of ending the war, and its involvement was the "only way you get things done."[63]

"Where Do We Go from Here?"

The fall of 1994 demonstrated that even the new team struggled to arrest the old cancer. In early November the CIA reported, "Grave humanitarian conditions loom in Bihac."[64] Located in northwest Bosnia, Bihac was one of the six designated UN safe areas and home to 200,000 residents cut off from food and other supplies by Serbian attacks. Despite desperate American pleas and plans for greater action after Bosnian troops launched an offensive to break the siege, European officials, who were worried about their UNPROFOR personnel on the ground, rejected a forceful intervention.

Many in European governments were also frustrated that the United States had so little personnel on the ground and skin in the game. As the British defense secretary said at the time, "Those who call for action by the world must match words [by] deeds, and that doesn't include just a few aircraft."[65] As Serbian forces dropped napalm and cluster munitions and took UNPROFOR troops hostage, a crisis was now growing in Brussels at NATO headquarters where the alliance, which had withstood the Cold War and Clinton had promised to expand, appeared at risk of collapse.

After a month of trying to come up with a plan for Bihac that was acceptable around Washington (at the Pentagon and State Department, as well as an increasingly vocal Congress) and in European capitals, the upcoming holidays must have looked like a welcome respite. But Vershbow was finding that the NSC staff's work does not stop, no matter the hour of night or even on holidays. Over Thanksgiving weekend 1994, he and Lake traded drafts back and forth of a memorandum on Bosnia for the president. Even though they both had long been in favor of an American-led solution to the problem, in light of the latest setback in Bihac, Vershbow and Lake were resigned to ask the president, "Where do we go from here?"[66]

The two offered a downbeat assessment of the options at hand. According to Vershbow and Lake, the "'stick' of military pressure seems no longer viable":

sending in American ground troops was still too unpopular for Clinton to consider, and airstrikes were too hard to get approved with the dual-key protocol and UNPROFOR personnel in harm's way. Given the courses available, Lake and Vershbow concluded that unless the United States could "come up with other forms of leverage, the chances of a political settlement will remain slim." Thus it was better to contain the violence than directly counter it.[67]

At a late November meeting of the National Security Council, all but Albright accepted Lake and Vershbow's conclusion. Despite the unfolding tragedy in the Balkans, the rift in Brussels had to take precedence: as one senior American official explained at the time, the principals had agreed that NATO was "more important than Bosnia."[68] The priority became mending the alliance while containing the violence. Lake recalled thinking, "Okay, there's not much we can do about Bosnia, let's keep it from flipping over, washing over into the rest of the Balkans."[69]

As 1994 wound down, Clinton was despondent. After two years in office, the promise with which he stormed the White House had faded, and the president was lashing out, blaming, among others, the "traitors on my staff."[70] Although he was still loyal to the president, it was "absolutely the low point" for Lake, who admitted later, "for a while there I threw up my hands" in December and January.[71] The national security advisor struggled to continue bringing Clinton bad news, explaining, "Every time I walked in for the morning brief, I had the big B for Bosnia written on my forehead."[72]

Yet as the new year began, there were a few changes in Lake's Bosnia briefings. With the failure of the last multilateral diplomatic push, the United States, Russia, United Kingdom, France, and Germany had established an informal "Contact Group" to pursue negotiations based on the promise of a map with 51 percent of Bosnia under Muslim-Croat control and 49 percent for the Bosnian Serbs.[73] Another small development was a little-noticed benefit of the team's dedication to prioritizing NATO. In early December, Clinton committed, in principle, to providing some of the military personnel required to stage an emergency evacuation of UNPROFOR troops.[74]

Vershbow recommended the plan to demonstrate the American commitment to put troops on the line for their allies, but the agreement ended up having additional consequences. Since any extraction would be a NATO-only operation, with no dual-key parameters, it helped set a precedent for NATO to retake control of military decisions. Even if American troops would only deploy in an evacuation, the agreement also helped break the seal, at lower levels of government, on consideration of sending military personnel to the Balkans as the Pentagon began planning and pre-positioning personnel in Germany for such an operation.[75]

"I've Given Your Name . . ."

As the Thanksgiving memorandum made clear, Vershbow knew that if anything was going to change, the United States needed to build leverage, particularly with the military. Fortunately, right around this time, the NSC staffer began to see a familiar face at the daily meetings of the interagency working group on Bosnia. As the Balkans demanded more and more time of the Defense Department and military, Nelson Drew, who had left Brussels in early 1994 and been slated to teach for a few years as an air force officer at the National War College in Washington, was instead assigned to the policy staff of the Joint Chiefs.

When Drew reported for duty at the Pentagon in January 1995, he joined in the NSC-led Bosnia policy discussions. At one session, Vershbow took a coaster and wrote Drew a note on the back. It read in part, "I've given your name . . . as someone I'd like considered in devising a list of candidates to replace" a military staffer who was leaving the NSC that spring.[76] The senior director saw in Drew someone who knew the issues, NATO, and the military, and also believed the United States could meet the test in Bosnia.[77]

On receiving the note, Drew was "in seventh heaven," according to his wife Sandra.[78] The air force colonel knew what an NSC assignment meant because he had spent a brief time on the staff almost a decade before. In 1988, Drew was handpicked to be the first Air Force Academy faculty officer to spend a summer on the Reagan NSC, where he worked on arms control and NATO military plans in the wake of the Iran-Contra scandal and in the last days of the Cold War.[79]

Though the Clinton administration lacked the screaming matches, scheming, and secrecy of the Reagan NSC, the policy process was failing the Bosnia test in 1995. Among Lake's frustrations that winter was that the White House–led system that relied on long discussions with the principals was not working.

On Bosnia and more, they were, according to the national security advisor, not "getting it done through the formal channels."[80] As a result, the deliberate choice was made to allow the deputies and staff-led groups to become the primary venue for policy development and debate.[81]

In one February 1995 discussion, Vershbow assessed the leverage of the United States and its allies in Bosnia. Sanctions, diplomatic pressure, and limited airstrikes had proved insufficient. The NSC staffer believed that more robust and flexible NATO airstrikes, freed from the dual-key, could change the dynamic on the ground. But such actions were unlikely with UNPROFOR in harm's way. Even more, Vershbow worried that if the United States took steps to "Americanize the war" without a real chance of success, failure would be a severe blow to the credibility of the president and the country.[82]

While Vershbow and Drew worked on the problem at the NSC, the bloodshed continued on the ground in Bosnia. By then more than 200,000 people had been killed, and the United States and the rest of the international community looked powerless to stop the violence.[83] As the informal Contact Group tried to induce Milosevic to join diplomatic talks, the Serb leader and his forces appeared to be emboldened. In May, despite some NATO airstrikes, Serb forces killed indiscriminately in Sarajevo, Tuzla, and elsewhere, and took hundreds of UNPROFOR peacekeepers as hostages.

In case daily intelligence briefings were not enough to keep Lake, Vershbow, and Drew focused on the problem at hand, Clinton would tear out newspaper articles, annotate them, and send the missives down to the NSC. One note on a Bosnia article said, "Tony [Lake], Do we need to say more about this . . . BC."[84] The Clinton NSC staff rarely got face time with the president, so the annotated media clips, like Clinton's venting and outbursts, gave the staff insight into the president's thinking and allowed him to light a fire under his team.

By June, the president's press articles were filled with stories of Bosnia's atrocities, US inaction, and Clinton's frustration. As Vershbow fretted over the nation's lack of leverage to stop the atrocities, Clinton worried about his own. According to journalist Bob Woodward, the president said, "Right now we've got a situation, we've got no clear mission, no one's in control of events."[85] After one of these outbursts, a National Security Council principal told Clinton he was right: the present "muddle-through" strategy made him "appear weak."[86]

"Blue Sky"

To take control, Lake thought it was time to do some "blue sky thinking" and to move policy discussion and development further outside of the formal channels.[87] The national security advisor made it a practice to have what he called "blue sky sessions," where he would invite people he considered smart to just talk informally about the world and the challenges facing the United States and Clinton team.[88] In spring 1995, Albright, who wanted the United States to take the initiative to end the crisis, was a regular partner for Lake in these conversations, and soon enough, so were Vershbow and Drew.

Taking the conversation outside of the principals and deputies committee meetings and relying on the NSC instead of the agencies were, in some ways, a surprise for Lake, who had taken a less heavy-handed approach as national security advisor up until that point. It was also a move laced with irony for Lake, who had lamented Kissinger's intrigues and micromanagement when the then-staffer resigned from the NSC in disgust in 1970. Although Lake's formal letter of resignation focused on Cambodia, an unsent draft he wrote with a colleague decried Kissinger's attempt to forge a rational foreign policy "single-handedly."[89]

Still, with violence worsening in Bosnia and Clinton upset, Lake felt he had to pull things further away from a process that had failed to that point: he and the National Security Council principals had tended to produce the types of "middle options" the national security advisor had once denounced, and Clinton had a hard time ensuring that even these policies were implemented.[90] On June 24, 1995, Lake called Vershbow, Drew, Berger, and another NSC aide to his office and told them, according to two recollections, "We can't let this drift" any longer. He said, "Let's think from the end backward. I don't want to hear about what's next."[91]

The group agreed that the Contact Group's map was the optimal endgame, but it might require tweaking to get a deal. Lake asked Vershbow to take the lead on an integrated strategy, one that considered all the tools—from so-called carrots to sticks—in the American and allied arsenal to bring an end to the crisis. Vershbow realized this was an opportunity to "really break loose from the shackles" of the present policy and the failing process. More than that, he was excited to be the person Lake turned to for the plan, and Vershbow in turn looked to Drew, whom he called a "real alter ego" in the process.[92]

After tasking Vershbow and Drew with the endgame, Lake raised the project with the president directly.[93] Although going to Clinton so early was, in the words of one member of the national security advisor's team, "highly unusual," the move allowed Lake to get the president in a place to make a decision and bolster him against hesitancy at the Pentagon and State Department, where one assessment said it was time to "write off the Bosnia policy."[94] Lake said, "Mr. President, tell me if you don't want to do this, stop me now because the risks are very clear." Clinton responded, "Do it."[95]

With the president's green light, Vershbow and Drew, working with others on the NSC and at lower levels of the agencies, tried to "think of all the angles," in Vershbow's words: how to get NATO deeper into the fight, how to manage the United Nations and the dual-key protocol, and how to tinker with the Contact Group's map to ensure agreement.[96] Although there was still a clear concern over whether or not to use force, it was becoming clearer that American troops were likely going to be involved one way or another because of the president's commitment to help should UNPROFOR decide to withdraw.[97]

The urgency of the planning increased as the violence in Bosnia did. From July 6 to July 16, 1995, amid late and ineffectual NATO airstrikes, Serbs assaulted Srebrenica, which along with other cities had been designated a safe area by the UN, took additional peacekeepers hostage, and killed more than 8,000 Muslims.[98] The fall of the city was, in Vershbow's words, a "galvanizing moment," eliciting a renewed European dedication, led in part by forceful French president Jacques Chirac, to ending the tragedy. However, Vershbow and Drew's drafting was not keeping pace with the emotions and outrage the Srebrenica attacks inspired in Washington.

On July 14, Clinton, furious at how much events were drifting out of control, took a momentary break to practice his golf swing on the Eisenhower putting green near the Oval Office. Amid the chips and putts, Berger, the deputy national security advisor, and another NSC staffer arrived with additional details of the horror in Srebrenica. In response, the president screamed: "This can't continue. We have to seize control of this." He wanted to know where the new ideas were. The NSC staffer said, "We're working on" the endgame plan, but Clinton responded, "That's not fast enough."[99]

"Lift, Arm, Train, and Strike"

When Lake heard about Clinton's outburst, the national security advisor made sure Vershbow and Drew knew about the president's urgency.[100] A few days later, they finished their draft which proposed an "all-out effort in the coming weeks" to push for a diplomatic solution and "restore" US and NATO leverage with more aggressive NATO airstrikes.[101] None of these were really novel ideas, all had been considered at some point in one way or another, but the two staffers and their agency colleagues had attempted to orchestrate all of them, based on a complex "schematic" of incentives and punishments, into a cohesive roadmap that would help respond to different events on the ground in the Balkans.[102]

With the "Bosnia Endgame Strategy" in hand, Lake invited the National Security Council principals to a breakfast on July 17, 1995. The national security advisor met with Christopher, Perry, Shalikashvili, Albright, and Berger in his White House office where Vershbow attended as notetaker. Most of the participants had prepared for a discussion only about how to respond to Srebrenica, but instead, Lake presented the NSC's much more ambitious paper and arranged for Clinton to stop by to voice his support for another push and to make his own urgency clear to the principals.[103]

Despite initial hesitancy aired at the breakfast, Lake asked each agency to prepare integrated papers similar to the NSC's.[104] Rather than trying to get everyone to agree to a plan, each agency was tasked with coming up with their own to achieve the endgame. This novel approach to honest brokering provided each National Security Council principal the opportunity to give the president what his or her department considered the best course of action; but it was also meant to try to protect Vershbow and Drew's plan, which was being further refined with a small group from the different agencies, from being watered down.[105]

On August 5, the combined endgame papers were submitted to Clinton with a cover note from Lake, and a paper each from the NSC staff, Albright's office, the State Department, and the Defense Department, which also included the Joint Chiefs' assessment. Vershbow and Drew detailed a plan to lift-arm-train-and-strike—lift the embargo, arm and train Bosnian forces, and continue non-dual-key airstrikes—to provide enough leverage for an American diplomatic push to get the warring parties to agree to a single Bosnia with a 51 to 49 percent map.[106]

Two days later, Clinton met in the White House Cabinet Room with Lake, the National Security Council principals, and Vershbow. In her paper and in the meeting, Albright argued that the United States could no longer treat Bosnia like a "tar baby," but instead had to provide the leadership necessary for a solution.[107] Meanwhile, the State Department proposed in its paper a more "limited approach" through multilateral diplomacy, and the Pentagon remained hesitant to put Americans on the ground for training amid a conflict, which for some continued to stir echoes of Vietnam and Lebanon.[108]

At the end of the conversation, Clinton said he wanted to sleep on the choice, but he suggested he liked the NSC's paper.[109] As they waited for the decision, Vershbow, Drew, and the rest of the team began to refine the plan for a new round of diplomacy that would launch the initiative and hopefully get European nations on board with the plan.[110] Lake agreed to go to Europe to speak with allies about the president's decision, but knew he could not be away from the White House for long. Holbrooke, who still believed in the need to end the bloodshed but had never been enamored with or adept at working the Washington policy process, which on Bosnia he called a "a gigantic stalemate machine," was tapped to lead what many expected to be intense shuttle diplomacy in the Balkans.[111]

"Watch"

With Clinton's final approval and his edits to the NSC-drafted talking points for Lake's trip, the national security advisor departed for Europe along with Vershbow and representatives from State, the Joint Chiefs of Staff, and the Defense Department. On the plane, Vershbow continued to bolster Lake, telling him: "Tony, this isn't going to be as hard as you think. It just isn't." When the national security advisor suggested that the Europeans might blanche, the NSC staffer who had been in Brussels at the beginning of the administration replied: "No, they're going to be more amenable. They're ready for change. Watch."[112]

Vershbow's prediction proved true. After productive meetings around the continent, Lake met with Holbrooke in London on August 14 to transition to what was expected to be dizzying rounds of diplomatic visits in the Balkans and around the world.[113] The Lake-Holbrooke handoff, with the considerable personalities involved and their personal history dating back to their days working for the State Department in Vietnam, was steeped in symbolism; but it was the quiet handoff between Vershbow and Drew, who had stayed back at the White House for the Lake trip, that proved more fateful.

The national security advisor had decided Vershbow needed to be in Washington rather than on the plane with Holbrooke. Although the staffer was disappointed to miss what promised to be a high-profile diplomatic show, Vershbow knew he had to be in the Executive Office Building to manage and monitor the government-wide, and NATO-wide, effort to make sure the plan—his plan—could be implemented if Holbrooke's diplomacy worked. In the end, the staffer saw himself as a "policy person first and foremost," and coordinating the complicated plan of military action, diplomacy, and other steps was the ultimate policy job.[114]

Of course, the diplomatic mission was also supposed to be in the hands of diplomats. Granted diplomacy had always been one operational area where the staff, including Lake during his time working for Kissinger, was expected to play a role; and even in the post–Iran-Contra era, when staffers were expected to stay in their lane, as Haass demonstrated, they were not required to stay put in the Executive Office Building. Although Lake's hesitancy appeared to have little to do with the common law against the staff taking part in operations, the decision was also supposed to be how government worked.

Lake, however, still wanted someone on the plane with Holbrooke. Drew got the assignment and immediately set off from London on the first shuttle. The American team, which included Deputy Assistant Secretary of State for European and Canadian Affairs Robert Frasure and Deputy Assistant Secretary of Defense for Europe and NATO Affairs Joseph Kruzel, traveled around the regions cajoling leaders of the various parties to negotiate. Many in the region were pleased to see the Americans' more visible leadership, but before Holbrooke and his team could make much progress, tragedy struck.

"Whooopppee!"

On August 19, 1995, Drew, Frasure, and Kruzel were riding in an armed personnel carrier when it skidded off the road on Mount Igman near Sarajevo. The three were killed in the resulting fire and explosion. Holbrooke and others on the American team, who were riding in a separate vehicle, survived but were left shaken by the accident and returned to Washington.[115]

Vershbow, out of the office that Saturday, was called with word of Drew's death. As he rushed back to the White House, CNN had begun to broadcast that some of the American team had been in an accident. After hearing the scattered media reports, Drew's wife, Sandra, at home in Virginia with their two teenage children, frantically and frustratingly called around the Executive Office Building looking for word on her husband. Soon Vershbow and Lake arrived at her home to deliver the sad news in person.[116]

In the tragedy's wake, Clinton reaffirmed his commitment to carry on with the plan. At the memorial service for the fallen at a chapel on Fort Myer near Arlington Cemetery, the president said of the NSC staffer, "The White House and the nation are better for his service."[117] In addition to delivering the eulogy, Clinton met with many of his advisors in a small room at the chapel. The group reviewed Holbrooke's progress and adaptations to the plan and discussed the steps needed to finally realize the endgame that Drew and the others had died to bring about.[118]

Holbrooke's second shuttle began only a few days later, and he was joined by, among others, Donald Kerrick from the NSC, who believed Lake wanted a staff representative on the team to keep an eye on the program.[119] Shortly after the diplomacy restarted, a Serb shell killed thirty-seven people in Sarajevo's market square, and the international community vowed to respond. On August 30, NATO launched the first wave of NATO bombings in Bosnia without a dual-key. When Lake told the president the news, Clinton replied, "Whooopppee!"[120]

NATO's "Operation Deliberate Force," which eventually included 3,400 sorties and 750 attack missions against fifty-six ground targets, degraded Serb positions even as it bolstered diplomacy. With the military progress, Holbrooke convinced the Bosnian, Croatian, and Yugoslav foreign ministers to accept the Contact Group map and a cease-fire to allow for talks. Holbrooke orchestrated the discussions at the Wright-Patterson Air Force Base near Dayton, Ohio, with support from Secretary of State Christopher, European representatives, and the Russian deputy foreign minister.

The resulting Dayton Accords were a historic achievement when they were concluded on November 21, 1995. The parties agreed to maintain a unified

Bosnia-Herzegovina as a single state with two parts—the Bosnian Croat Federation (51 percent) and the Bosnian Serb Republic (49 percent)—and that Sarajevo was to remain the capital of the central government. To preserve this fragile peace, a 60,000-member NATO Implementation Force was going to be deployed at the end of December.

After ruling out such an option in spring 1993, Clinton agreed to deploy 20,000 US ground troops as part of the NATO force, though he also established a deadline for their withdrawal, promising the mission "should and will take about one year."[121] Despite the deadline, only 41 percent of Americans approved of US troops in Bosnia at the time, with a clear majority disapproving.[122] Clinton's own polling, however, improved with the Dayton deal: a majority of Americans approved of the job he was doing as president.[123]

In the end, Clinton's deadline went unmet: US forces remained in the Balkans for almost a decade though the size of the operation decreased. Like the Gulf War before it, Americans proved more tolerant for the low-casualty military intervention in Bosnia and less affected by the Vietnam syndrome than Bush, Clinton, and other presidents had assumed. Without arousing political opposition at home, the military and diplomatic success also reaffirmed a model of American leadership of NATO and other multinational initiatives in the post–Cold War era.

"Just Getting Started"

Though the NSC and Lake played little role at Dayton itself—Vershbow and the national security advisor only traveled to the negotiations once—completing the deal required the work and ideas of nearly everyone on the Clinton team.[124] The president, of course, despite much venting and indecision, ultimately launched the initiative that brought the parties to Dayton. The State Department, including Holbrooke and Christopher, kept the parties talking through shuttle diplomacy around the Balkans and during the sessions at Dayton. And Lake kept Clinton focused and pulled the process into the White House.

Yet after the national security advisors called for an "endgame" several times over the first two years of the administration, Vershbow, whom Lake calls an "unsung hero" in the process, and Drew were critical to developing the plan that helped realize it.[125] Without the NSC staff's conviction, knowledge of

NATO, and strategic planning, Lake's call for an endgame in June 1995 might have been just as fruitless as his first in February 1993.

Buoyed in no small part by the success in Bosnia, Clinton went on to victory in his reelection campaign the next year. With it, some on his foreign policy team moved on or moved up. Lake, who was nominated to head the CIA only to withdraw in the face of Republican opposition, left the White House, and Berger replaced him. Although the Clinton process remained about the same, its management benefited from the new national security advisor's close relationship with the president.

The NSC, which would grow to almost one hundred staffers working on policy, was also further empowered by the success in the Balkans.[126] Like Haass's advocacy for ideas during the Gulf War, Vershbow and Drew's work on Bosnia helped underline the post–Cold War need for a strong and engaged staff. Yet the success of the intervention masked what had been a risky choice and some aggressive policy advocacy done outside of the formal system. It suggested that even in the post–Iran-Contra era, the NSC staff would be tempted, and occasionally asked, to take on a bigger strategic role, especially when blessed by the national security advisor and faced with dysfunction in Washington and conflagrations abroad.

The post–Cold War world was not short of the crises one Clinton team member called the "brown blobs" marring the new era's promise.[127] As the Clinton NSC sought to manage these blobs, the so-called "integrated planning" in the Bosnia endgame process, with staffers like Vershbow and Drew at its center, further solidified the NSC's centrality in the national security process and Clinton's management of foreign policy.[128] NSC staffers leveraged the Bosnia model in 1999 to ensure that NATO responded forcefully when Balkan violence erupted again, this time in Kosovo.

By then Vershbow was back in Brussels. After he stayed at the NSC for a time in Clinton's second term, the president named Vershbow US ambassador to NATO in 1998, another stop in a well-timed career. Still, he looked back on his time at the NSC fondly, where together with Drew, he had not just helped to defeat some of the new barbarism in the post–Cold War world but also to establish a model for American leadership in the new era.

Drew, the only NSC staffer ever to die in the line of duty, did not live to enjoy the end to a conflict he had foreseen as an intelligence officer in the late

1970s. When he perished on Mount Igman he was, in Vershbow's words, "just getting started."[129] Drew was buried in Section 6 of Arlington National Cemetery; his grave is one of the few related to the wars in the Balkans. But it was not the only way Washington and the NSC chose to remember his service. In 1996, Clinton created the Colonel Samuel Nelson Drew Memorial Award for a staffer, or any other public servant, who exemplified the dedication of the late service member and member of the NSC and, like him, made contributions to a more peaceful world.

CHAPTER SIX

A "Wartime" Staff

"This Is Too Damn Hard, Too Risky"

In January 2007, President George W. Bush announced in a speech to the nation that he had decided to send 30,000 additional troops to Iraq, where sectarian violence had divided the country and engulfed its capital. The president had made the choice despite division in the White House Situation Room, frustration from voters, and a new Congress intent on ending the war. With so much opposition, it is fair to assume Bush felt alone when he decided to pursue what became known as "the surge."

Yet, a week after the speech, Bush invited the aides who had helped develop the plan, including NSC staffer Meghan O'Sullivan, to the Oval Office to thank them. After photographs were taken, Bush said of the decision, "There's pressure to say, 'Oh, well, this is too damn hard, too risky, let's not do it.'"[1] But as everyone in the room knew, the president was not talking about O'Sullivan, who had fought for almost a year to give Bush the push, the plan, and the personnel to be able to say, "Let's do it."

Of course, it was not supposed to be this way. Bush won the presidency after explicitly ruling out the sort of "nation-building" that Bill Clinton, Tony Lake, and Sandy Vershbow had launched in Bosnia, yet the surge aimed to help a struggling Iraqi government build its credibility.[2] The president had also promised that his team—full of bold-faced names from the Republican foreign policy establishment—would make the United States safer, only to see his advisors locked into disagreement.[3] And although Bush had long believed the "government micromanaged" the Vietnam War, the president was now regularly questioning commanders in Baghdad via video-teleconferences.[4]

Few embodied just how much had changed over the course of the Iraq War more than the red-haired O'Sullivan. After growing interested in the world as a second grader in Lexington, Massachusetts, she had joined the State Department in the weeks after September 11, 2001, to focus on matters wholly unrelated to the attacks of that day. Yet like many in her generation of foreign policy professionals, O'Sullivan soon went to war herself, serving in Iraq as a civilian and then joining the NSC where she explained, "My real job was trying to shape the winds of policy."[5]

By the time O'Sullivan arrived at the Executive Office Building, the Bush National Security Council had been upset by personal and bureaucratic rancor. Those divisions and the evolving nature of the Iraq War, which had been launched to remove the threat posed by Iraq's purported weapons of mass destruction, made finding solutions nearly impossible. Amid disagreements and attempts to change course in Iraq, O'Sullivan and her colleagues became what the president's first national security advisor called a "wartime" NSC.[6]

In the aftermath of the September 11th attacks, as the country and the commander in chief went to war, the NSC went right along. When Iraq and the wider war on terror went badly, the common law struggled to keep up and keep staffers like O'Sullivan in line. With his speech and surge, Bush doubled down on a war many thought had already been lost while his decision further empowered the NSC's warriors to do what was necessary to fight for their ideas and the president in Washington.

"Real Experts Who Shared the President's Policy Instincts"

O'Sullivan was still an undergraduate student at Georgetown University when NSC staffer Richard Haass was writing the ultimatum that led the United States into war against Iraq. During the Clinton administration, Haass and O'Sullivan worked together at the Brookings Institution think tank in Washington and wrote alone and together about the evolving nature of sanctions. For a case study, the two reviewed the economic constraints the United States imposed on Iraq after the Gulf War that, along with a US military presence in and above the Gulf, helped keep Saddam Hussein in check after Desert Storm's messy end.

The two continued their collaboration at the Bush State Department in the weeks after September 11th. Haass, who had been named head of the policy planning staff in the new administration, hired his former coauthor O'Sullivan to his team. Once at Foggy Bottom, she joined a still young administration rushing to respond to the terrorists' attacks and their implications for nearly every facet of American foreign policy.[7] But in those busy and anxious days, O'Sullivan and many others in Washington were aware of the tension in the Bush national security team, which had simmered in some ways since its delayed inception following the long recount battle after the 2000 presidential election.

When the memorandum on Bush's NSC and interagency process was finally distributed almost a month after he took the oath of office in 2001, it showed how the new president wanted to make the most of a national security team of heavyweights.[8] The Bush National Security Council included Vice President Dick Cheney, who had served as defense secretary during the Gulf War; Secretary of State Colin Powell, returning to national service after his term as chairman of the Joint Chiefs of Staff had ended in 1993; and Defense Secretary Donald Rumsfeld, another veteran of Washington and the Pentagon.

A former NSC staffer, Condoleezza Rice, was named national security advisor and tasked with keeping those principals productive. Like the Scowcroft-designed organization she and Haass had worked in the decade before, Rice relied on Principals and Deputies Committees; but the system struggled as the team disagreed about foreign policy for a new century and then for the new era that began on September 11, 2001. The disagreements eventually grew so pronounced and publicly known that unnamed "colleagues" took pains to deny one observer's comparison of the Bush team to the quarrelsome Reagan administration.[9]

Given the relatively peaceful world at the outset of the administration, Rice designed what she called a "peacetime" NSC.[10] As national security advisor, Rice considered herself to be "staff—rarified staff, to be sure, but staff nonetheless," and she thought the same of the NSC, which was reduced in size by about one-third from a Clinton team that grew by 28 percent during his presidency, and similar in seniority to the Scowcroft NSC.[11] Rice's deputy national security advisor, Stephen Hadley, a lawyer and former NSC staffer who had also worked for Scowcroft as counsel on the Tower Commission's investigation into the Iran-Contra affair, explained the plan: a "smaller organization, a flat organization of real experts who shared the President's policy instincts."[12]

Even a peacetime NSC, however, soon became the subject of bureaucratic brinkmanship. Although vice presidents had had aides, including their own national security advisors, for years, Cheney built a rival to the NSC, with upwards of thirty-five members, some of whom Rice accused of playing "bureaucratic games" to get the upper hand and get the vice president's way in policy debates.[13] Meanwhile, over at the Defense Department, Rumsfeld combated any interventions on what he thought was the Pentagon's turf. The defense secretary complained the NSC was too tardy in sending papers and a "bit of a black box," where too many decisions were made without the consultation of principals like him.[14]

The tensions only worsened after the attacks of September 11, 2001, as the nation invaded Afghanistan, launched a broader global campaign against terrorism, and soon enough began another war in Iraq. The very nature of the terror threat was a challenge to the entire government, including the smaller NSC staff. Cheney asked in an interview, "What bureau does that fit in?"[15] Congress soon answered, creating a new Department of Homeland Security as well as a Homeland Security Council staff, or HSC, in the Executive Office Building, which was designed on the NSC staff's precedent and model.

Meanwhile, Rice explained that with a wartime commander in chief, the staff had to lean forward to get Bush the intelligence he needed and his orders implemented.[16] The further the staff leaned, however, the more it dabbled in operations and bent the common law. As the staff began operating in war zones, conferring with military officers, and advocating for ideas, Rumsfeld pushed back hard. A year into the war in Afghanistan, the defense secretary wrote Rice a pointed reminder that neither the national security advisor nor the NSC were in the military's chain of command.[17]

"Iraq Envy"

Bush, the NSC, and the US military were not the only ones going to war. In her time at the State Department, O'Sullivan had an eclectic portfolio, working on matters related to Northern Ireland, Libya, Syria, and Iran, but as the rest of the government fought terrorism, O'Sullivan was on the outside of the team working on Iraq—and increasingly looking in. When the war drums on Iraq began to grow louder, the young policy planner, who had studied and written about America's contentious post–Gulf War standoff with the country, confessed to a supervisor that she had developed a case of "Iraq envy."[18]

Unfortunately, the internal tensions that had plagued the administration's first two years also frustrated planning and strategy for the Iraq War. Following the Gulf War, Bosnia, and Kosovo, the latter where the U.S. military suffered few losses, many in the defense world, including Rumsfeld and others at the Bush Pentagon, assumed the US technological advantages had created a revolution in military affairs, as it became known. Cutting-edge tactics and technology would allow the United States to take risks, and even shock and awe adversaries, necessary to win the twenty-first century's wars while putting fewer troops and assets in harm's way.

In the wake of the September 11th attacks, however, the purveyors of this revolutionary way of war were confronted with a strategy old as time. In the face of a modern, technologically advanced US military, opponents in Afghanistan, later Iraq, and elsewhere in the so-called global war on terror took to the tactics used by insurgents throughout history, including Vietnam. As urgent as the campaign against terrorism was, the defense establishment struggled to find the right approach to fight it, let alone win.

The same was true for what came after combat. Before the Iraq War began, the State Department and the Defense Department could not get on the same page about so-called "Phase IV," or postcombat stabilization and reconstruction operations. As the increasingly hands-on NSC failed to force the two to come together, no one was able to develop a comprehensive, interagency plan.[19] The breakdown signaled that bureaucratic and personal prerogatives were trumping the war before it had even begun.

After her Iraq envy won out, O'Sullivan volunteered for the war effort, only to get caught up in the behind-the-scenes fights. With Haass's support, she was assigned to deploy with a Defense Department–based team on a five-week tour in postwar Iraq to provide reconstruction and humanitarian assistance. But shortly after reporting for duty, O'Sullivan was told to go back to the State Department because some at the Pentagon did not believe—due in part to her work on Capitol Hill for a Democratic senator and her pre–September 11th arguments against using force in Iraq—that she was, as O'Sullivan recalls, "politically appropriate" or committed enough to Iraqi democracy.[20]

Despite the pressure to quit, O'Sullivan was eventually allowed to stay on the team and arrived in Baghdad in a civilian convoy shortly after US forces took the Iraqi capital on April 9, 2003.[21] In the chaotic days after Hussein's ousting, frustrated Iraqis and foreign extremists stoked tensions and violence against US forces and between the nation's Sunnis and Shia that no one—not the remaining Iraqi government, the American military, or its civilian advisors like O'Sullivan—appeared capable of stopping. The spiraling violence soon took another casualty: O'Sullivan and her team's reconstruction and humanitarian mission was impossible to do safely.

In the face of the developing chaos, unprepared teams in Washington and Baghdad, including some of Rice's NSC staffers working in the Iraqi theater, struggled to rewrite a postwar strategy on the fly as sectarian violence broke out. Although O'Sullivan had done field research amid Sri Lanka's civil war and helped Democratic US senator Daniel Patrick Moynihan write a book on ethnic conflict, she was still excluded by more conservative members of the American team working on the war. For a while, O'Sullivan had little to do but help fuel convoys and then wander around the US headquarters in Baghdad looking for a way into the action.[22]

The White House eventually sent help to Baghdad in L. Paul Bremer III, the head of the Coalition Provisional Authority (CPA). Bremer had worked for then–secretary of state Kissinger and later watched, from his position as the State Department's executive secretary, the dysfunction of Reagan's National Security Council. Reflecting the lessons he learned in both assignments, Bremer brought to Baghdad a direct line to the White House, which was approved despite objections from Rumsfeld, and a seven-step plan for aggressively building the Iraqi government, political system, and security forces.[23]

The establishment of the CPA also brought changes for O'Sullivan, who, after being discovered by a member of Bremer's team, decided to stay on in Iraq.[24] There she watched the envoy make fateful decisions to ban nearly all of Hussein's Ba'ath Party members from the new government and to disband the Iraqi army.[25] As violence rose in the aftermath of these orders, Iraqi security forces struggled to respond, and American troops were left picking up the slack. O'Sullivan, meanwhile, found herself assigned to helping reboot the Iraqi government and write its new constitution amid deepening violence.[26]

A "Camouflage Plan B"

With Iraq in chaos, Rice made some changes to how Washington, and the White House, were managing the war. In light of Bremer's direct line to Bush, the national security advisor decided to further strengthen the wartime NSC, which had also begun to grow in size. Rice hired Robert Blackwill, who had served as an ambassador to India and had been her boss on the first Bush administration's NSC. Though known to be a "bull in a china shop," Blackwill was hired in 2003 in part because the national security advisor believed he could ensure the staff "had a voice" in the contentious postwar interagency debates and decisions.[27]

With that voice, the NSC staff began to more strongly assert themselves. Rice later wrote that the NSC staff "should intervene when there is a policy disagreement among the departments or when they cannot coordinate among themselves."[28] In October 2003, as the team in Baghdad struggled and the agencies in Washington bickered, the national security advisor tasked Blackwill and the NSC with intervening and developing a "camouflage plan B," to be used should the existing strategy finally be deemed a failure.[29] But when the camouflaging failed, and word of the plot leaked, both Rumsfeld at the Pentagon and Bremer in Iraq complained, and the White House's initiative fizzled.

Far from agreeing on a new plan, the Bush team could not even agree on the problem. In mid-November one CIA briefer told Bush and the NSC principals, "We are seeing the establishment of an insurgency in Iraq." To which Rumsfeld inquired, "Why do you call it an insurgency?" Even though Bremer agreed with the briefing, the president cautioned against the term. Bush said: "I don't want to read in *The New York Times* that we are facing an insurgency. I don't want anyone in the cabinet to say it is an insurgency. I don't think we are there yet."[30]

The debate about the term *insurgency* betrayed several deeply held, if rarely voiced, concerns in those days, as the pretext for the US invasion of Iraq fell away when the United States did not find the ostensible Iraqi stores of weapons of mass destruction. Bush was right to worry about the term since its use would churn up bad and bloody memories, around the Situation Room table and the country, of America's past encounters with insurgencies, especially in Vietnam. Such a comparison was particularly worrying as more and more Americans were coming to see the war as a mistake.[31]

At the Pentagon, an insurgency was a particularly unwelcome development. After Vietnam, the more traditional parts of the Defense Department had tried to ignore and avoid counterinsurgency at all costs, preparing and innovating for bigger fights like a potential hot war with the Soviet Union and then other nations. That did not mean there was no one thinking about insurgencies, it is just that most in the Defense Department assumed, as the saying around the Pentagon went, "if you can lick the cat, you can lick the kitten."[32] If the military could win a big war, it could surely win the small ones too.

Since the Gulf War and the Balkans, the United States looked as if it could win any war. With the revolution in military affairs, the Defense Department had relied on technology and superior firepower to keep its fights, like those in Bosnia, at arms' length, its engagements quick, and casualties low. The US military had purposefully gone to Iraq with a small force and a plan to get out hastily lest the United States be seen as occupiers. The Defense Department did not have the people or the plans needed for counterinsurgency, which promised a much longer, more expensive, and deadlier fight.

The semantic debate also demonstrated how differently the war looked from the Situation Room. For O'Sullivan, the reality of the insurgency had already hit her home-away-from-home. Baghdad's Hotel al-Rashid, where she and many coalition officials lived, was struck by a rocket attack that left one American soldier dead and more than a dozen people injured. The assault, another of O'Sullivan's brushes with the burgeoning violence in Iraq, left her stranded in a room when debris blocked the door. O'Sullivan had to escape by crawling out a tenth-floor window and along the ledge to safety.[33]

Back in Washington, two members of the NSC worried about the disconnect. Franklin Miller, who had served in the Pentagon for twenty-two years, and Marty Sullivan, a Marine colonel detailed to the Executive Office Building, had become convinced that the military and diplomatic teams in Baghdad were not giving the White House, and the commander in chief, the full story quickly enough.[34] To try and keep up with those in the war zones, more of the staff gained access to the Defense Department's classified email system.

Even if it required going around the Pentagon leadership or chain of command, Rice encouraged them to use their email and other channels, whether around Washington or in Iraq, to get Bush a better picture of the situation on the ground.

"End the Insurgency"

On June 28, 2004, Rice wrote her own piece of intelligence to the president. During an international conference, she handed Bush a slip of paper that read, "Mr. President, Iraq is sovereign." At the top, Bush handwrote, "Let freedom reign!"[35] The transfer of sovereignty in Iraq brought about changes to the American team in Baghdad. As the CPA was shuttered and Bremer returned home, John Negroponte, a seasoned diplomat and well-connected veteran of the Reagan NSC, became US ambassador in Iraq, and Army General George Casey was named commander of Multi-National Force–Iraq (MNF-I).

After fifteen months in Iraq, O'Sullivan's life changed as well: she joined Blackwill's NSC team in July 2004. Tired from being in country but not tired of working the war, O'Sullivan, age thirty-four, was named senior director for strategic planning and Southwest Asia. In her office on the second floor of the Executive Office Building, itself a sign of how large the staff was growing to meet war's demands, O'Sullivan also continued the efforts to get Rice and the president the best information available on the war.

The result was a nightly memorandum, often called the "POTUS Iraq Note." Written by O'Sullivan and other NSC senior directors and directors without review, or approval, by the Defense and State Departments, the classified briefings, which contained top secret and sensitive compartmented information, were meant to give Bush a nightly unfiltered digest of intelligence from the frontlines.[36] The report was due by the end of the business day and allowed to be no longer than four pages. The president read the notes in the morning and often followed up with O'Sullivan and other NSC writers with additional questions and requests for data.[37]

A few months after O'Sullivan's arrival, Blackwill, Rice's bull in the china shop, resigned unexpectedly after being accused of abusing a US Embassy employee in Kuwait—a charge he denied.[38] With his departure, O'Sullivan, whom Bush liked because, according to White House colleagues, she was "succinct, unpretentious, full of facts and cheerful," became the president's point person on the war.[39] O'Sullivan had also spent time on the ground in Iraq and kept in touch with an operational network of Iraqis, which allowed Bush to pepper her with questions: "What are you hearing from people in Baghdad? What's it like in Baghdad? What are people's daily lives like?"[40]

More than on-the-ground knowledge, the new staffer brought a mission to the Executive Office Building. She believed that simply "chasing paper was not my real job."[41] Instead, for much of O'Sullivan's time at the NSC, the staffer kept a simple reminder of her bigger purpose: a Post-it note stuck to her computer read simply, "End the insurgency."[42] At the time of O'Sullivan's arrival at the Executive Office Building, one military analysis said the 8,000-to 12,000-strong insurgency was "stronger than it was nine months ago," as a violent cycle of attacks and reprisals played out between sectarian groups in neighborhoods throughout the Iraqi capital and towns across the country.[43]

Most in Washington and Baghdad hoped that as the Iraqi political process matured enough to provide an outlet for sectarian disagreements, the violence would eventually ebb. Until then, US and coalition militaries planned to hold the line, attempt to contain the violence, and train the Iraqi security forces to be able to handle the job themselves.[44] Bush and his team viewed the Iraqi elections, three of which were scheduled for 2005, as critical to progress in the country, and Bush sent in additional American troops, in small surges, to provide security for voters going to the polls.[45]

Despite growing American public concerns about the Iraq War, Bush himself was reelected at the end of 2004, and for his second term, the president brought on a second team. Powell left government for the last time, and Rice was named secretary of state, completing a career climb that began on the NSC staff in 1989. Even with the change, the philosophical and personal disagreements between her and Rumsfeld, and to some extent Cheney, persisted. Those testy relationships were left to Hadley, the new national security advisor, to manage.

Hadley, who gave the first-term staff a "B" for policy planning but a "D-minus" for execution of the president's decisions, sought to strengthen the NSC.[46] To improve its grades on the wars in particular, the new national security advisor recruited staffers who, like him, had deeper relationships with Rumsfeld and the Pentagon. J. D. Crouch, an assistant secretary of defense in the first term, was named Hadley's deputy, while another Rumsfeld associate and a former naval aviator, William Luti, became senior director for defense policy and strategy.

To focus on the president's priorities, Hadley created another level of deputy national security advisors, who outranked senior directors but still reported to his main deputy Crouch, to manage presidential priorities, including the war on terror. O'Sullivan was promoted to special assistant to the president and deputy national security advisor for Iraq and Afghanistan, and her seven-person team included many of the staffers working the economic, diplomatic, and military portfolios on the conflicts.

Hadley also established a new directorate for long-term Strategic Planning and Institutional Reform under Peter Feaver, a Duke University professor and former Clinton NSC staffer. He was charged in part with thinking about the policy legacy the president would leave at the end of his term.[47] Feaver explained that the "typical NSC operation was shooting at the zappers in the wire, after they had already reached the walls," but he and his team were to focus the zappers, or problems, still way out on the horizon.[48]

"False High"

Several months into 2005, Feaver caught sight of one of the first-term NSC innovations. The Iraq team had begun to track US strategic progress, or lack thereof, in Iraq on a spreadsheet using color codes (red, amber, and green) for progress on various objectives so that the chart looked like a rainbow.[49] Yet as the year dragged on, one chart of the number of attacks in Iraq, which had risen in the spring and summer, took on greater weight for many on the Bush team, including O'Sullivan, whose night notes contained the number, and Hadley, who kept a copy in a folder for his meetings with the president.[50]

Despite increasing violence on the chart in 2005, the US military remained committed to withdrawing troops and transitioning responsibility to Iraq's security forces, which still could not control all the country's provinces.[51] The plan reflected a belief at the highest levels of the Pentagon that the US military's presence, which most Iraqis opposed (82 percent in one poll), inspired the violence.[52] More than simply rousing opposition, military leaders were also convinced that the performance of American troops was delaying the development of Iraqi forces. To Rumsfeld, the time would come, and soon, for the United States to take its "hand off the Iraqi bicycle seat."[53]

Many in Washington, including Hadley and O'Sullivan, hated the paternalistic analogy.[54] After all, they, the president, and many others on the NSC and at the State Department believed in what Bush himself had said in June 2005, "As the Iraqis stand up, we will stand down."[55] More than simply a rhetorical and even philosophical difference, members of the NSC saw the sequencing as a critical difference in strategy. They believed the United States had to leave eventually, but with Iraqi forces and government so fragile, it was imprudent to take on too much risk too early because Iraq might never recover if the handoff did not work.

Still, for much of 2005 and even into the next year, this difference of opinion and discussions about strategy in general were stifled by the personal and bureaucratic disagreements that had hampered the Bush team from the start, as well as a more fundamental question of just who should call the shots in war. After Rice suggested an alternative strategy for Iraq in a speech in the fall, Rumsfeld publicly spiked the idea and complained privately to Hadley about the strategic meddling.[56] The defense secretary wrote, "Please ask someone [to] figure out where it is coming from, who is doing it, why they are doing it, and ask them to stop."[57]

As the national security advisor knew well, this was not a new concern for Rumsfeld. Earlier in the year, Hadley and O'Sullivan had themselves been taught a hard lesson about pushing the Pentagon. In the face of violence and continued struggles in Iraq, they had asked a young army lieutenant colonel detailed to the staff for "some ideas of how the military could do some things differently."[58] After the staffer worked for a while, the national security advisor asked the president's permission to share the results with the Pentagon.

When Bush agreed, Hadley called Rumsfeld and said: "Don, I know that we don't do military planning at the NSC, and nobody wants to do that, but we've got some smart people over here and they've got some ideas. Can I bring them over and give a briefing to you?" When Hadley and O'Sullivan, who had been pushing for strategic changes, went to the session, the national security advisor recalled it felt like they had walked "into a freezer." According to his recollection, Rumsfeld said, "If you don't think we can do military planning over here and you don't like what you're getting, then get a different secretary of defense and get a different Joint Staff."[59]

In 2005, however, the most significant impediment to change was that for every bad day in the NSC's Iraq note, every red light on its tracker, and every uptick in the chart of attacks, there was just enough progress, especially toward the end of the year, to suggest, as one American military analysis from the time concluded, that there were "clear grounds for optimism."[60] The December 15 general election, with low violence and nearly 70 percent turnout from all sects in the country, set the stage for a permanent Iraq government.[61] At the end of 2005, it looked to Bush as though the strategy was working.[62]

"Meghan, Um, Where's the President?"

Those hopes turned out to be, the US commander in Iraq later said, a "false high."[63] On February 22, 2006, the golden dome of the al-Askari Mosque in Samarra, one of the holiest sites in Shia Islam, was bombed. In the aftermath of the attack, as violence swelled, O'Sullivan and one of her directors, Brett McGurk, a Columbia-educated lawyer who had clerked on the Supreme Court and served as a civilian legal advisor at the US Embassy in Baghdad, explained in their nightly notes that some in Iraq were talking openly of civil war.[64]

At one point, Bush asked O'Sullivan, "How are your friends in Iraq?" The NSC staffer replied, "They're scared, they're terrified, they've never been more fearful, and they've never been more pessimistic."[65] The president's public optimism—at one point he told Americans in a radio address, "Our strategy is getting results"—contrasted sharply with private thoughts of the military and his staff.[66] In the face of the staggering violence, the US military pushed to take their hands off the bicycle seat and start withdrawing troops: one commander in the region said privately, "We need to get the fuck out."[67] Meanwhile, O'Sullivan was one of the "loudest internal critics" of the race to transition, according to an NSC colleague.[68]

In the early part of 2006, O'Sullivan traveled to Baghdad to help form the Iraqi government, a process that had stalled amid the violence, and later recalled that nearly every one of her meetings was "interrupted or punctuated by some security problem."[69] With everyone so scared, no one could focus on the conversations, let alone the compromises required to govern. Returning to the Executive Office Building and the Post-it note reminder on her computer about the insurgency, she became convinced the delay in political progress was not causing security to deteriorate, but fighting was trumping politicking as frightened Iraqis chose to settle their differences in the streets.

Those at the NSC were not the only ones trying to figure out what to do in Iraq. In fact, the war had become the subject of a robust round of introspection by the US foreign policy establishment. At think tanks and policy conferences, and in private conversations across Washington, those who had served in Iraq and just about everyone else appeared to have an opinion about what should be done in the war, and their advice spanned partisan affiliations and strategic persuasions. Congress had even established a ten-person "Iraq Study Group," composed of former government officials, including a couple of former NSC staffers, to make recommendations on a path forward.

In the military, the Iraq War was an obsession, particularly among junior officers who had been serving in combat since the attacks of September 11, 2001. To try and understand the fight they faced, these service members were devouring the classics, like the writings of Prussian theorist Carl von Clausewitz, as well as the Middle East canon, including T. E. Lawrence's *Seven Pillars of Wisdom*. Insurgency literature was in particular demand: dog-eared books and annotated articles were shared from the Pentagon's E-ring to Baghdad's Green Zone.

Since Vietnam, as counterinsurgency was mostly ignored by much of the Pentagon, a dedicated group of defense scholars and thinkers had studied and written about the strategy. As the war entered its third year, the so-called "coinistas," who focused on counterinsurgency (known as COIN in military conversations), were gaining credibility in military circles. Few had a higher profile than Army Lieutenant General David Petraeus, a West Point graduate and Princeton PhD. After leading a campaign in Iraq earlier in the war and getting to know O'Sullivan when their paths crossed in Baghdad, he was assigned in 2005 to write a new army counterinsurgency field manual.

Of course, the coinistas were not just reading and writing about counterinsurgency; some were trying it out in Iraq. In 2005, Army Colonel H. R. McMaster, a PhD who had written a well-reviewed book on Vietnam, deployed with the Third Armored Cavalry Regiment to clear insurgents out of Tal Afar, a town in northern Iraq. Using many classic counterinsurgency tactics, like emphasizing foot patrols and establishing bases throughout the city to develop relationships with the local population, McMaster and his unit slowly turned many local leaders against the insurgents and produced security and governance gains in the city.[70] Eventually, President Bush promoted the campaign as one sign of progress in the war in his speeches.[71]

Still, as the violence worsened elsewhere in the country in 2006, O'Sullivan and her NSC colleagues, with Hadley's support, tried to restart the strategic conversation in government.[72] In mid-June, the NSC and national security advisor arranged two days of meetings for Bush and his advisors at Camp David to review the latest campaign plan and the steps ahead. Although the first day's schedule included what a staffer called an "unusual session," one in which the NSC staff brought outside voices from think tanks and universities to debate the current strategy in front of the president, Bush had muted the deliberations by pronouncing early in the day that the existing plan needed more time to work.[73]

Disappointed that the president's pronouncement had stalled the discussion, O'Sullivan held out hope for more introspection during the review's second day. Before it began, she called McGurk at the White House to discuss the program; but during the conversation, he glanced at the television and found a live broadcast of Bush arriving in Iraq. McGurk asked, "Meghan, um, where's the president?" O'Sullivan, who was at Camp David, replied: "He's here. We're about to get started." McGurk then said, "He just landed in Baghdad." A shocked O'Sullivan replied, "What?"[74]

"8,000-Mile Screwdriver"

Unbeknownst to his NSC staffer, Bush had flown to meet with the new Iraqi prime minister Nouri al-Maliki, who had managed to form a government, and reaffirm his commitment to Casey's military transition plan. Despite the concerns over rising violence in Iraq and the NSC's efforts to open up the debate in Washington, O'Sullivan's conference had turned into a "PR session," as she called it.[75] The president and the rest of the team had made, according to Feaver, a "renewed commitment to plan A."[76]

Although frustrated, O'Sullivan and others on the NSC decided to test plan A's underlying assumptions, which seemed increasingly mismatched with events in Iraq. After a visit to Baghdad, McGurk wrote O'Sullivan a trip report in which he called for a radical strategic shift "to match the facts as we find them" and delay Casey's planned troop withdrawals.[77] Because the national security advisor, worried about leaks, preferred that the NSC limit the sensitive analysis committed to paper, O'Sullivan, who had herself earlier written to Bush and Hadley about the need to change the strategy, asked McGurk to tone down his memo and sent the new draft to Hadley.[78]

The national security advisor was also concerned with the sense of drift in Washington and the feeling that events there as well as in Iraq were spiraling out of control, but he was hesitant about another review. On policy grounds, he thought the Iraqi security forces, not the US military as O'Sullivan believed, would be a better arbiter amid sectarian unrest.[79] Hadley also worried, given the icy reception that met the NSC's previous meddling in the Pentagon's business, that any initiative for a strategic review would be more successful if it came from the military command in Baghdad rather than from the Executive Office Building in Washington.

But the staff did not think there was time to wait. In July, Bush read in one of O'Sullivan's Iraq notes that the violence had "acquired a momentum of its own."[80] In the face of the spiraling bloodshed, the NSC believed the military's commitment to withdrawing troops proved how many assumptions were going unchallenged and questions unasked. Opinions about the same challenge varied so widely, O'Sullivan even suggested in one memorandum that an "additive" strategy, one that increased troops, should be considered.[81]

By July 2006, the national security advisor agreed to ask some hard questions of Rumsfeld, Casey, and US Ambassador to Iraq Zalmay Khalilzad, himself a former NSC staffer from earlier in the administration. Hadley believed that if done right, and taken seriously, the questions could "plant the seed for a full strategy review," according to one account.[82] In all, O'Sullivan and her team drafted and distributed fifty hard questions for a scheduled July 22 video-teleconference that Hadley would lead from the White House.

To those on the other side of the video-teleconference in Baghdad, however, the questions felt like attacks. According to reports, a "flabbergasted" Casey, along with Khalilzad, found the list "demeaning."[83] For the American commander, the interrogation was more evidence Washington was trying to micromanage the war with what he called an "8,000-mile screwdriver." Busy in Baghdad, the general and the ambassador did not even attempt to answer all the inquiries before the meeting.[84]

In mid-August, the National Security Council principals met with the president to discuss the question-and-disappointing-answer session. After being briefed on O'Sullivan's summary of the conversation, Bush chose to keep firing questions at the team in Baghdad, whose responses left the president unconvinced.[85] Demonstrating how much the president's perspective had changed in a few months, Bush said of the Iraqi security forces: "If they can't do it, we will. If the bicycle teeters, we're going to put the hand back on."[86]

As dramatic as the declaration was, at that point it was a difficult commitment for the president to make. At home, more than 50 percent of Americans believed the war had been a mistake and disapproved of the president.[87] For the upcoming congressional elections, scheduled for early November, Democrats were leveraging growing opposition to the war and the commander in chief to try to make significant gains in Congress. Even more, Bush had no plan for how to change course in Iraq, and developing one would not be easy.

"You Better Be Damn Sure"

Autumn 2006 was a difficult moment for an honest conversation about the war. The White House was cautious about divulging internal concerns that the strategy was not working, particularly while troops were in harm's way. At the same time, every congressional candidate, think tank scholar, and member of the vaunted Iraq Study Group, which was slated to share its recommendations publicly after the election, was questioning the current plan.

In addition, even if a better strategy were available, it was unclear that the United States had the manpower to do anything differently. In August, Hadley's deputy, Crouch, had taken a piece of paper and drawn a crude graph illustrating a temporary increase in troops. Speaking with NSC staffer Luti, Crouch admitted he did not know the duration, the size, or the purpose of the increase, but he wanted to know if something like the graph was possible. Based on the already taxed deployment cycles, the Pentagon had told others, including the State Department, there were no additional personnel available; but Luti, as well as some others at the NSC and the Pentagon, believed there were enough troops available in the system.[88]

Although Hadley, who as a member of the Tower Commission had reviewed some of the NSC's worst overreach, still had concerns about the NSC taking the lead on a new plan, in September, he did not have many alternatives. The State Department had only grown more pessimistic since Rumsfeld had pushed back so hard the year before on Rice's strategic proposal; and for the Pentagon leadership and the command in Baghdad, the strategy remained the same: the military leadership was willing to slow the transition down if the president wanted and the situation warranted, but the plan was still to let go of the bicycle seat and get out of Iraq.[89]

With few options in September and the attacks chart in his folder, the national security advisor decided to unleash the NSC on two tracks. He tasked O'Sullivan with assessing whether the prevailing assumptions were still plausible. After "distressingly few" passed muster, according to Feaver, she was encouraged to develop some new strategic options to be presented to Hadley. O'Sullivan was prepared for the assignment: she and her team had been quietly drafting all summer for such a moment or request to arrive.[90]

Meanwhile, Luti was asked, "If you had a clean sheet of paper, what would you do?"[91] After crunching the numbers and the capacity of the US forces, he thought there were enough personnel available to send extra troops to the war. The NSC staffer wrote up a new operational concept called "Changing the Dynamics in Iraq: Surge and Fight" that required up to five more brigades, or 20–25,000 troops, which Luti believed were available for deployment.[92]

O'Sullivan, Luti, and the rest of the NSC were not the only ones trying to figure out the next steps. The Joint Chiefs of Staff recruited some of the military's up-and-coming officers, like McMaster, who had made counterinsurgency a success in Tal Afar, to debate strategy in the post–September 11th wars. The so-called Council of Colonels did not develop many new ideas, but its assessment, "We are losing because we're not winning," would have caused heads to nod in the military's ranks and around Washington, including at some think tanks, like the conservative American Enterprise Institute. There scholars and former policymakers were working on recommendations for a surge in Iraq.[93]

On October 21, 2006, O'Sullivan and her team presented Hadley with a memorandum on "The Way Forward." Betraying the title, the staffer outlined four different paths: (1) adjusting "at the margins"; (2) focusing on counter-

ing al-Qaeda and other terrorist entities; (3) supporting the new Iraqi government; (4) and, doubling down, which required an infusion of 30,000 additional
American troops. O'Sullivan did not make a formal recommendation in what
was a first cut at an options memorandum; but she wrote that "double down"
ensured the "highest likelihood of security success as we have defined it."[94]

After the national security advisor was briefed on the paper, Hadley told
the NSC team to work through the problem again. When O'Sullivan suggested
they had already done the work, Hadley snapped: "Hey, guys! Do you get it?
This is it! You want the president of the United States to send more Americans
into Iraq, betting everything on it. . . . You better be damn sure." Hadley continued: "I'm the one in the Oval with the recommendation. So you better be
sure." O'Sullivan replied: "We're sure. We understand, and we're sure." To
which Hadley said: "You better be damn sure. Go back to the table and run
the analysis again."[95]

The "Hardest and Worst Memo I Ever Wrote"

Although many of the NSC had never heard Hadley curse before, the outburst
was a sign of the immensity of the challenge in Iraq, where more than 5,500
attacks occurred in October, and the stress in Washington, where Democrats
took control of both houses of Congress in November 7th elections that Bush
himself called a "thumping."[96] The next day, the president announced he was
replacing Rumsfeld with former NSC staffer Bob Gates, who had become the
president of Texas A&M University after serving as deputy national security
advisor and then CIA director in the first Bush administration.

Two days later, George W. Bush met with Cheney, Rumsfeld—who
stayed on while Gates prepared for his upcoming congressional confirmation
hearing—and the rest of the National Security Council principals to announce
a formal Iraq review to be headed by Crouch and include O'Sullivan, Luti, and
representatives from the various departments with a role in the war. As the
review began, each of its participants was given a copy of O'Sullivan's "Way
Forward" memorandum with instructions from Hadley explaining that her
alternatives could be augmented or combined, but that a surge option had to
be included in the review's final product.[97]

Any potential surge, however, required troops. Despite what Luti was hearing about availability, the Pentagon's leadership continued to tell a different story. At one of the first sessions Crouch hosted, Army Lieutenant General Douglas Lute, the Joint Staff representative to the review, was asked directly if the military could add five brigades as suggested by the NSC plans. When Lute said no, echoing what the military had told others earlier in the fall, McGurk pushed back. Lute replied: "You could do it. You just won't have an American Army left. So, you know, it's kind of up to you."[98]

Apart from the formal review, Hadley worked to convince the military brass, particularly the chairman of the Joint Chiefs of Staff, Marine General Peter Pace, to not just be open to a potential surge but to propose one themselves.[99] When the national security advisor shared Luti's surge concept with Pace, the national security advisor, who remembered Rumsfeld's previous rebuff, said, the "last time I tried to do anything like this, I got my head handed to me by the secretary of defense."[100] Pace was far more open to reviewing the plan, and eventually asked the other military chiefs whether a surge was a good idea.[101]

At the time, the military was of many minds about the value of additional troops in Iraq. There were supporters, including a few retired general officers who were pushing hard publicly and behind the scenes for more troops and a shift to a counterinsurgency strategy.[102] In Iraq, Casey, who had not participated in the review even though he was commander of US forces, found the 30,000-troop proposal excessive and suggested a smaller increase.[103] Meanwhile, Pace and some others could not figure out what more a relatively small addition of troops (whether Casey's or the NSC's proposal) would be able to do compared with the 140,000 Americans already in Iraq.[104]

The most concerned, however, were those at the Pentagon who worried about the surge's impact on the military's ability to handle other threats. At one of the Joint Chiefs' discussions of the surge, the army chief of staff reportedly said, "This is not just about Iraq!"[105] For one thing, 20,000 American personnel were still in Afghanistan, which was in better shape than Iraq but fragile, and others were combating terrorism elsewhere.[106] In order for the Defense Department to meet the personnel demands of the surge proposal, some of its other missions in Europe, the Asia-Pacific, and even Afghanistan would surely suffer.

In late November, Bush called a meeting to discuss the result of the strategy review. Before the session, Hadley had asked O'Sullivan to summarize the group's discussions in a memo to be titled "emerging consensus," but there was no such thing. Although the NSC supported a surge and a shift to a full counterinsurgency strategy, State's representatives preferred one of them, the fallback option of selective counterinsurgency, while the Pentagon again proposed transitioning responsibility to Iraqi security forces in 2007.[107]

O'Sullivan admitted later that the consensus summary was the "hardest and worst memo I ever wrote."[108] Even more than the bad briefing, Bush, who said at the time he was "inclined to believe that we do need to increase our troops," had to confront several additional hurdles to the surge.[109] At home, the American people had turned against the war, while in Iraq, the government was not yet supportive of another influx of American troops.[110] Around the Situation Room table, the National Security Council was split, with Cheney and Hadley actively pushing for the surge, but both Rice, to the frustration of the president, and the soon-to-be Pentagon chief Gates remained cautious.[111]

"Not Alone"

At the end of 2006, just as the 3,000th American service member died in the war, Bush decided he was going to send the 30,000-troop surge to Iraq.[112] The number alone made headlines when the president announced it in a speech to the nation on January 10, 2007; but the surge's objective (security of Iraqis) and comprehensive strategy (counterinsurgency, with support for political and economic development), were perhaps the bigger news. The significance of the change in course was reinforced by Bush's selection of Petraeus as the new commander in Iraq.[113]

The assignment confirmed that the US military's coinistas were ascendant. The surge was an opportunity for those who believed in the potential of counterinsurgency to demonstrate its value, in theory, in Iraq, and in the broader war against terrorism. As such, Bush's decision was a boon to the COIN cottage industry growing in Washington and military circles, though more often than not the military part of counterinsurgency got celebrated instead of its diplomatic and economic components.

Another group of warriors were rising at the White House. Hadley and the NSC had fought to provide Bush the opportunity to make the decision and to ensure the president knew, as O'Sullivan told him in the Oval Office before the surge speech, that he was "not alone."[114] The national security advisor had orchestrated a full-court press on the Joint Chiefs of Staff, including a presidential visit to the Pentagon, to bring the military on board. After developing the surge concept, the staff had stood firm for the choice, working in Baghdad to convince the Iraqi prime minister to accept the additional troops and in Washington to kill less ambitious ideas proposed over the course of the month.

Bush's decisions did not immediately change much on the ground. The violence continued in Iraq: there were 4,000 attacks per month through the winter and spring, and 126 Americans were killed in May 2007 alone.[115] The lag in success worried some in Washington, including a few White House staffers who started asking about back-up options, and some in the new Democratic Congress, like US Senator Harry Reid of Nevada, who said, "This war is lost and the surge is not accomplishing anything."[116] By September, however, the violence had ebbed, with Iraqi civilian deaths declining by 70 percent in Baghdad and 45 percent across Iraq.[117]

The progress was the result of several factors. The additional troops and Petraeus's new strategy did help measurably improve security, especially in Baghdad. Still, the surge, as one of its close observers recalled, may have had more of a "psychological impact than an actual physical impact."[118] Even before Bush's decisions, Iraqis began to step up in some of the most dangerous parts of the country like Anbar Province, taking responsibility for their neighborhoods, siding with US and Iraqi forces, and confronting extremist elements. Overall, as envisioned by O'Sullivan and others on the NSC staff, when Iraqi security improved, the nation's government and political processes began to function better.

Yet despite the gains, the worries about the investment of troops in Iraq grew less acute but no less profound. When Bush traveled to the Joint Chiefs' tank at the Pentagon in December before his final decision, he was warned the additional deployment could "break" the army.[119] The president, and others on the team, were convinced a loss and retreat from Iraq would be worse for the army and the rest of the military, and thus the surge was worth the risk. However, when considering the investment in light of the inattention to the war in Afghanistan, where the United States was losing the initiative, the Iraq surge was not the success some have made it out to be.

Completed in 1888 as the State, War, and Navy Building, the now Eisenhower Executive Office Building is home to the National Security Council staff. But the office still shows its warrior past: the cannon, one of two guarding the building's Pennsylvania Avenue Entrance, was captured during the Spanish-American War. *Courtesy of John Gans*

The National Security Council staff offices are distinguished by simple nameplates along the checkered hallway of the Executive Office Building's third floor. *Courtesy of John Gans*

"The Men Who Guard the Nation's Security" was the headline when this photo of an early National Security Council meeting ran in a 1947 issue of the *New York Times*. The first NSC executive secretary, Sidney Souers, is seated third from left; President Harry Truman is seated second from right; and the first secretary of defense, James Forrestal, is fourth from right. *National Park Service, Abbie Rowe, courtesy of Harry S. Truman Library*

The first national security advisor—Robert Cutler, a Republican lawyer—takes the oath of office for another assignment in February 1960 as President Dwight D. Eisenhower looks on. *National Park Service, courtesy of the Eisenhower Presidential Library*

Kennedy White House aides, including National Security Advisor McGeorge Bundy, far right, and NSC staffer Bromley Smith, second from right, pose for a portrait in 1963 along the White House colonnade near the Oval Office. *Robert Knudsen, White House Photographs, courtesy of John F. Kennedy Presidential Library and Museum*

One of the "bright young men" on the NSC, staffer Michael Forrestal, meets with President Lyndon Johnson, on right, in 1964. *Cecil Stoughton, courtesy of Lyndon B. Johnson Library*

The "center of the foreign policy universe in America": National Security Advisor Henry Kissinger, leaning on chair, meets in the White House Cabinet Room with President Richard Nixon, seated; Al Haig, first from right; and other members of the NSC in February 1970. Staffer Anthony Lake, sixth from right among those behind the table, resigned in protest a few months after this picture was taken. *Courtesy of the Richard Nixon Presidential Library and Museum*

Former staffer Mort Halperin, one of the accomplices in Kissinger's "coup d'état at the Hotel Pierre," is pictured in 1976 after suing over the wiretap on his home telephone line. *Bettman / contributor / Getty Images*

The "best we could do": Reagan NSC staffers Phil Dur, left, and Howard Teicher, center, speak in the White House Cabinet Room with Chairman of the Joint Chiefs of Staff General Jack Vessey during a heated meeting on Lebanon in September 1983. *Courtesy of the Ronald Reagan Library*

Back in his Navy dress blues, Dur, right, receives a gift from National Security Advisor Robert "Bud" McFarlane in November 1984 after departing the White House and the NSC staff. *Courtesy of the Ronald Reagan Library*

Below: NSC staffer Richard Haass, in borrowed blazer, stands next to President George H. W. Bush as he meets with reporters on the White House South Lawn and declares Iraq's invasion of Kuwait "will not stand" in August 1990. *Courtesy of the George Bush Presidential Library and Museum*

Bush meets with some of the "reluctant generals" at Camp David in August 1990, joined by National Security Advisor Brent Scowcroft, second from right; Chairman of the Joint Chiefs of Staff General Colin Powell, third from right; and others. Haass is at the table, fifth from right. *Courtesy of the George Bush Presidential Library and Museum*

Alexander "Sandy" Vershbow, who as an NSC staffer helped President Bill Clinton find an "endgame" in the Bosnian War, is pictured as a US ambassador in 2006. *US State Department*

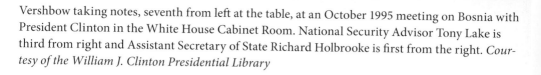

Vershbow taking notes, seventh from left at the table, at an October 1995 meeting on Bosnia with President Clinton in the White House Cabinet Room. National Security Advisor Tony Lake is third from right and Assistant Secretary of State Richard Holbrooke is first from the right. *Courtesy of the William J. Clinton Presidential Library*

NSC staffer Meghan O'Sullivan, one member of President George W. Bush's "personal band of warriors," in the Oval Office in May 2007. *Dennis Brack-Pool / Getty Images*

O'Sullivan along with National Security Advisor Stephen Hadley, center; Deputy National Security Advisor J. D. Crouch, second from left; and Vice President Dick Cheney, left, listen as Bush makes an announcement about Iraq from the White House Rose Garden in June 2006. *Brendan Smialowski / AFP / Getty Images*

Army Lieutenant General Douglas Lute testifies before the Senate Armed Services Committee in June 2007 on his nomination to become the "war czar" on Bush's NSC staff. *Saul Loeb / AFP / Getty Images*

Lute, first from right, tells President Barack Obama the proposed Afghanistan surge "still smells to me like a gamble" in late November 2009. The meeting includes several other members of the NSC, including John Tien, fifth from right; Denis McDonough, third from right; and Ben Rhodes, fourth from left. *Courtesy of Pete Souza, the White House*

At his Mar-a-Lago resort in Florida, President Donald Trump meets in April 2017 with members of the National Security Council, along with National Security Advisor H. R. McMaster, second to Trump's right at the table, and political advisor Steve Bannon, fifth from right along the back bench with some NSC staffers. *Shealah Craighead*

In Washington, the decision on the surge was ultimately a product of the strategic meddling and the 8,000-mile screwdriver that Rumsfeld, Casey, and others in the military had bemoaned. Bush and Hadley, however reluctantly, had to shed their previous preference for delegating strategy to the military leadership and decide to be more hands-on. For White House war management to work, the common law was a real burden. O'Sullivan, one of those the president called a "warrior," along with a whole band of warriors on a "wartime NSC," had spent time in Iraq trying to turn the mess around, advocated for a change of course, and written the type of operational plans that were a rarity earlier in the staff's history.

"Meghan-ize the Problem"

Many in Washington and Baghdad noticed the NSC's evolution—and few outside the White House liked it. Some of the displeasure is hard to distinguish from the personal and bureaucratic disagreements that plagued the Bush team from the beginning. It is no surprise that wars, especially ones going badly, would exacerbate preexisting tensions. Still the administration's dysfunction provided not just a motive but an opportunity for the NSC to intervene even as it set off a pernicious cycle, where disagreement led to indecision and then drift, which the staff felt compelled to fix—but their involvement only set off another round of frustration.

In addition, the wartime NSC was clearly operating outside Washington common law not just with its advocacy for the surge but also its prominent role on the ground in warzones. As part of the war on terror, the US government, particularly the military and intelligence agencies, had operations going in every corner of the world, most notably Afghanistan and Iraq. The NSC staff was charged with coordinating and developing policy for a more operational government and, perhaps most important, an increasingly operational president, which Hadley explains should be expected of a wartime staff.[120] None of that, the national security advisor contends, made the NSC "operational" in the way of Iran-Contra since it was not running operations out of the White House.

But the staff was doing more than simple coordination. Bush's warriors, including O'Sullivan, had by the time of the surge decision spent weeks in Iraq as a staffer, not just observing but trying to help turn the war around. They were pulling intelligence through separate channels up to the Executive Office Buildings for notes and briefings that were only shared with the president and not reviewed by anyone outside the White House. And they not only developed a military plan but advocated for a surge that was opposed by the military.

The resistance to the NSC and O'Sullivan in particular was also deeply personal. Such is the nature of Washington staffing, where the people behind the principal often take the flak about decisions and process, especially when both are unpopular. But the judgmental nature of many of the complaints about O'Sullivan's youth, supposed naiveté, and lack of military experience—some on the American team in Iraq suggested anyone who tried to simplify the disorder there was trying to "Meghan-ize the problem"—suggest that something else was driving the discontent with Bush's staffer.[121]

More than a few people appear uncomfortable with a young woman questioning professional warriors about the direction of a war. In 2004, when O'Sullivan arrived at the Executive Office Building, the Situation Room remained a relative boys' club. When she took over as the NSC lead on the wars, she was one of only a few women serving as senior directors among nearly twenty directorates.[122] With Bush's leadership, Rice, O'Sullivan, and others helped change that, but it was not always easy on them or their reputations.

"Increased, Focused, Full-Time, Real-Time Support"

After more than five years in government, including fifteen months in Iraq and more than two-and-a-half years on the fast track at the White House, O'Sullivan decided after the surge speech in January 2007 that she did not have the energy to give Bush or the war the effort required until the end of the administration. O'Sullivan, exhausted after fighting for Iraq and for the president, told Bush that it was time for her to move on.[123]

Even though O'Sullivan was departing, the president and the national security advisor still wanted a warrior at the NSC. With Hadley busy addressing issues and crises in the rest of the world, the national security advisor proposed hiring someone to oversee the wars. The decision reflected another attempt to improve on the poor grade he had given the first-term NSC on ensuring policy implementation. Washington soon became abuzz with recruitment of a new "war czar," as many took to calling the position, to serve as the president's go-to person responsible for the Iraq surge and the war in Afghanistan.[124]

The problem was, no one wanted the job. Three retired military leaders turned it down, with one saying publicly that the White House did not "know where the hell they're going."[125] Eventually a uniformed officer accepted on a direct appeal from the secretary of defense. After Gates "twisted the arm" of Lute, who liked his job and—as he made clear when he joined the NSC's fall 2006 review—disliked the idea of a surge, the army lieutenant general agreed to become the deputy national security advisor and report directly to Bush.[126] With the war czar's arrival and access, the "wartime" NSC, which had grown to almost two hundred staffers working on policy, was further empowered to help a more hands-on president execute the surge.[127]

Regardless of his personal opinion, Lute, who with gray hair, broad shoulders, and intense eyes looked like Hollywood's idea of a war czar, now had to try to help make the surge a success, a job for which there was no real precedent. He explained at the time that his fundamental purposes were to advise the president and ensure that the wars, and those in harm's way, had "increased, focused, full-time, real-time support" in Washington.[128] Although counterinsurgency was the order of the day, it was not always the first priority at a Pentagon that still was preparing, and arming, for classic country-on-country wars.

Such bureaucratic intrigues were one reason that Bush leaned even farther forward after he bet his presidency on the surge and became a far more hands-on manager. Lute helped him do so. He met with the president alone every day at 7:00 a.m. to review the previous twenty-four hours in the wars, and he spent the rest of the day ensuring Bush's orders and the warfighters' needs were met. As a result, Gates believed the new NSC staffer was an "important asset" in the Bush administration, but some at the Pentagon worried about Lute's White House role and military rank, which allowed the NSC staffer to reach deeper into military operations and the chain of command.[129]

In addition to a new war czar, Bush still needed his departing warrior. Although O'Sullivan was rumored to be a candidate for other positions, and even an ambassadorship, the president ordered her to return to Iraq. Petraeus, who thought he could never have enough people like the "brilliant, focused, tireless, and personable" O'Sullivan on his team, had asked for her help as the troops and the plan came online.[130] Though she had left the Executive Office

Building and the computer with her Post-it reminder, O'Sullivan continued to try to "end the insurgency."[131]

The surge did just that, buying time for the Iraqi political process and government to come online. By the time she left Baghdad in September 2007, O'Sullivan had seen the insurgency ebb in real time. Before heading off to a fellowship at Harvard that fall, O'Sullivan turned in her White House badge at the Executive Office Building where her fight for a change of course in Iraq, along with the work of Feaver, McGurk, and others, had established a model for a post–September 11th NSC. The arrival of Lute signaled that a wartime staff, and the frustrations its warriors could inspire, was the new way of Washington.

CHAPTER SEVEN

"When You Work for the President, You Work for the President"

"Giddy Up"

Although most of official Washington was at home the Saturday after Thanksgiving 2009, there was a crowd around President Barack Obama in the Oval Office. The commander in chief had called in his closest advisors, some dressed casually for the holiday weekend, to talk about the war in Afghanistan, which had just entered its eighth year. With the aides seated in a horseshoe around him, Obama asked for opinions on his options as the Taliban's insurgency gained strength and the American military pushed for more troops.

In the discussion about one of the president's first major decisions as commander in chief, only two of the staffers sitting before him had ever served in the US military. Doug Lute, nine years older than the president and with decades of service in the army and more than two years on the NSC, sat to Obama's right, and John Tien, a forty-five-year-old army colonel, combat veteran, and NSC senior director, was a few seats down the line. After they both had said their piece and left Obama with his choice, Lute, knowing the weight of the opportunity to counsel a president, looked at Tien as they returned to their offices and said, "Well, you know, giddy up."[1]

Just a year before, as Lute and Tien were working on the NSC, Obama and his campaign had won the White House during their own insurgency. The young candidate and his campaign had promised to change not just who controlled the White House but also the way of Washington itself, which the candidate and many of his young staff blamed for misleading the nation into an unnecessary war in Iraq. Yet, as he converted from candidate to commander in chief, Obama—needing experienced talent and worrying about unnecessary mistakes—came to rely on a cadre of advisors, including some from President George W. Bush's White House.

Even with that change of perspective, Lute, who grew up in Michigan City, Indiana, was a surprise Bush holdover in Obama's world. Hungry for more than the blue-collar jobs of the industrial Midwest and inspired by the television program *The West Point Story*, which dramatized the real stories of US Military Academy cadets, Lute himself graduated from and later taught at West Point before going on to two decades of army command and staff jobs.[2] After getting his arm twisted into taking the war czar assignment in 2007, Lute was getting ready to leave the White House before being asked to stay on by the new president and his team.

Ten months after Obama first walked into the Oval Office, Lute was sitting there, at his right hand, and offering impassioned advice about what to do in Afghanistan. Lute knew better than most how badly the war there was going, and he had included more Afghanistan content in night notes he wrote for Bush and then Obama. By November 2009, the 67,000 US troops and a relatively small embassy staff looked powerless to stop Afghanistan's downward trajectory as the Taliban and assorted militant groups, including al-Qaeda, grew more emboldened in their attacks and the Afghan government and security forces struggled in response.

As the new president sought to bring some order to the war that would soon be America's longest, Lute earned Obama's trust. Like the wartime staffers before him, the three-star-general-turned-NSC-staffer ensured the young commander in chief had what he needed to make his decisions on the war, including the big one facing him over Thanksgiving weekend. But on the way to the Oval Office that Saturday, Lute's fight had frustrated many of his long-time Pentagon peers and, far worse to many in Washington, set a precedent for the aggressive and hands-on staff that would serve Obama throughout his term, lead to a new round of calls to reform the NSC, and come to serve the unconventional president who followed.

"War Czar"

The vote was one of dozens cast by then–US senator Obama in 2007. After taking charge of Capitol Hill in the 2006 elections, congressional Democrats like the junior senator from Illinois tried everything they could—threatening funding cuts, imposing deadlines, and more—to force a new direction on the unpopular Iraq War and the surge itself. When the Bush White House decided to establish a war czar on the NSC and appoint a serving general officer to the position, Congress, and in particular the Senate Armed Services Committee, had a legal say in the matter.

On Capitol Hill, deference is typically given to the president's picks for the NSC and other White House staff positions, which do not require Senate confirmation, as well as to the Pentagon's plans for the senior officer corps, even if each appointment is subject to congressional approval. The war czar position, however, was too high-profile for a pro forma vetting. In early June 2007, Lute, dressed in his army green uniform, three stars on his shoulders and six rows of campaign and commendation ribbons on his chest, sat in front of his wife, herself a former Clinton NSC staffer, and faced a withering interrogation by the Armed Services Committee.

In the tense hearing, senators of both parties questioned the wisdom of the surge in Iraq and its lack of results at that point. They also took the opportunity to criticize Bush's war management: to some the job for which Lute was being considered felt like either an abdication or a replication of responsibilities held in some way by the president, the national security advisor, the secretary of defense, and the chairman of the Joint Chiefs of Staff. Even US Senator Jack Reed of Rhode Island, a fellow West Point graduate and a friend of Lute, called the war czar position a "devastating critique of the national security apparatus."[3]

Despite the condemnation of the job, Congress deemed Lute qualified for it: Obama joined ninety-three other senators in voting to confirm him.[4] With Congress's blessing, Lute took over O'Sullivan's team and her portfolio on the NSC. But Lute, who wore a business suit to the NSC, did not sit at O'Sullivan's desk in the Executive Office Building; instead he got a West Wing office around the corner from the White House Situation Room.[5] From there, Lute sent the nightly war notes to President Bush and walked up to brief him first thing every morning.[6]

Even with this considerable access, Lute had promised Congress he would not issue orders in the military's chain of command.[7] Regardless, everyone in Washington, Baghdad, and Kabul knew the war czar had a direct line to the president, and Lute liberally gave out his White House business cards and encouraged people to call him personally if there was a problem.[8] As a result, Lute's calls and video-teleconferences on a secure desktop Tandberg system were returned more quickly and his suggestions carried greater authority with commanders, like General David Petraeus in Iraq, and diplomats in Baghdad and Kabul as well as those at the Pentagon and State Department.

Over the last two years of the Bush administration, Lute and his team, which grew to twelve members, prioritized requests from the frontlines, troubleshot presidential orders, and reminded the bureaucracy of the wars Washington sometimes forgot. Defense Secretary Bob Gates, who himself worried the Pentagon bureaucracy did not prioritize the warfighters, felt he owed Lute "big-time" for reluctantly taking the White House post.[9] To the Pentagon chief and others in the military leadership, the war czar was an "important asset" in the Bush administration as the tide slowly started to turn in Iraq, but there were others who took issue with the way he fought in Washington and for whom: some considered him so beholden to those on the frontlines that Lute was sometimes called "Petraeus's guy."[10]

"Holding Action"

Lute, however, had another war to worry about. Even before the war czar arrived at the NSC, Bush's staff had begun warning the president about the deteriorating situation in Afghanistan, where the Taliban, the Sunni Muslim fundamentalists who had hosted Osama bin Laden, and al-Qaeda had been pushed out of power after September 11th.[11] Since then, the Taliban and other militants had been attacking coalition forces and Afghan targets with impunity, aware of what everyone from Washington to the war zones knew: as the chairman of the Joint Chiefs said, "In Afghanistan, we do what we can. In Iraq, we do what we must."[12]

In 2008, the American military could not do very much in Afghanistan.

Lute, and others in the military who had opposed the Iraq surge, had been right about the availability of forces. With any extra troops sent to Iraq, the 31,000 Americans in Afghanistan at the end of the year were fighting a "holding action," in the words of vice chairman of the Joint Chiefs of Staff James Cartwright, a Marine general.[13] According to him, the US military simply did not have the resources, whether it was troops or technology, like the new and deadly predator drones, to "make it much more."[14]

More than manpower and matériel, few in Washington had dedicated much intellectual muscle to Afghanistan. While O'Sullivan and her team had done review after review on Iraq, and General Petraeus and other military thinkers were reinvigorating counterinsurgency scholarship with an eye on that war, Afghanistan had just not received the same level of attention. As important a fight as it remained in the eyes of Americans, whose anger over the September 11th attacks still burned, to many in Washington it felt like an impossible war to manage.[15]

Compared with Iraq, Afghanistan was less modern, more rural, and perhaps even more aggressively resistant to outsiders. No central government in Kabul had ever completely controlled the country's vast territory, and the US-backed regime under President Hamid Karzai was not promising to do so any time soon. Meanwhile, Afghan security forces, about 150,000 strong in 2008 but weakened by sectarian division and corruption, also struggled to hold ground against the resurgent Taliban and the remnants of al-Qaeda leveraging access to and tacit support from Pakistan.[16]

In summer 2008, as Iraq continued to improve, Bush ordered Lute to take a hard look at Afghanistan. To develop, as the staffer called it, a "soup-to-nuts" review of the war as well as a way forward, Lute traveled twice to Afghanistan and met for over forty hours on the fourth floor of the Executive Office Building with NSC colleagues and representatives from all the departments with responsibilities in Afghanistan.[17] The war czar came away believing the United States, along with its NATO allies and Afghan partners, was fighting several different battles in the country, and yet no one seemed to have authority or a plan for the whole war.

Around the time of Obama's victory, Lute put the finishing touches on his twenty-five-page report and delivered it to Bush. Lute told the soon-to-be-former president, "I know this is kind of bad timing, but here it is." The briefing said, "We're not losing, but we're not winning, and that's not good enough," and Lute and the rest of the team saw three core reasons why: Afghan governance was spoiled by corruption, the nation's opium trade was fueling the insurgency, and a Pakistani safe haven allowed the Taliban and al-Qaeda to operate freely.[18]

Although several on the Bush team, including Secretary of State Condoleezza Rice, believed Lute's report was too pessimistic, the president chose to let it serve as a transition document to the incoming administration. It was Obama's, and his team's, war now, and the recommendations for more military, civilian, and economic commitments and decisions—including one on the bulk of an outstanding request for 30,000 additional troops from the US commander in Afghanistan, who wanted the personnel to help secure the Afghan election scheduled for August 2009—were the new president's to make.[19]

"Not on Reason but on Passion"

More than leaving a memorandum and a troop request, Bush also sent his war czar to brief the Obama transition team. When Lute arrived at the Obama team's office in downtown Washington, the NSC staffer found a substantial operation, boosted by new federal support for post–September 11th handovers between administrations.[20] Teams of young staffers and seasoned national security policymakers were hard at work studying the wars and what had become of government since Democrats last held the White House in 2001.

The well-established transition was a long way from the early days of Obama's unlikely path to the White House. In 2002, years after his bleeding-heart battles under then–national security advisor Kissinger and blue sky conversations with then–NSC staffers Sandy Vershbow and Nelson Drew, former NSC staffer and national security advisor Tony Lake was asked after a speech in Chicago to give some advice to Obama, then a state senator. As one phone call led to more, and as Obama's campaign for the US Senate in 2004 led to another for president four years later, Lake encouraged young foreign policy professionals to work for a candidate he believed was the "most talented person I've ever met."[21]

Some came to share Lake's opinion, in part because Obama had been right about the biggest foreign policy decision of the post–Cold War era. In October

2002, Obama rejected the proposed invasion of Iraq, a conflict he said was "based not on reason but on passion, not on principle but on politics."[22] What Obama called the "dumb war" was more than simply Bush's fault, however. The candidate later explained, "The American people weren't just failed by a president—they were failed by much of Washington."[23] The press, the foreign policy establishment, and Congress had not questioned the rush to the war, and to Obama, each deserved a share of the blame.

Many of the young campaign aides now working at the transition offices and preparing to join the White House had been attracted to Obama's rejection of Washington's conventional wisdom. Denis McDonough, who grew up in a big family in small-town Minnesota, had worked his way up on Capitol Hill, becoming a foreign policy advisor to a Democratic leader before the September 11th attacks. In the years after that day, the young aide labored and listened with concerns as Iraq War fever took over Washington.[24] Five years later, he found himself in Chicago after helping elect Obama, and ready to join the NSC staff, at the age of thirty-nine.

Despite Obama's unease with the ways of Washington and his promise of a "new dawn of American leadership," he still appreciated the value of some of the town's old hands.[25] US Senator Joe Biden, a fixture of the Senate Foreign Relations Committee, had been Obama's pick for vice president in part because of his more than three decades of congressional experience. To join Biden on the National Security Council, Obama built what was called at the time a "team of rivals," based on a book of that name by historian Doris Kearns Goodwin about President Abraham Lincoln's diverse and disagreeing cabinet. Obama convinced Gates, Bush's secretary of defense, to stay on, and US Senator Hillary Rodham Clinton, Obama's opponent for the Democratic Party's nomination, to become secretary of state.[26]

The president-elect also selected a former Marine commandant, General James Jones, to be national security advisor on a strong recommendation from Brent Scowcroft, still a Washington wise man and the godfather of the modern NSC.[27] In his interview with Obama, however, Jones admitted he was not naturally suited to be an aide to a principal. To make up for it and his still developing relationship with the soon-to-be president, the retired general hired several professional staffers and Obama loyalists to the NSC.[28] His team included longtime Democrats such as Deputy National Security Advisor Tom

Donilon, a lawyer and Washington operator who had been chief of staff to one of President Bill Clinton's secretaries of state; and McDonough, who became the NSC director for strategic communications.

At transition headquarters, as Lute briefed a collection of senior and more junior members of the Obama team on what worried him about Afghanistan, the war czar was also worrying about his own future. Like everyone on the Bush team, the Obama transition, and the rest of Washington, he presumed his White House tour was over and had even started packing up his office. Lute expected to return to his army career after the inauguration, although no assignment had been finalized, and the lieutenant general's years out of uniform—and fighting as "Petraeus's guy" with the Pentagon bureaucracy to prioritize the surge in Iraq—put him in a delicate and likely diminished position for promotion.

Yet weeks after Lute's first briefing to the transition, Jones asked him to stay at the NSC. The decision to keep a knowledgeable and respected staffer regardless of who hired him was "classic Obama," according to McDonough.[29] Looking at their inheritance, which included a global financial crisis that had begun in 2008 and staggered the American and international economies, the president-elect and his team had decided that Lute, who knew every detail of the two wars, could help the new commander in chief avoid unnecessary errors.

But not everyone on the new team was as ready to accept Lute, whom some derisively called "Bush's guy." These were heady days for an Obama cohort that came from nowhere to win the White House. Even more, many believed the victory had been a triumph over not just the Washington conventional wisdom but also its purveyors, who had taken the country down many wrong paths, including in the Iraq War Lute had helped manage. Eventually, the persistent questions about Lute's loyalties led Jones to say, "He's not a Bush guy, he's a lieutenant general in the United States Army."[30]

"Regular Order"

As Obama attended inaugural festivities after being sworn in at the US Capitol, Lute and others on his team showed up at the White House and the Executive Office Building on January 20, 2009, to continue to keep an eye on the wars. While a few Obama staffers started looking around for their new offices, Bush's war czar and other holdovers were providing, by design and by the decision of the new president, continuity from one wartime staff to another.

Slowly, however, change came to the NSC and to Lute's role in particular. The reform reflected some lingering distrust of Bush's guy, but it was mostly about a commitment to a disciplined process, or "regular order," a shibboleth brought from the Obama campaign to his White House. With a lot to do in the world, like facing the global financial crisis, and too little time to do it, the new team believed, as one member said, "regular order is your friend."[31] Jones wanted a "strategic," "agile," "transparent," and "predictable" operation as a way of bringing reason to Washington and, according to one official, of "improving the quality of decisions" and avoiding mistakes like the Iraq War.[32]

To impose regular order, the Obama team had studied the Bush NSC and how its post–September 11th exertions abroad and the emphasis on homeland security at home had given rise to a wartime staff. Lute's war czar position was exhibit A in how irregular the NSC had gone. As a result, Lute got a new title and became a senior advisor and coordinator for Afghanistan-Pakistan. With the new role, the staffer's responsibilities were curtailed (after a few months Iraq went back to its regional home in the Middle East directorate), his status was lowered (he was no longer an assistant to the president, a cherished rank), his access shrank (he did not meet alone with the president first thing in the morning as he had under Bush), and his office moved from the West Wing to the Executive Office Building.

The Obama team, however, was not done changing the NSC. In May, the White House announced it was renaming and reforming the staff itself. The NSC was merged with the Homeland Security Council's staff to create a single "National Security Staff," or "NSS" for short, with more than two hundred members working on policy.[33] The name change, which required new email addresses and business cards, sought to demonstrate a unity of effort and mission to both those inside the Executive Office Building and around government, but the new initials never caught on in Washington.*

The unified staff and regular order were meant to support Obama, who believed Iraq was an unnecessary war not just because of its consequences, but

---

* "NSS" will not be used in this book since few in government used it and the name later reverted back.

because the math on the decision to invade had never added up. Accordingly, the president wanted every question asked, every assertion examined, and, as Jones explained, everyone on his team to have the opportunity to voice their opinions before a decision was made.[34] If the president and his team played their respective parts, it was assumed, policy would improve and Washington might just come to make decisions based on reason and principle.

Along with Jones, Donilon—who had worked in and out of government since an internship in the Carter White House, including in the Clinton State Department during some of the darkest days of the Bosnia War—policed the process.[35] He drove a system with exhaustive paper production and inclusive meetings: the two related features reflected the president's (and Donilon's) legal background as well as the Democratic administration's commitment to full representation.[36] But the punishing workload overtaxed and overscheduled National Security Council principals at the agencies, who had their own work to do and departments to manage, and grew to resent the heavy load.

The burden, of course, included the two conflicts, which frequently reminded Donilon and the rest of the Obama team that war does not always run on a regular order. Although Bush had sent 6,000 additional troops to Afghanistan before leaving office, he had deferred outstanding requests for an additional 24,000. After the Pentagon asked about the troops in late January, Obama reminded the National Security Council principals he had promised during the campaign to add personnel to Afghanistan, but the new president also explained, "When we send them, we need to announce it in the context of a broader strategy."[37]

"Integrated Military-Civilian Insurgency"

To write such a plan, Obama, a few days in office, ordered a sixty-day, top-to-bottom review of the war and brought in an outsider to run it.[38] When the new president telephoned Bruce Riedel on January 30, 2009, the thirty-year CIA veteran and former NSC staffer was three years into retirement, content to help put someone in the White House but never serve in it again.[39] During the presidential campaign, Riedel was an early Obama advisor who helped develop the candidate's promises on Afghanistan.[40]

Riedel, who had published a widely read think tank report on Afghanistan and Pakistan in August 2008, had a good idea what he was going to write for the new president, but time was of the essence and he only had a small team drawn from the agencies to help with the drafting. Although Lute and his staff were still managing both wars and a separate review of Iraq, Riedel took him up on the offer for support from NSC staff, some of whom had been working on Afghanistan for months and in some cases years. Since Riedel did not plan to stick around to implement his recommendations, it also made sense for the NSC to help with development and drafting in order to follow through on implementation.

On February 11, 2009, Riedel, Lute, and some staffers met in the Executive Office Building conference room with the other members of the review, who had all been given a copy of Lute's Afghanistan briefing from the previous administration. From the Defense Department, Michèle Flournoy, a respected defense wonk and the newly sworn-in undersecretary of defense for policy, was a cochair for the review. Petraeus, who, after the perceived success of the Iraq surge, had been named commander at the department's Central Command (CENTCOM), was also present.

The review's other chair was Richard Holbrooke, who had delivered on the Bosnia endgame in the Dayton Accords and had been named by Clinton the State Department's special representative for Afghanistan and Pakistan. Eager to make history again, Holbrooke had ambitiously stocked his team with diplomats, scholars, and former military officers to end another conflict complicated by ethnic tensions. For those familiar with Holbrooke, or like some at the White House suspicious of his motives and his longtime support for Clinton, it appeared the new special representative was trying to build an NSC-like team to take control of the war.

Even though the review's first session had begun with the still new team introducing themselves to their colleagues, Riedel promised a draft of the report would be written in two days. That speed surprised many in the room—including Lute, who had spent months writing his own report—and belied just how complicated the war, and strategy for it, had become.[41] As would become clearer in the months ahead, the individuals around the table had subtle disagreements about almost every word of the eventual objective to "disrupt, dismantle, and eventually defeat al-Qaeda and its extremist allies, their support structures and their safe havens."[42]

More than the ends, the members of the review struggled to find a novel way to achieve them. Even if most, including Lute, agreed with then-candidate Obama, who had said, "The solution in Afghanistan is not just military—it is political and economic," those charged with solving Afghanistan, still plagued by pervasive corruption and governance issues, only had so many options to consider.[43] After more than seven years of war, the military had come not just to dominate much of the discussion of national security policy but also its implementation, even jobs better suited to diplomats because US forces had greater capacity to take action in dangerous war zones.

With the perceived success of the surge, counterinsurgency had taken on a near miraculous status in military, as well as the broader foreign policy, conversations. It appeared to be the cure-all for every one of a tough war's ails. Reflecting the military's recent experience in Iraq and the State Department's push to strengthen Afghan governance and economic development, Riedel eventually recommended the president pursue an "integrated civilian-military counterinsurgency."[44]

"They Know What the Hell's Going On"

But a full and honest accounting about what was needed to realize such a strategy was preempted by the military's hard push in early February for the White House to approve a pending request and send an additional 13,000 troops to Afghanistan in time for the August elections. To Lute, something about the request and its urgency did not smell right. The Pentagon's numbers looked suspicious, since he did not see enough of what are known as "enablers," the personnel who provide transport, surveillance, and evacuations.

After catching the paperwork for the decision on its way to the president for signature, Lute cried foul and told Donilon, "These numbers are really soft," and encouraged him to question the military's math.[45] When the deputy national security advisor did so, the chairman of the Joint Chiefs of Staff, Admiral Michael Mullen, responded to the White House doubts by saying, "We've done our homework."[46] But it soon became clear the numbers and the military's homework had indeed been wrong. In short order, the Pentagon sent a revised proposal, and Obama approved an additional 17,000 troops, a decision announced in a lone White House statement.[47]

Contrary to regular order and Obama's commitment in one of his earliest meetings with the military, the president had sent more troops before the broader strategy was established. The entire incident, from proposal to press release, was an eye-opener for the new war managers in the White House, who worried about the bad math. Even more troubling, the staff thought it was their job to protect the president's space and process for making decisions, which the rush for approval had curtailed.

The incident was also a bad first step in the civil-military relationship. The Pentagon's sloppy work and insistence for approval struck many of the new Obama team as an attempt to take advantage of a new president, while the White House doubts and double-checking offended some in the brass. The incident had also proved the value of Lute, and the three-star general's willingness to question the military, to his new NSC colleagues. As Donilon later said of him and other holdovers, "This is exactly why we kept these guys, because they know what the hell's going on."[48]

By mid-March 2009, the 44-page Riedel review, which included 20 recommendations and 180 subrecommendations, was complete. Although initial discussion of the report elicited further disagreements among the National Security Council principals—including those like Vice President Biden who worried the plan committed the United States and the new president to a long-term nation-building effort—the president accepted it. A few days later, Obama announced that he was sending an additional 4,000 military personnel to join the previously approved 17,000 troops as well as what became known as a "civilian surge" of agricultural experts, educators, and engineers to help develop the Afghan economy, infrastructure, and political and social institutions.[49]

"Tally Up the Bill"

With some trust earned, Iraq off his desk, and Riedel, who kept his vow to stay out of government, gone, Lute was charged with helping implement the new Afghanistan strategy. This was in some ways familiar territory: as he had done on the Iraq surge, Lute inherited a plan he had not written and tried to keep the president's, and everyone else's, eye on the ball by knowing the objectives, measuring progress, and keeping the policy on track.[50] As the new strategy sought to apply some of the lessons of Iraq, Lute convinced John Tien, an army colonel detailed to the NSC the year before to work on that war, to again delay his return to an active regular service post and take on more responsibility on Afghanistan.

A child of Chinese immigrants and a graduate of West Point, Tien was part of a unit that had assumed responsibility for security in Tal Afar in 2006 after then-colonel H. R. McMaster had demonstrated the value of counterinsurgency in pacifying the Iraqi city.[51] While on a fellowship at the Harvard Kennedy School a year later, Tien was recommended to Lute as a potential addition to the war czar's team. Rather than returning to uniform and his command tour, Tien found himself an active-duty army colonel wearing a business suit and working at the Old Executive Office Building in 2008.

A year later but under a new president, Lute and Tien took a page out of the Bush NSC's playbook. That staff had developed a system to comprehensively track progress, or a lack of it, on the war's objectives. These strategic implementation plans, which tried to establish and measure benchmarks at regular intervals, had become a useful tool at the White House, but the NSC had never formally adopted the practice on Afghanistan. With Jones's permission, Lute developed a strategic implementation plan for the president's new Afghanistan plan.

The minute the new strategy was exposed to metrics, however, the practice revealed some of the differences that had gone underexamined before Obama's announcement of the strategy. After Lute shared the draft document with the Pentagon, members of Gates's team changed one objective, from "disrupt" the Taliban, to "defeat."[52] It could have seemed a minor edit, as much a semantic point as a bureaucratic tiff playing out in track changes, but it concerned Lute, who worried that the Pentagon was pushing for the most expansive and thus most troop-intensive definition of the mission. Regardless, Jones and Donilon told Lute to go with "defeat."[53]

But simply accepting the edit did not resolve the disagreement behind it. According to Lute, in part because the Pentagon's February troop request and the president's approval had preempted the discussion of what means the new strategy required, "We did not really get to the last step which is to tally up the bill."[54] Now charged with implementing counterinsurgency, the Defense Department, where Mullen said at the time, "The under-resourcing of Afghanistan was much deeper and wider than even I thought," was looking for more: more troops, more intellectual energy, and more financial resources.[55] The State Department as well was pushing for more personnel to go to Afghanistan.

Meanwhile, many in Washington, especially at the White House, got sticker shock as the bill started growing in terms of troop totals and economic commitment, at a time when the United States was reeling from a financial crisis. Obama himself was doing the math; he said, "A six-to-eight year war at over fifty billion dollars a year is not in the national interest."[56] The White House made a point of considering the costs in its strategic conversations and communications. More than just dollars-and-cents considerations, the president explained at the time, "My strong view is that we are not going to succeed simply by piling on more and more troops."[57]

"Whiskey, Tango, Foxtrot"

Trying to get the ground truth on what was needed, Jones and Lute dispatched Tien to Afghanistan in April 2009. The NSC staffer, a few years out of combat, knew the best way to see war's reality and determine what was needed was to go outside the wire, or beyond the safety of the base. So the NSC staffer pulled back on his army combat uniform, grabbed a rifle, and went on patrol with several units in Southern Afghanistan.[58] In the vast, ungoverned and unsecured swaths of the country, Tien saw how the United States was losing the initiative and how additional resources and troops might be required to realize a true counterinsurgency plan.

Many at the Pentagon agreed. Even more, they thought the entire operation required "fresh thinking."[59] In May, Mullen and Gates recommended that the American commander in Afghanistan be replaced by Army General Stanley McChrystal, who had become a legend in national security circles for leading counterterrorism raids in Iraq. At McChrystal's confirmation hearing in May, the new commander said of the 21,000 additional troops Obama had approved, which took the total of American personnel in Afghanistan to 67,000: "You might properly ask if that is enough. I don't know. It may be some time before I do."[60]

With Obama's decisions on the new strategy and troops only a few months old, Jones grew concerned about the Pentagon's changes, McChrystal's suggestive testimony, and whispers elsewhere in Washington that another troop request was coming the president's way. When the national security advisor traveled with Tien and others from the NSC in late June to Camp Leatherneck in Afghanistan's restive Helmand Province, Jones tried to send a message. He said if Obama heard about any new requests, the president was going to have a "whiskey, tango, foxtrot moment," referring to the acronym for "What the fuck?"[61]

The colorful remark, which was reported on the front page by the *Washington Post*'s Bob Woodward, whom Jones had invited on the trip, reflected the unease in the Obama team and its Afghanistan policy. Despite Riedel's review, its strategy, as Obama later said, had "retained ambiguity about what our central mission was."[62] Because of the failure to fully air opinions about the ways and the means and tally the bill, when the military and State fought to implement their respective interpretations of the plan, it frustrated those at the White House and NSC who had their own perspectives.

Regular order took a further hit when everyone tried to take their case, as Jones had done with Woodward at Camp Leatherneck, to the press instead of the Situation Room. At the White House, all the leaks other than their own were seen as not just politically damaging, but as attacks on the president, his policy, and the process. The Obama team believed the military was trying to "jam" the president and limit what some at the White House called his "decision space" or freedom to make the choice he thought was best.[63] Obama eventually felt compelled to ask Gates about the military's leaks, "Is it lack of respect for me?"[64]

"We're Being Fed a Pack of Bullshit"

Upon arriving in Afghanistan, McChrystal had set about drafting an assessment of the war and the way forward. After the general sent the sixty-six-page report to the Pentagon at the end of August, it was leaked, in full, to the *Washington Post*.[65] With a click on the paper's website, readers from the District of Columbia to Kabul learned that the new commander believed that if the United States failed to "gain the initiative and reverse insurgent momentum in the near-term (next 12 months)," it may no longer be possible to win.[66]

That explosive conclusion and the leak itself shocked many in the Obama administration and contributed to the sense that events had drfited out of the control of everyone at the Pentagon, the Executive Office Building, and the White House. Even before the assessment leaked, the president had concluded, "We've got to get everybody in a room and make sure that everybody is singing from the same hymnal."[67] To try to find what he called "something that we could all agree to," Obama, over the course of the next two-and-a-half months, would spend almost twenty-five hours in meetings with his team about Afghanistan.[68]

More than just the president's time, the effort also required Lute to become Obama's guy. Working with Jones, Donilon, Tien, and others at the White House, he helped organize a months-long conversation on Afghanistan that included draft after draft of papers and agendas and dozens of principals, deputies, and interagency sessions. As violence in Afghanistan remained worse than it had been the year before, Obama and the National Security Council principals debated every detail of the policy from whether the opponent was al-Qaeda, the Taliban, or both; whether "defeat" was better than "degrade"; how to define and measure both; and who should do the fighting.

After his assessment leaked, McChrystal submitted, in hard copy only, a formal request for additional troops. Though he included both a more limited and a higher option, the Afghanistan commander recommended the middle path: 40,000 additional troops for a counterinsurgency campaign. The president's team, however, thought McChrystal was boxing in the president with what are known as Goldilocks options: two unpalatable paths that make the planner's preferred one look just right. In late October, Obama, who wanted a choice of three distinct options, called out the maneuver and said: "We don't have two options yet. We have 40,000 and nothing."[69]

Some of this difference of opinion, and the resulting tension, was healthy and natural for a high-stakes policy debate among dedicated, passionate professionals. The military and the State Department were expected to give their best advice; but Obama, and those on his team, did not believe any agency's judgment alone should be the only consideration when the president faced a decision. As Obama explained, he had "extraordinary commanders on the ground and a lot of good advisers who I have a lot of confidence in, but the president has to make a decision: will the application of military force in this circumstance meet the broader national-security goals of the United States?"[70]

Obama wanted—and he believed the Constitution bestowed on him the responsibility—to be the one to answer that question, but by the beginning of the review, the relationship on Afghanistan between the White House and Defense Department was rife with distrust. After the Pentagon's bad math in February, the public hints about needing more troops, and all the leaks, the benefit of the doubt had evaporated to the point that innocent missteps were assumed to border on insubordination. More than hurt feelings, the result was a nasty cycle, according to one Pentagon official, of "second- and third-order effects."[71] When the NSC, including those with military experience like Jones, Lute, and Tien, began to more forcefully manage the Pentagon, there were additional frustrations and leaks at the Defense Department, which only led to stronger White House arm-twisting.

"Ghosts"

Of course, the arms being twisted were not always in a uniform. Holbrooke's outsized ambitions for his job and outsized public persona, ruffled feathers at the White House. The special representative could never get in step with the NSC and Obama team, who distrusted him as Clinton's guy. As Obama was settling into the role of commander in chief, some also saw the diplomat, with a way of making the story and history about himself, as a show-off.

Yet perhaps the biggest difference was generational. As they took on responsibility for managing the war in Afghanistan, many at the White House had taken to reading Gordon Goldstein's *Lessons in Disaster* to learn about the NSC's role in the escalation in Vietnam. But Holbrooke had lived it: as a young Foreign Service officer, he had dined with McGeorge Bundy in 1965 on one of the Kennedy and Johnson national security advisor's fateful trips to Vietnam. Holbrooke saw lessons worth learning in the book and the broader history of Vietnam, but the president himself was less certain that the war, let alone the Vietnam syndrome, could shed much light on his Afghanistan deliberations. At one point in the Situation Room when Holbrooke made a point about Vietnam, Obama simply whispered to no one in particular, "Ghosts."[72]

Lute, more than anyone, stood in the middle of these growing divides. To the dismay of Gates and Mullen especially, the former war czar chose to fight for his boss in the Oval Office, not the chain of command at the Pentagon.[73] Lute warned those on the NSC not to participate in a scheduled war game since he believed it would by design end up boosting the Pentagon's proposal.[74] He worked to get fresh intelligence from Afghanistan and military sources outside the chain of command to arm and inform the White House.[75] And Lute was willing to tell the president and others at the White House, as he did after one military briefing, "We're being fed a pack of bullshit."[76]

Beyond whom Lute chose to fight for, several in the national security team believed he fought dirty. The NSC staffer could wield invitations to meetings as weapons to exclude and send messages to those like Holbrooke.[77] Even more, Lute was a magnet for information, particularly from those on the frontlines in Afghanistan, which many in Washington readily agreed was one of his jobs on the NSC. But rather than sharing the intelligence and keeping everyone at the NSC and elsewhere on the same page, Lute had a habit of giving it to his White House bosses alone, who would then discuss the information in meetings to the surprise of military leaders.[78]

At one point, according to Bob Woodward, Lute called Mullen and said directly, "Mr. Chairman, the president really wants another option."[79] When no additional proposals were presented by the Pentagon, save further tweaks to the number of troops, the White House tried to develop its own alternatives. Vice President Biden and his team, with help from Lute, others on the NSC, and the vice chairman of the Joint Chiefs of Staff, took the initiative to develop a more restrained concept, one with fewer troops targeting a smaller number of terrorists over a more modest patch of Afghanistan.

As the military options developed fitfully, the president and his team also looked for ways to improve the Afghan government, which was struggling after its August elections had been consumed by fraud. As one aide later said of Obama, he "believes the military can do enormous things, it can win wars and stabilize conflicts. But a military can't create a political culture or build a society."[80] Yet with the State Department and Holbrooke's civilian surge slow to get on the ground and show results, the Obama team considered how a troop surge could be used to entice the Karzai government to take the steps to improve governance, reduce corruption, and build its security forces.

"It Still Smells to Me like a Gamble"

Of course, because this sort of leverage, and even Biden's more limited plan, required some additional troops, the White House began to discuss how long the supplemental personnel needed to be in country. With Lute and Donilon's encouragement, the president pushed on the military's timing. When a Pentagon graph showed it would take fifteen months for 40,000 additional troops to arrive in Afghanistan, Obama pointed to the chart and asked why it would take so long. Unsatisfied, the president said he wanted the whole graph shifted to the left, so the troops would arrive earlier and depart sooner, by a specific date.[81]

Obama knew the argument against a deadline was that it could reward a patient adversary, but the president still believed it necessary to "show some light at the end of the tunnel" to Americans, specifically those in Congress, who were worried about the costs of the war.[82] Many in the military leadership were uncomfortable with the end date, but Gates, who appreciated that it might help signal that the United States was not planning a long-term occupation, convinced the White House to make the deadline contingent on "conditions on the ground."[83]

Before the Thanksgiving holiday, the president made clear to Lute and the White House team he was likely to order a surge in Afghanistan. Obama also admitted, "I've got more deeply in the weeds than a president should."[84] After another round of confusion and frustration over the exact number of troops in the surge, the president thought he needed to go deeper still and told his team, "We should get this on paper and on the record."[85]

Working with Donilon and leveraging the notes taken of all the conversations from the preceding months, Lute and his team drafted a remarkable six-page decision sheet, which became known as a "terms sheet," to remove any ambiguity.[86] Part war plan, part order, part tallied bill, and part contract, the terms sheet more tightly defined the US goal in Afghanistan: "to deny safe haven to al Qaeda and to deny the Taliban the ability to overthrow the Afghan government."[87] It also explicitly detailed the number of troops, how many enablers were to support their operations, when they would start coming home (July 2011), how much the whole operation would cost, and who would track the monthly progress (Lute's NSC team).

As the president's team finalized the terms, Obama spent most of the Saturday after Thanksgiving talking about Afghanistan. Sitting by the fireplace in the Oval Office, the president asked Lute, Tien, Donilon, McDonough, and other White House and NSC staffers for each of their opinions. Tien, who punctuated his comments with the perspective of having deployed outside the wire in Iraq, supported committing troops to counterinsurgency, since he believed it was based on the best military advice to achieve the mission the president had articulated earlier in the year. If Obama preferred to change the mission, Tien, who added that any new strategy should be given the resources to succeed, believed the military would faithfully back their commander in chief whatever his final decision.[88]

When it came time for Lute to speak, he was direct. "Mr. President, you don't have to do this." He had concluded that the review had not justified the surge. If all the months of discussion had done anything, it had made plain the various risks in the plan, and Lute did not see how the military's proposed plan would overcome all of them by the deadline. Of the decision, Lute said, "It still smells to me like a gamble." The terms sheet, which provided among other things an audit trail, was meant in part to check the amount wagered and provide a way to leave the table if necessary.[89]

"I Am Giving an Order"

After some more conversation, the president thanked Lute, Tien, and the others and continued to weigh the decision, the draft terms sheet, and the delicate act of being commander in chief. The day before, he had called upon a retired and even more reluctant general: Colin Powell. That Friday, the former national security advisor, chairman of the Joint Chiefs of Staff, and secretary of state walked into the Oval Office for a private audience with Obama. It was not their first meeting; the president had called on Powell earlier in the fall for advice on how to get the decision right. Now that it was made, the once-reluctant general told him, "You're the commander in chief. These guys work for you."[90]

The commander in chief called a Sunday evening meeting in the Oval Office with his principal military advisors Gates, Mullen, Cartwright, and Petraeus. After giving each a copy of the terms sheet, Obama asked if they had objections, and when none were raised, the meeting began to break up. Before it did, however, according to one recollection, Vice President Biden interjected that the military "should consider the president's decision an order." A moment later, Obama said, "I am giving an order."[91] Gates, who was "really disgusted" with the review, felt the same way about the directive: he later wrote it was "unnecessary and insulting, proof positive of the depth of the Obama White House's distrust of the nation's military leadership."[92]

Two days later, on December 1, Obama traveled to West Point with most of his National Security Council principals. Speaking to somber cadets dressed in the gray wool uniform Lute himself had worn decades before, the president made the case for a surge that Lute did not think was worth the risk. The onetime war czar traveled to his alma mater, but he did not help much on the speech; instead, the pen was in the hands of his NSC colleague Ben Rhodes.

Rhodes, a New York native and ghostwriter, had become interested in foreign affairs after September 11th. More than simply sharing a frustration over Iraq, Rhodes had gotten to know then-senator Obama while working on legislation that would have precluded the surge in Iraq.[93] After that, Rhodes joined Obama's campaign and then his NSC, at the age of thirty, all the while developing what many called a "mind meld" with the president and his voice.[94]

The West Point remarks were not the only speech Rhodes was helping the president draft that week; the staffer had also begun to write the address Obama would give the following week in Oslo, Norway, upon accepting the Nobel Peace Prize. In his lecture, Obama tried to make the most of the symbolic incongruity of a war president, a relatively new one at that, accepting a peace prize. He explained how a commander in chief must wrestle with "two seemingly irreconcilable truths—that war is sometimes necessary, and that war at some level is an expression of human folly."[95]

To many, including Obama, Lute, and the rest of the team, the drawn-out conversations before his surge decision were a reminder of both of those truths. As Obama had said, Afghanistan was a "war of necessity," but that did not make figuring out how to win any easier.[96] After more than a year in office, Obama had concluded, "War is hell." Perhaps worse for a president and his team who had wanted to bring reason to management of Afghanistan, Obama also concluded, "Once the dogs of war are unleashed, you don't know where it's going to lead."[97]

A "Guy without a Country"

The Obama team had also hoped to bring regular order to wartime Washington, yet the challenges of changing course in Afghanistan, not to mention Iraq, which was winding down, put such a goal out of reach. Instead, the White House relied on Lute, Tien, and others to continue to be wartime staffers to get the policy the president wanted even if it required working around, and breaking with, the common law and the chain of command to get the president operational details and deliverables.

For Lute, the war in Afghanistan, and the fights over it, led to bureaucratic confrontations with the Pentagon that often grew personal in the first years of the Obama administration. Like previous NSC staffers, Lute believed "when you work for the president, you work for the president."[98] Mullen, however, contends the NSC staffer "lost his way," attracted by power at the White House.[99] From the Bush administration to Obama's, Gates's judgment of Lute flip-flopped: the staffer was a help on the Iraq surge as Bush's war czar, but during Obama's Afghanistan review Lute had become an "advocate rather than a neutral party, contributing to a damaging split in the government."[100]

Aside from personal accusations and partisan affiliations, the underlying disagreement appears to have been about what Lute was fighting for: it was one thing, in the minds of those at the Pentagon, to work to get a policy like the surge implemented, but it was another—and contrary to the military's definition of honest brokering—for a staffer to push that hard to get a policy made. Regardless of why, McDonough explained, the lieutenant general had become a "guy without a country": though he had been promised a return to uniform, the bridge, according to Gates, had been burned.[101] Instead, Lute chose to retire from the army after thirty-five years and accept an offer to continue on at the NSC managing the war as a civilian political appointee.

Even with Lute out of uniform, the broader battle of attrition between the White House and the Pentagon continued. Though there were some areas of positive collaboration, whenever NSC staffers like Lute pushed hard on senior officers to get what the president and the warfighters needed, Defense Department officials accused them of micromanaging. The Pentagon's frustrations grew so severe that at one point when Gates was at an air base in Afghanistan, he caught sight of a direct line to Lute at the White House, which of course meant the command was calling the NSC, not the other way around. Regardless, the irate defense secretary ordered it removed, and told the commander there, "You get a call from the White House, you tell 'em to go to hell and call me."[102]

The continued disagreements even after the surge decision were worsened by how difficult changing events on the ground proved to be. The surge's spotty success led some on the Obama team to question whether a war in Afghanistan could be won at all. Even Lute admitted as much when he said, of Obama's Afghan surge: "When you ask people what makes this a sustainable plan, they just look at you. Because there's nothing to say."[103] Although the additional troops helped deliver some security gains, Afghanistan continued to struggle with limited economic development, failing governance, and persistent corruption.

The surge's mixed results brought to an end the counterinsurgency boomlet in Washington. Although Afghanistan is a tough test for any strategy, the failure to bring peace to the country meant the Pentagon once again relegated counterinsurgency to rather-not status. More than even the virtues of COIN in particular, any troop-heavy, time-intensive operations quickly became, in the years after the financial crisis and the two surges, harder sells for policymakers in general and the Obama team in particular.

Eventually, McDonough, Lute, and others from the NSC and around the interagency began to work to determine just what the United States and Obama could live with in Afghanistan. The quietly held sessions, where hard questions and trade-offs were considered (for example, just how much corruption was sustainable?), became known as the "Afghan good enough" project.[104] The group's discussion helped shape Obama's decision to begin pulling American troops out, against the military's recommendations, in 2011 and transitioning security to Afghan forces.[105]

"Don't Do Stupid Shit"

Although Lute continued to work the wars as a civilian appointee, another retired general left the Obama NSC in 2010. Jones, who had never been fully in sync with Obama loyalists or the staff responsibilities of the national security advisor position, departed. Donilon replaced him, McDonough became deputy, and together they ran the largest NSC in history: by 2012, with the merger of the HSC staff complete, more than four hundred staffers worked in the Executive Office Building and elsewhere.

As in previous administrations, the total number of staffers was a misleading indicator, as not every individual on the Obama NSC worked exclusively on policy issues. A quarter of them, more than one hundred, were mostly technical specialists, who ran the White House Situation Room and maintained the technology that allowed the president to speak to anyone on Earth at any time of day. There were also dozens of administrative service staffers who handled secretarial work, maintained records, and provided human resources support. Still, in 2012, more than 215 staffers worked on policy, including those who focused on the war in Afghanistan under Lute.[106]

Although smaller in practice than the headlines suggested, for those in Washington who wanted to complain about the staff's influence on policy or Obama's decision-making, the size of the NSC became a target of convenience. Over the course of the administration, the large NSC staff was publicly accused of moving "far beyond its original advisory role," symbolizing an "overbearing and paranoid White House," and producing a process that was "sclerotic at best, constipated at worst."[107] Within government, the reviews of the NSC staff were more caustic, personal, and colored by four-letter words.

In many ways, that reputation found its start in Lute's role, which of course had been created in the Bush administration, and in Obama's management of the review that produced the Afghan surge. The Pentagon's military and civilian leadership, under Gates and his successors, remained on guard against any perceived NSC overreach. At the State Department, some had been frustrated during the Afghanistan discussions, saying that the NSC formed a "Berlin Wall" that kept diplomats like Holbrooke and their ideas away from the president.[108] In the diplomatic corps, many continued to blame the staff for Obama's unwillingness to intervene to stop atrocities like those in Syria.

Despite the frustrations the staff inspired in the agencies and the flak it brought the White House, Obama clearly wanted a strong NSC to pursue his agenda. When the president was looking for everyone in the Situation Room to give their opinion about the decision, he called on the staff along the backbench. The result was that staffers, some like Rhodes who had arrived at the NSC directly from Obama's campaign, gave their advice while cabinet secretaries listened on.

To many in Washington, it appeared the Obama NSC was not only developing but also seeking to implement its own agenda, breaking with common law. The NSC staff had become much more involved in actually carrying out the policies and operations, whether going on patrol in Afghanistan like Tien, reviewing targets and plans for drone strikes and counterterrorism raids, or doing some of the diplomacy to negotiate Iran's nuclear deal. In the lead-up to Obama's renewal of diplomatic relations with Cuba in 2014, Rhodes, with the support of another staffer, had on the president's orders done most of the secret diplomacy.

To the administration's defenders, however, the Obama team found in Lute, and his more operational approach, a hands-on wartime staff waiting in the Executive Office Building when they took office. It turned out to suit a hands-on president who felt hard questions were to be expected for a commander in chief. Lute's role, and the precedent it represented, also came in handy for those who wanted to defend the president's and NSC's probing: as McDonough said of the complaints, "One man's micromanagement is another person's civilian control of the military, which happens to be a constitutional prerogative of the president."[109]

A strong NSC also made sense for a president who distrusted the way Washington usually made decisions, especially risky ones. After the Afghanistan review, Obama said, "I can sum up my foreign policy in one phrase, 'Don't do stupid shit.'"[110] In minding the regular order and fighting for rational choices, as Lute had in the Afghanistan review, the Obama NSC staff reviewed, requested, tested, and edited options for the president to consider and then monitored implementation aggressively. The staff also kept a tight leash on National Security Council principals and their agencies to avoid stupid mistakes.

Ironically, Lute soon became one of those the NSC staff kept an eye on. In 2013, Obama nominated the now retired general to be US ambassador to NATO. Six years after joining the Bush NSC amid questions about the White House's ability to manage its wars, Lute left an Obama staff accused of micromanaging the nation's warriors. In the years ahead, Ambassador Lute found himself on the other side of the video-teleconferences, as the Obama NSC developed responses to Russian provocations, the rise of the Islamic State, and more.

"Right-Sizing"

Although the president's manner and ambitions did not change much in his last term, the staff did with the departures of Lute, Donilon (who left the administration), and McDonough (whom the president named White House chief of staff in 2013). In July 2013, Susan Rice became national security advisor. Rice, a staffer on Bill Clinton's NSC and Obama's first US ambassador to the United Nations, brought unique experience to the job as a former member of both the staff and National Security Council.

As a staffer reporting to Clinton National Security Advisors Lake and Sandy Berger, Rice laid the foundation for a policy career that would take her to the highest levels in government. She also came to appreciate the NSC, a small, collegial, flat institution made up of policy wonks like Sandy Vershbow and Nelson Drew. In the 1990s, according to Rice, when there was a debate or disagreement about a decision, "You walked down the third-floor hallway of the Executive Office Building, and you knocked on the door for whoever was the issue and you sat with them until it was resolved."[111]

Upon her return to the NSC, Rice was heartbroken to discover the NSC had lost its "intimacy and collegiality."[112] The sheer number of staffers and the overreliance on email and desktop video-teleconferences made meetings rarer and deliberations far less personal. The creation of new layers of management, like Lute's positions of deputy national security advisor and then coordinator, made the institution more hierarchical. Although Rice's youth on the Clinton NSC had been an exception, the younger and less experienced Obama staffers also had fewer relationships at the Pentagon and the State Department and within the intelligence community.

The staff, in Rice's opinion, had also been "bastardized" when its name was changed to the NSS in 2009. The advisor recalled: "I knew the meaning of being an NSC staffer. It had a name, it had a point, it had a certain cachet."[113] Many staffers missed it, and some complained about the name to the new national security advisor on her return. So Rice and the president changed it back, rebranding with an executive order in 2014.[114] The reversal was a rare Obama White House surrender to the ways of Washington: as Rhodes admitted at the time of the earlier change, "Frankly, everyone kept calling us the N.S.C. anyway."[115]

More consequential than the name change was Rice's commitment to recalibrating, or as the effort became known, "right-sizing" the staff.[116] Driven by Rice's personal concerns rather than Washington's complaints, the national security advisor launched a review in winter 2015 to determine how the NSC could better serve both the president and national security policy. The months-long process included interviews and focus groups with staffers, their counterparts at the agencies, and cabinet secretaries in order to establish what was working and what was not.

In May of that year, Rice stood before a full South Court Auditorium, a drab theater-style room in the Executive Office Building that looks and feels like the setting for a high school musical, and explained the way ahead for the NSC. Rather than firing staffers, the review determined which directorates could shrink, and as staff billets expired, replacements were not appointed, while Rice and her team added staff to directorates that needed more manpower. At the end of the administration, the NSC had fewer than 180 policy staffers.

More than simple numbers, Rice and her team aimed to right-size the role of the NSC. The national security advisor sought to pull the remaining staffers back within the common law and from the more operational, wartime posture the Bush team and then Lute and his staff had adopted. In June 2015, she issued a memorandum instructing the staff that they could no longer directly contact ambassadors, military commanders, and CIA station chiefs, unless it was an emergency.

In addition to Rice's own prerogatives, the White House was facing increased calls for NSC reform on Capitol Hill. Members of Congress and their staffs had taken aim at the NSC, partly because of complaints from the Pentagon. Various size limits (at one point it was 100, then 150) were considered—and Rice's team briefed congressional representatives on the right-sizing effort—before Congress finally included a 200-person restriction on staffers in "policy roles" in the defense authorization bill signed by Obama in December 2016.[117]

The new limit was an important moment for the NSC, which had so often escaped congressional reform in its seventy-year history. Yet Congress's bark was worse than its bite: the "right-sized" Obama NSC met the limit at the end of the administration, and the only regulation on staff behavior remained a matter of common law. Besides, Lute's service had been a reminder of just how consequential only one staffer, with support from the president, the capacities of the wartime NSC, and the willingness to bend and break the restraints, could be.

"From the Top Down"

The *New York Times* headline from February 12, 2017, said it all: "Turmoil at the National Security Council, From the Top Down."[118] After just a little more than three weeks in the White House, President Donald Trump had managed to turn the NSC, one of the most secret parts of government, into one of the most discussed topics of his very tumultuous first month in office. With changes the new president and his team had made, the staff became the subject of celebrity tweets, newspaper editorials, and congressional action.[119]

The reaction to Trump's decisions was as much a testament to the perceived importance of the NSC as it was to concerns about the president himself and his newly appointed national security advisor Michael Flynn, a retired lieutenant general turned consultant-for-hire and campaign supporter. Flynn, who grew up in Rhode Island the son of a soldier, had risen quickly through the army's ranks to lead the Defense Intelligence Agency before Obama fired him for insubordination.[120]

Despite an unusual warning from the outgoing president, Trump named Flynn national security advisor, and the controversial choice quickly brought controversy to the job.[121] In the administration's first weeks, Flynn reorganized the staff, hired several aggressive and unconventional staffers, known to some in Washington as "Flynn Stones," and gave Steve Bannon, the president's political advisor, a seat on the high-level Principals Committee.[122]

Then after less than a month in office, Flynn was forced to resign over misleading White House officials about his meetings and communications with foreign governments during the transition. As the news media was still digesting Flynn's stormy tenure and departure, Trump quickly named Army Lieutenant General H. R. McMaster to be national security advisor. McMaster, well known in national security circles for—among other career highlights—leading the counterinsurgency campaign in Tal Afar, Iraq in 2005, was introduced to the country wearing his army uniform and sitting next to Trump in a gilded room at the president's Mar-a-Lago resort in Florida.

Shaved-headed and straight-laced, McMaster was an unconventional choice for an unconventional president. The three-star army officer did not have a preexisting relationship with Trump. McMaster was also stepping into a political position in Washington, a city with which he was familiar enough but had never worked in during all his years in uniform. And national security advisor was a role in which few active-duty military officers had served. With Congress's approval of his new assignment, McMaster chose to stay on active duty, even if he spent most days in a business suit, making the lieutenant general the fourth active-duty officer in the job after Brent Scowcroft, John Poindexter, and Colin Powell.

Even with a new advisor, Trump's election had unleashed forces intent on changing Washington, the NSC included. As in previous administrations, much of the staff serving Trump in his first year had arrived under his predecessor. Like Lute, Tien, and hundreds of others before them, these career nonpartisan officials, often loaned to the NSC from their home agencies, were meant to ensure continuity during the change in administration. Yet to some Trump loyalists outside of government and even a few in the White House and Executive Office Building, these career public servants were called "Obama holdovers" and targeted as part of a "deep state" opposed to the new president.[123]

Amid this contentious environment, McMaster, who had written a well-received book, *Dereliction of Duty*, about the Vietnam decision-making of President Lyndon Johnson, spoke with every living national security advisor about the NSC to determine what worked, what did not, and what might help a president like Trump. After some reflection, McMaster got to work on fundamentals: bolstering a demoralized staff, refining policy products to work for Trump, and establishing a policy process that had barely gotten underway. One of his first steps was writing and distributing to the staff an NSC mission statement: they were to help the president "plan and execute integrated national security strategies to protect United States citizens and the homeland while prioritizing American interests and values."[124]

"Thanks NSC Staff!"

At his first all-hands meeting in the Executive Office Building's auditorium, McMaster made clear that the staff not only needed to be "valued and trusted as an honest broker," but that they also needed to trust each other.[125] By not using the terms "holdovers" and "Flynn Stones" himself, the new national security advisor made clear the labels, and the divisions each represented, were not to be tolerated.[126] In new hires, McMaster worried less about political background than competency: he brought on several staffers who had worked in the Obama administration and even its NSC. McMaster also had little patience for those who continued to stir intrigues on the staff, including one Flynn hire who was removed for seeking to spy on his NSC colleagues, and another who was fired after circulating an extraordinary memo arguing some in the government, including the very NSC on which he served, were bent on subverting Trump's agenda.[127]

McMaster knew that each of the NSC's "products have to serve the president not the other way around."[128] To better serve Trump, McMaster and the staff helped draft some of the commander in chief's tweets. They also sought to get the president more digestible information: as a result, the NSC shortened their briefings from the long tracts preferred by Obama, and they prioritized creative ways, including charts, graphs, and photographs, to communicate important points, some of which tested assumptions Trump had brought to the White House.

For example, after tweeting before running for president that the United States "should leave Afghanistan immediately," Trump had to confront many of the same issues on the war Obama did in his own first year.[129] As the new president considered his options, McMaster and his team presented him with over sixty photographs—some from before the Soviet invasion in 1979, twenty after the Taliban took over, and others that were more recent—to demonstrate that US investments in Afghanistan had made the country demonstrably better.[130]

Although much of the deliberation behind Trump's choice in August 2017 to halt Obama's scheduled drawdown in Afghanistan is still cloaked in secrecy, the NSC's fingerprints and photographs can arguably be seen on the president's decision. In his announcement speech, Trump admitted that his instinct had been to "pull out." But he had been reminded that "decisions are much different when you sit behind the desk in the Oval Office; in other words, when you're President of the United States."[131]

Afghanistan was one of many challenges facing the new commander in chief, so McMaster and the staff sought to "develop strategies and action plans in key regional and functional areas to shift the global balance of power in favor of US interests and values."[132] Doing so for Trump, who had little governing or national security experience, required changes to the policy process established in Flynn's early administration memorandum. With the president's approval, Bannon, whose political position caused an outcry when he was appointed to the Principals Committee, was removed from it.[133] Compared to the deliberative Obama NSC's heavy schedule of meetings, McMaster called far fewer Principals and Deputies Committee meetings and tried to keep sessions focused at the strategic level, while leaving tactical details to the agencies.

Even with fewer meetings, McMaster and his team sought to restore what he called "strategic competence" and to set, and often reset, the government's course for a list of challenges determined in consultation with the president.[134] In the first year of Trump's presidency, the NSC staff developed and the president approved more than a dozen integrated strategy documents, on both regional (the Asia-Pacific) and functional (like US nuclear posture) areas as well as on acute matters like the civil war in Syria and longer-term issues like the rise of China.

Though nearly all remain classified, Trump's National Security Strategy, a version of which has been required by law since 1986, is an example of both the ambitions and efficiency of McMaster and the NSC team, including his deputy Nadia Schadlow, a longtime defense hand with a doctorate from the Johns Hopkins University's School for Advanced International Studies. The strategy, which for the first time ever was completed in an administration's first year, fundamentally realigned US policy to engage in what some took to calling "great power competition" with China and Russia.[135] The NSS, as it is known in Washington, was also widely commended upon its release in December 2017: one NSC veteran, who had previously criticized Trump, called the document "first-rate."[136]

With McMaster's management, Trump's decision on Afghanistan, and products like the National Security Strategy, the NSC staff in the Executive Office Building were a source of some regular order in a chaotic Trump world.

For much of its first year, the administration was marked by turnover at the White House, including Flynn's departure, and turbulence at the agencies where then–defense secretary Jim Mattis's Pentagon was understaffed, and the State Department, due in part to a heavy-handed reorganization launched by then–secretary of state Rex Tillerson, was in crisis despite the arrival of Secretary of State Michael Pompeo. Still, steady leaks about friction between the agencies and the NSC and rumors about McMaster's future made any calm feel fragile.[137]

In March 2018, Trump chose to replace McMaster with firebrand and former US ambassador to the United Nations John Bolton. The wily new national security advisor moved to reform the NSC, even as staffers worked to coordinate the cancellation of the Iran Deal as well as diplomatic overtures to North Korea. Among other changes, Bolton got rid of the NSC's cyber defense coordinator and downgraded its team focused on global health issues.[138] Complicating NSC-Pentagon relations, the new national security advisor also cut down on coordination meetings and hired a deputy who was known to have a contentious relationship with other senior Defense Department leaders.[139]

As in much of the rest of his unlikely administration, Trump's national security management has been hard to predict. No one knows whether Bolton will continue as advisor or be fired over Twitter tomorrow. As the world and Washington wait and interpret Trump's tweets for the latest on who's up and down in a mercurial White House, the NSC's history, with its tendency to fight for the president and capitalize on disorder in government, makes the Trump and Bolton staff worth watching closely, particularly as the president pushes for more aggressive policy on trade, Iran, and more.[140]

Although much about Trump's Washington is unclear, one thing is certain: the NSC has won another fight. After suggesting early in his term that some officials in Washington were part of a "deep state" working against him, by September of his first year, Trump had changed his tune some about at least a few public servants in Washington. He tweeted: "70 years ago today, the National Security Council met for the first time. Great history of advising Presidents-then & now! Thanks NSC Staff!"[141]

EPILOGUE

What the NSC's Warriors Have Won

O ver the years, the ornate Executive Office Building, called by one president and amateur architecture critic the "greatest monstrosity in America," has been targeted several times for razing or at least a renovation.[1] Congress even appropriated money to reface the building to fit in better with its more traditional neighbors. Still, despite complaints and plans for remodeling, the building has survived, a granite testament to government inertia and the triumph of the good enough.

Similarly, the NSC staff has been targeted for reform time and again, only to continue to work, and fight, on the Executive Office Building's third floor. The reason is relatively simple, and the same for presidents from Harry Truman to Donald Trump. When an interviewer asked the thirty-third president whether the office was, as the cliché claimed, the "loneliest job in the world," Truman replied without hesitation, "Oh yes, it's true."[2]

It still is. Commanders in chief like Trump feel they face the highest stakes and make some of the hardest decisions in the world; but thanks to Truman, none of them has had to do so alone. For over seventy years the NSC staff has been right next door. As a result of his successors' decisions, the men and women of today's NSC stand ready at the Executive Office Building to help the president with everything from his biggest choices to his most bilious tweets.

Like Michael Forrestal, Mort Halperin, Phil Dur, Richard Haass, Sandy Vershbow, Meghan O'Sullivan, Doug Lute, and hundreds of others, today's

NSC staff has been entrusted and empowered to serve the president. With that responsibility, the NSC staff has the opportunity to fight for ideas that can change the course of wars, their own lives, and history. But at a time of profound public mistrust in government and doubts about those serving in it, it is worth considering what these White House warriors have won.

Today's NSC staffers, like nearly everyone in government, want to be in the room where decisions are made, even if few know just what they will do with the privilege. Trusted to be in the Oval Office and White House Situation Room, Forrestal, Halperin, Dur, Haass, Vershbow, O'Sullivan, and Lute were driven to speak up—and write up a memorandum—when the moment was right, and more than a few times when it was wrong. The staff do so for several reasons.

O'Sullivan had personal beliefs on her mind and the Post-it note on her computer when she advocated for the surge. Like many on the NSC before and after, Bush's staffer had spent her career developing opinions about every matter of national security from how to win a war to how to keep the peace in Iraq and elsewhere, and once in the position to advocate for what one believes, it is human to do so. In addition, it was in O'Sullivan's own interest, as it is for many staffers, to raise her voice: if done at the right time, an assignment on the NSC can be a career maker and the staffers themselves can make history, as Bush's warrior did with the surge.

Even though staff members like Halperin have worked under leaders for whom they did not vote, nearly all are driven, regardless of personal politics, to serve—and speak up to support—their commander in chief. Seeing the demands on the president, the NSC staff, like Lute who signed up to report to one president only to continue under another, not only work a little harder, but most want him to succeed, sometimes despite even the commander in chief's own judgment, if more out of patriotism than partisanship.

In addition to serving personal and presidential interests, the NSC staff speak up, like Forrestal on Vietnam, Dur in Lebanon, and Haass during the Gulf War, Vershbow in Bosnia, and O'Sullivan on Iraq, because they worry that events abroad and conversations in the Situation Room are quickly drifting out of control. Those who work at the White House are not accustomed, in their careers or days, to feeling at a loss for control. For many, who after all have climbed to the apex of the US government, powerlessness in the face of world events and stalled deliberations can be a disorienting experience, especially when they fear a crisis of drift could become a catastrophe.

As the clock ticks, the staffers' frustration can grow as each feels a responsibility, for progress or postponing disaster, but none of the authority required to just order or implement their desired changes. For many on the NSC it can, as one former staffer explained, feel a "bit like trying to execute policy with a remote control. You don't own troops, diplomats, or a budget."[3] Instead, the NSC staff has the opportunity to try to convince either the proper owners in the military, diplomatic corps, and elsewhere, or the president himself that a change is needed. If persuasion proves impossible—and sometimes before it's even tried—the NSC's warriors have proven more than willing to fight for what they think is right.

Fans of television's *The West Wing* would be forgiven for expecting that once in the Oval Office, all a staffer needs to do to change policy is to deliver a well-timed whisper in the president's ear or a rousing speech in his company. It is not that such dramatic moments never occur, but real change in government requires not just speaking up but the grinding policy work required to have something new to say. A staffer, alone or with NSC and agency colleagues, must develop an idea until feasible and defend it from opposition driven by personal pique, bureaucratic jealousy, or substantive disagreement, and often all three.

Granted none of these fights are over particularly new ideas, as few proposals in war are truly novel. If anything, the staff's history is a reminder of how little new there is under the guise of national security. After all, escalations, ultimatums, and counterinsurgency are only innovative in the context of the latest conflicts. The NSC staff is usually proposing old ideas, some as old as war itself like a surge of troops, to new circumstances and a critical moment.

Yet even an old idea can have real power in the right hands at the right time, so it is worth considering how much more influence the NSC brings to its fights today.

To even make it to the Executive Office Building, the staff has demonstrated considerable political and bureaucratic skill, but the cold truth of

Washington is that what you can say, and who will listen, depends on where you sit. If Forrestal, Halperin, Dur, Haass, Vershbow, O'Sullivan, and Lute had worked anywhere other than the Executive Office Building, their voice would not have carried as far. The NSC staff's ability to fight for ideas has grown because the institution has been empowered over the last seventy years.

After all, even though Forrestal had far greater access and encouragement than his predecessors on the Truman and Dwight Eisenhower NSCs, he still had to resort to using like-minded colleagues at State and the Pentagon to send his ideas fingerprint free up the chain of command to the president. Later staffers like Halperin could recommend their own options only to face the national security advisor's heavy edits; while Dur and his teammates could come up—and cover in silver—their own proposals, they had to leverage dysfunction to get a decision made. Then, from Haass to Vershbow and O'Sullivan on to Lute, NSC staffers have taken—and been expected to exert—greater and greater strategic and operational control, crafting military plans and orders, conducting diplomacy, and coordinating operations.

The NSC has been able to do more as it has gotten bigger. Today's staff remains dramatically larger than originally intended and bigger than even the most influential NSCs in history needed to be. Although there are surely efficiency losses on larger staffs, the greater the number of staffers in the Executive Office Building, the freer they are to take on more, whether it is to write another draft of a war plan, brainstorm ideas for what to do next, or videoteleconference with those on the frontlines.

A larger staff can do even more thanks to technology. With the establishment of the Situation Room in 1961 and its subsequent upgrades, as well as the widespread adoption of email in the 1980s, the classified email system during the 2000s, and desktop video teleconferencing systems in the 2010s, White House technology upgrades have been justified because the president deserves the latest and the fastest. These same advances give each member of the staff global reach, including to war zones half a world away, from the safety of the Executive Office Building.

The NSC has also grown more powerful along with the presidency it serves. The White House, even in the hands of an inexperienced and disorganized president like Trump, drives the government's agenda, the news media's coverage, and the American public's attention. The NSC staff can, if skilled enough, leverage the office's influence for their own ideas and purposes. Presidents have also explicitly empowered the staff in big ways—like putting them in the middle of the policymaking process—and small—like granting them ranks that put them on the same level as other agency officials.

Recent staffers have also had the president's ear nearly every day, and sometimes more often, while secretaries of state and defense rarely have that much face time in the Oval Office. Each has a department with tens of thousands (and in the Pentagon's case millions) of employees to manage. Most significantly, both also answer not just to the president but to Congress, which has oversight authority for their departments and an expectation for regular updates. There are few more consequential power differences between the NSC and the departments than to whom each must answer.

Even more, the NSC staff get to work and fight in anonymity. Members of Congress, journalists, and historians are usually too busy keeping track of the National Security Council principals to focus on the guys and gals behind the national security advisors, who are themselves behind the president. Few in Washington, and fewer still across the country, know the names of the staff advising the president let alone what they are saying in their memos and moments with him.

Today, there are too many unnamed NSC staffers for anyone's good, including their own. Even with the recent congressional limit on policy staffers, the NSC is too big to be thoroughly managed or effective. National security advisors and their deputies are so busy during their days that it is hard to keep up with all their own emails, calls, and reading, let alone ensure each member of the staff is doing their own work or doing it well. The common law and a de facto honor system has also struggled to keep staff in check as they try to handle every issue from war to women's rights and every to-do list item from drafting talking points to doing secret diplomacy.

Although many factors contribute to the NSC's success, history suggests they do best with the right-size job. The answer to better national security policy and process is not a bigger staff but smaller writs. The NSC should focus on fewer issues, and then only on the smaller stuff, like what the president needs for calls and meetings, and the big, what some call grand strategic, questions about the nation's interests, ambitions, and capacities that should be asked and answered before any major decision.

It is no surprise that the 1990s staffs, with between fifty and one hundred policy staffers, or around half of the current total, probably did the best work and had the best relationships with their peers. Those staffs did fewer jobs day to day but a better job overall. They did not try to do everything and left much of the day-to-day planning and management of everything in between the small stuff and grand strategy to those in the military, diplomatic corps, and intelligence communities.

In all, committed and talented staffers—with the freedom, technological reach, access, and anonymity of the modern NSC—bring more than a voice to conversations in the Oval Office and Situation Room. Today, they are players with ideas and influence of their own, and often more clout than commanders in the field and cabinet secretaries on the National Security Council. When the NSC speaks, presidents, even unconventional ones like Trump, listen.

Now, it does not always feel that way. NSC staffing can be a frustrating slog. There are days at the Executive Office Building when members of the staff believe they are making no difference at all. Regardless of the number and passion of the NSC's memos, the president might just choose to rely on instinct or the advice of others. Even more, the operators in the agencies, who often doubt and even denigrate the staff contributions, can seem to have all the fun fighting the battles, negotiating the deals, and making all the subsequent headlines.

Still, history is a reminder that if an NSC staff member is patient and focused, he or she can be a force for change, though not always for the good.

Time on the NSC has transformed the lives of staffers. Haass, for example, managed to get married a couple of weeks after President George H. W. Bush decided to issue the Iraq ultimatum the NSC staffer helped develop.[4] Haass recalled, "The good news . . . is I went to Paris on my honeymoon. The bad news is I went with the President."[5] When on a trip that took Haass to Europe and then Saudi Arabia, Bush heard his staffer was missing his honeymoon, the president grabbed a piece of paper and wrote the new bride a note, "Dear Susan, Richard was with me today in the desert. Please forgive us."[6]

For some staffers, such dedication and sacrifice have helped make their careers. Since leaving government, Haass's leadership of the Council on Foreign Relations think tank, his books, and his punditry on morning television have ensured that his influence continues. His is just one NSC career success story, among many others: staffers Al Haig, Tony Lake, Bob Gates, Steve Hadley, Madeleine Albright, Condoleezza Rice, and Susan Rice have all climbed from the Executive Office Building's third floor to the highest levels in Washington.

Yet, for every best-selling author and cabinet secretary the NSC has produced, staffers like Forrestal, Dur, O'Sullivan, and Lute have seen their careers frustrated by their time at the Executive Office Building. Though it did not stop him from serving in government again, Halperin's story is a cautionary tale of how costly, for the individual and the country, staff fights can be. And although it remains to be seen what an assignment at the Trump NSC will mean for its staffers, at present the White House does not appear to be the resumé line it once was.

In addition to transforming their own lives, NSC staff have helped change history. The Gulf War and the Bosnian War are two of the NSC staff's and the United States' most successful military interventions. Although neither was particularly necessary or nearly as cut-and-dry as promised, each was successfully conceived and prosecuted. If the first goal of national security policy is doing no harm, both conflicts did plenty of good with relatively few downsides.

Those two examples, however, look like absolute triumphs compared to the NSC's worst hits. Forrestal's campaigns for counterinsurgency and a coup in Vietnam, the Nixon NSC's work to build a credible threat to expand the war and then to help Henry Kissinger finally hit hard, and the Reagan staff's proposals to join the fight in Lebanon demonstrate how wrong seemingly good ideas—not just for the country but for those Americans and others in harm's way—can go in war. Of course, despite the fleeting benefits of the Iraq and Afghanistan surges, shaped as much by the NSC staff as anyone else in Washington, the United States continued to fight in both countries.

In addition to changing the course of wars, these staffers have also changed the institution in which they served. Because staff practices are mostly the product of tradition and trial and error, one cannot imagine Haass's influence without Haig's earlier power or Lute's war czardom should Dur never have reported for duty at the NSC. Each staff—even, with great irony, the mischievous Nixon and Reagan teams—has begat a more powerful institution to the next, and along the way the NSC evolved from being a part of the president's team to serving as assistants to superstar national security advisors, including Kissinger, and then from process players like Haass to wartime managers, including Lute.

Along the way, the staff has taken on greater responsibilities from agencies like the departments of state and defense as each has grown more bureaucratic and sclerotic. Starting in the 1960s, the NSC dethroned the State Department in providing analysis, intelligence, and even some diplomacy to the diplomat in chief. In the years after September 11th, the staff also began to take greater responsibility, especially for planning, from the military and the rest of the Pentagon. Both departments have struggled and often failed to reclaim lost ground and influence in Washington.

As a result, today the NSC has, regretfully, become the strategic engine of the government's national security policymaking. The staff, along with the national security advisor, determine which issues—large and small—require attention, develop the plans for most of them, and try to manage day-to-day the implementation of each strategy. That is too sweeping a remit for a couple hundred unaccountable staffers sitting at the Executive Office Building thousands of miles from war zones and foreign capitals. Such immense responsibility also does not make the best use of talent in government, leaving the military and the nation's diplomats fighting with the White House over policies while trying to execute plans they have less and less ownership over.

Although protocol still requires members of the NSC to sit on the backbench in National Security Council meetings, the staff's voice and advice can carry as much weight as those of the principals sitting at the table. Just as the staff has taken on more of each department's responsibilities, the NSC are expected to be advisors to the president, even on military strategy. With that charge, the staff has taken to spending more time and effort developing their own policy ideas—and fighting for them.

Yet war is a hard thing to try to manage from the Executive Office Building. Thousands of miles from the frontlines and far from harm, the NSC make recommendations based on what they come to know from intelligence reports, news sources, phone calls, video-teleconferences, and visits to the front. Even with advice based only on this limited and limiting view, the NSC staff has transformed how the United States fights its wars.

The American way of war, developed over decades of thinking and fighting, informs how and why the nation goes to battle. Over the course of American history and, most relevantly, since the end of World War II, the US military and other national security professionals have developed, often through great turmoil, strategic preferences and habits, like deploying the latest technology possible instead of the largest number of troops. Despite the tremendous planning that goes into these most serious of undertakings, each new conflict tests the prevailing way of war and often finds it wanting.

Even knowing how dangerous it is to refight the last war, it is still not easy to find the right course for a new one. Government in general and national security specifically are risk-averse enterprises where it is often simpler to rely on standard operating procedures and stay on a chosen course, regardless of whether progress is slow and the sense of drift is severe. Even then, many in the military, who often react to even the mildest of suggestions and inquiries as unnecessary or even dangerous micromanagement, defend the prevailing approach with its defining doctrine and syndrome.

As Machiavelli recommended long ago, there is a need for hard questions in government and war in particular. He wrote that a leader "ought to be a great asker, and a patient hearer of the truth."[7] From the Executive Office Building, the NSC staff, who are more distanced from the action as well as the fog of war, have tried to fill this role for a busy and often distracted president. They are, however, not nearly as patient as Machiavelli recommended: they have proven more willing, indeed too willing at times, to ask about what is working and what is not.

Warfighters are not alone in being frustrated by questions: everyone from architects to zookeepers believes they know how best to do their job and that with a bit more time, they will get it right. Without any of the responsibility for the doing, the NSC staff not only asks hard questions but, by avoiding implementation bias, is willing to admit, often long before those in the field, that the current plan is failing. A more technologically advanced NSC, with the ability to reach deep into the chain of command and war zones for updates, has also given the staff the intelligence to back up its impatience.

Most times in history, the NSC staff has correctly predicted that time is running against a chosen strategy. Halperin, and others on the Nixon NSC, were accurate in their assessments of Vietnam. Dur and his Reagan NSC colleagues were right to worry that diplomacy was moving too slowly in Lebanon. Haass and Vershbow were correct when they were concerned with how windows of opportunity for action were shrinking in the Gulf and Balkans respectively, just as O'Sullivan was right that things needed to change relatively soon in Iraq.

Yet an impatient NSC staff has a worse track record giving the president answers to what should come next. The NSC staff naturally have opinions and ideas about what can be done when events and war feel out of control, but the very distance and disengagement that allow the NSC to be so effective at measuring progress make its ideas less grounded in operational realities and more clouded by the fog of Washington. The NSC, often stridently, wants to do *something more*, to "go big when we can," as one recent staffer encouraged his president, to fix a failing policy or win a war, but that is not a strategy, nor does that ambition make the staff the best equipped to figure out the next steps.[8]

With their proposals for a new plan, deployment, or initiative, the staff has made more bad recommendations than good. The Diem coup and the Beirut mission are two examples, and particularly tragic ones at that, of NSC staff recommendations gone awry. The Iraq surge was certainly a courageous decision, but by committing so many troops to that country, the manpower was not available for a war in Afghanistan that was falling off track. Even the more successful NSC recommendations for changes in US strategy in the Gulf War and in Bosnia did not end up exactly as planned, in part because even good ideas in war rarely do.

Although presidents bear the ultimate responsibilities for these decisions, the NSC staff played an essential, and increasing, role in the thinking behind each bold move. In conflict after conflict, a more powerful NSC staff has fundamentally altered the American way of war. It is now far less informed by the perspective of the military and the view from the frontlines. It is less patient for progress and more dependent on the clocks in the Executive Office Building and Washington than those in theater. It is far more combative, less able to accept defeat, and more willing to risk a change of course. And it is characterized by more frequent and counterproductive friction between the civilian and military leaders.

Such a way of war is a recipe for frustration and failure on the frontlines, as the United States has found since September 11th. Fighting a global war against terrorism was never going to be easy, but in debates about Iraq, Afghanistan, and elsewhere, the NSC staffers, for all their good intentions and perhaps because of them, have preferred to go big and go now, rather than aim for more realistic objectives or their pragmatic pursuit. Instead, good money and many good men and women have been thrown into fights that were impossible to win.

Through it all, as the NSC's voice has grown louder in the nation's war rooms, the staff has transformed how Washington works, and more often does not work. The NSC's fights to change course have had another casualty: the ugly collapse of the common law that has governed Washington policymaking for more than a generation. The result today is a government that trusts less, fights more, and decides much slower.

National security policy- and decision-making was never supposed to be a fair fight. Eliot Cohen, a civil-military scholar with high-level government experience, has called the give-and-take of the interagency process an "unequal" dialogue—one in which presidents are entitled to not just make the ultimate decision but also to ask questions, often with the NSC's help, at any time and about any topic.[9] Everyone else, from the secretaries of state and defense in Washington down to the commanders and ambassadors abroad, has to expect and tolerate such presidential interventions and then carry out his orders.

Even an unfair fight can have rules, however. The NSC common laws kept the peace in Washington for years after Iran-Contra. The restrictions against outright advocacy and outsized operational responsibilities were accepted by those at the White House as well as in the agencies during Republican and Democratic administrations. Yet as many in Washington believed the world grew more interconnected and the national security stakes increased, especially after September 11th, a more powerful NSC has given staffers the opportunity to bend, and occasionally break, the common laws, as they have been expected to and allowed to take on more responsibilities for developing strategies and new ideas from those in the bureaucracy and military.

The NSC staff has gotten away with it because presidents have not just endured but rewarded such behavior. Commanders in chief encouraged warriors on their staffs especially when matters looked lost. A bigger, more technologically advanced staff is also harder to constrain by should-be managers like the national security advisor, who has his or her own responsibilities advising the president and chairing many of the national security process's meetings.

The rest of Washington has, despite the occasional contretemps, looked the other way. As with other parts of what has been called the imperial presidency, Congress, driven by partisan politics, deference to commanders in chief, and disinterest in foreign policy oversight, has chosen not to referee the NSC's fights. The 2016 reform of the staff proves the point: the proposed limit on the NSC was so broadly written that the very NSC it meant to rein in— Obama's—would not have required any significant changes.

Self-interest also appears to drive the judgments of others in the nation's capital as well. Journalists, think tank denizens, and former officials appear more interested in preserving access to the NSC than in questioning its members publicly. Meanwhile, National Security Council principals, who have the greatest interest in checking the staff, have demonstrated it is hard to say "no" to the commander in chief and those on the NSC who appear to speak on his behalf. Even more, these cabinet secretaries prefer to try to either co-opt the staff or confound them rather than calling them out, especially to the president or in public.

The result has been the death of the common law. When the president wants some intelligence or insight, staffers are expected, even by those frustrated by their overreach, to go to great lengths, sometimes all the way to a war zone, to get it. At the same time, honest brokering, which was never as easy in practice as it was in the prose of scholars who expect ambitious policymakers to become opinion-less eunuchs after walking into the Executive Office Building, has proven impossible as politics and government itself grew more divided and fractious. Today, few expect the NSC to keep their opinions to themselves or are surprised when staffers aggressively advocate and fight for their ideas. After all, warriors make terrible brokers.

Without the common law, a decade-long bureaucratic battle of attrition has broken out in the nation's capital. As in the George W. Bush and Barack Obama administrations, when faced with a problem over a policy matter or process, the NSC staff reacts (and sometimes overreacts) to fix it, which frustrates those in the agencies, most often the Defense Department, and feeds a nasty cycle of reaction and counterreaction. To avoid further micromanagement, the bureaucracy will grow less cooperative, more combative, or both, which only leads to more forceful NSC intervention. In the end, relationships are burned, processes slow down, and governing becomes near impossible without a fight.

Despite this counterproductive cycle, Washington has time and again either ignored, absolved, or begrudgingly accepted the NSC staff and all but its most egregious overreaches. The result is the unprecedented evolution of a powerful and opinionated institution at the heart of government with little legal foundation, oversight from Congress, or exposure to the press and the American public. Such a development is remarkable in its own right, and but downright risky in the Trump presidency, which has exhibited so little sound management and so much discord. No one should be surprised if, during whatever time is left in the Trump administration, his NSC creates another uproar or real scandal and provides further reasons for Americans to distrust their government.

When a staffer raises his or her voice, different people hear different things. For some, their arguments represent good staffing. For others, they can sound like a micromanager wielding an 8,000-mile screwdriver. Still some may label the interventions as the heroic work of public servants stepping forward to save a war before it goes any further wrong. And then there are those who hear the whispers of a conspiracy of unaccountable bureaucrats pursuing their own interests over the nation's.

The rise of the NSC has not gone unnoticed in Washington. Among the frustrated, few have more experience than Bob Gates, the former NSC staffer, CIA director, and defense secretary, who believed the last staff with whom he worked had become "an operational body with its own policy agenda."[10] Gates is not alone: scholars, members of Congress, and journalists have in recent years begun to question the NSC, even if its perceived influence is difficult to decipher from outside the Executive Office Building.[11]

No matter the criticisms, history suggests the NSC will live to fight and speak up another day. For one, if the NSC did not exist, the staff would need to be invented. Someone needs to help bring regular order to national security decision-making, and the NSC staff is as good as any other option. One of the early designers of the National Security Council admitted how impossible it was to come up with a single plan that made sense for all the nation's interests and traditions. The same is true today: the president and the process need some support, and imperfect as the staff may be, at least they do that much.

Besides, the NSC staff is better than nothing. Even if it should be smaller, better managed, and less aggressive, the staff play a necessary role in coordinating national security players and policy, one that is not missed until it goes missing, as it has at times in the Trump administration. The staff are also now considered an indispensable piece of the fabric of Washington—so much so that changing one letter of its name proved impossible—and it is unlikely to disappear for as long as there is a president and a presidency. Commanders in chief want staffers, and even warriors, exactly where they are.

Still, the NSC must make some changes because even as the staff has grown more powerful, it has lost control of its own story. Indeed, the reason the NSC must change is not the threat of congressional reforms or even oversight, a step that has been considered at times and feverishly fought by White House after White House. Nor is the potential for a bad decision in war or even another scandal like Iran-Contra the reason for adjustment. No, the biggest reason the NSC must itself change course is the perception that like others in the federal bureaucracy, the staff is part of what some call a "deep state."

The NSC has grown in power, and its fights more intense, just as Americans have lost trust that government works and become increasingly fixated on the belief that a shadowy group of unelected officials secretly manipulate policy to pursue their own interests. Though the "deep state" is foreign to American ears, the term was torn from Turkey, where a self-appointed group of military and civil officials have tried to protect the nation's democracy from those intent on less secular government, the fear of an unaccountable government is even older than the United States itself.

Today, different parties in the country have appropriated, and misappropriated, the concept. To Trump, who has suggested he does not like the term but still tweeted about the "deep state," and some of those he brought into government, it is a culprit that has stymied progress on his agenda at times.[12] Meanwhile, others, including the anonymous author of the infamous September 2018 *New York Times* opinion piece, believe government officials who comprise a "steady state" amid Trump's chaotic presidency are "unsung heroes" resisting his worst instincts and overreaches.[13] Thus, it is no surprise that more and more Americans are concerned: a 2018 poll found that 74 percent of Americans feel a group of officials are able to control government policy without accountability.[14]

In an era when Americans can see on reality television how their fish are caught, meals are cooked, and businesses are financed, it is strange that few have ever heard the voice of an NSC staffer. The Executive Office Building is not the only building out of reach: most of the government taxpayers' fund is hard, and getting harder, to see. With bigger security blockades, longer waits on declassification, and more severe crackdowns on leaks, it is no wonder some Americans have taken to assuming the worst of their public servants.

The American people need to know the NSC's war stories if for no other reason than each makes clear that there is no organized deep state in Washington. If one existed, there would be little need for the NSC to fight so hard to coordinate the government's various players and parts. However, this history also makes plain that though the United States can overcome bad decisions and survive military disasters, a belief in a deep state is a threat to the NSC and so much more.

For all the NSC memoranda and Situation Room debates about the defense of the nation's security, few crises have ever been as dangerous to the future of the NSC staff than the collapsing trust in the government it helps manage. Americans' faith that elected officials and public servants are dedicated to every citizen's interest is the foundation of not just the National Security Council and the entire US government but the American way of life. A breakdown in this trust and the pervasive belief in a conspiratorial deep state threatens the nation's representative democracy.

Amid the whispers, some in Washington have come to treat the label as an inside joke, a badge of honor, or unworthy of serious consideration. But the accusation that some in government and the NSC itself are part of the deep state, which is gaining momentum of its own, is too serious to brush off and too far out of Washington policymakers' control. The NSC needs to respond to this threat in the same way it reacts to other national security risks: by taking action to change course—and change the perception that the staff and others are secretly pulling the strings in government—before it is too late.

If the greatest trust is giving counsel, the NSC needs to rebuild trust with the American public by opening up and demonstrating that they serve the public as much as the president. One easy way to do so would be for the current and future national security advisors and NSCs to volunteer for some level of congressional oversight. For example, the staff could, like presidential nominees for senior appointments at the agencies, respond to background questionnaires and disclose their financial obligations. Although the president himself may prefer otherwise, and there is some reason to doubt whether Congress can or even wants to handle the responsibility, the power of the NSC has increased to the point that anonymity no longer makes sense.

Besides, the NSC's history is full of ironies—whenever it appeared destined for reform, it only seemed to gain power—and welcoming public scrutiny may provide another: the NSC might just find a few admirers after opening up, not just for themselves but for the president's decisions. If Americans knew how hard these choices are, and how bad the other options can be, they might better appreciate and support the policies made in their name. Even more, the public might also come to know the hardworking staff not as a deep state but as the dedicated government servants most are.

Each member of the NSC staff needs to remember that their growing, unaccountable power has helped give evidence to the worries about a deep state. Although no one in Washington gives up influence voluntarily, the staff, even its warriors, need to remember it is not just what they fight for but whether a fight is necessary at all. Shortcuts and squabbles may make sense when every second feels like it counts, but the best public servants do what is necessary for the president even as they protect, for years to come, the health of the institutions and the very democracy in which they serve. As hard as that can be to remember when the clock in the Oval Office is ticking, doing things the right way is even more important than the latest crises, war, or meeting with the president.

Right now, on the third floor of the Executive Office Building, there is an NSC staff member figuring out what to say when he or she next sees the president. Most Americans will never hear the staffer's voice, step foot in his or her cipher-locked office, or read one of their classified memoranda. Instead, when an American walks by the Executive Office Building, they must trust the staff on the third floor is fighting for them.

Although no organized deep state exists in Washington, the American people are not wrong to worry about one. Too many in Washington, including at the Executive Office Building, have forgotten that public service is a privilege that bestows on them great responsibility. Although the NSC has long justified its actions in the name of national security, the means with which its members have pursued that objective have made for a more aggressive American way of war, a more fractious Washington, and more conspiracies about government.

Centuries ago, Plato argued that civilians must hope for warriors who could be trusted to be both "gentle to their own and cruel to their enemies."[15] At a time when many doubt government and those who serve in it, the NSC staff's history demonstrates just what White House warriors are capable of. The question is for what and for whom they will fight in the years and wars ahead.

DEBTS

I got debts that no honest man can pay . . .

—BRUCE SPRINGSTEEN, "ATLANTIC CITY"[1]

One of the first public servants I remember seeing was a scoundrel. As rain ruined a family vacation day in 1987, I was eight years old and sitting in a hotel room with my mother and siblings captivated by the Capitol Hill hearings into the Iran-Contra scandal. Like millions of Americans around the country, I watched as Marine Colonel Oliver North sat upright in his olive uniform and tried to explain to a crowd of congressmen his and the NSC staff's misadventure.

As I have learned since, North was not a true reflection of those who serve their nation. Year after year, in good times and wartimes, remarkable men and women have shown up in Washington with a dream to serve their country. Their service has been one of the secrets of America's success, and their dedication and diligence, even when leading to errors, shows why it is unwise to thoughtlessly doubt America's future or blindly criticize Washington.

In the preceding pages, you have met a few of these public servants, NSC staffers like Michael Forrestal, Mort Halperin, Phil Dur, Richard Haass, Sandy Vershbow, Meghan O'Sullivan, and Doug Lute, whose work and fights sit at the heart of this book. For this project, I have been trusted with telling the story of their service, including not just the highlights but some of the lows. If I have told their stories right and done them justice, it is because I have been blessed with a great deal of help and accumulated a great number of debts along the way.

Although this book does not reflect any of the history I lived through in government, how I think about public service, and public servants, was shaped by the talented, humble, and dedicated people I have served alongside at the Pentagon, at the Treasury Department, in the navy, on Capitol Hill, and elsewhere in Washington. To know the NSC is to be saved or scolded by its staffers; I have done both and been fortunate to learn from cabinet secretaries and members of Congress, and from quiet career government employees and junior military officers, what it means to dedicate a day and a life to one's country.

This book started as a dissertation at the Johns Hopkins University's School of Advanced International Studies (SAIS), a one-of-a-kind institution that remains my kind of place. There Eliot Cohen, Erik Jones, John Harper, David Calleo, James Mann, Dan Markey, Dana Allin, Ken Keller, Michael Plummer, Jessica Einhorn, and Vali Nasr and more have been good friends to me and my writing. The rest of my dissertation committee, Kurt Campbell, Tom Keaney, Mort Halperin, I. M. Destler, and Eric Edelman shaped the initial study and the many revisions that led to this book.

My writing was also nurtured under the roof of the German Marshall Fund. A few blocks from SAIS in Washington's Dupont Circle, the GMF mansion is a home for civilized conversations and committed thinkers, which I occasionally diverted on the hunt for distraction or another shot of espresso. Karen Donfried, Derek Chollet, Sophie Arts, Nicola Lightner, and many others were kind and generous hosts.

The volume was finished as I joined Perry World House at the University of Pennsylvania, which, under its leader, William Burke-White, is an exciting new venture at one of the country's oldest schools. I was born at the University of Pennsylvania, but joining the team at Perry World House has felt like a homecoming because of the generosity of Richard and Lisa Perry and the dedication of Bill, Michael Horowitz, LaShawn Jefferson, Amy Gadsden, Tony Sorrentino, Leah Popowich, Debbie Rech, Itai Barsade, Lisa Jourdan, Brian Yansak, Ashley Napier, Carter Goodwin, and especially Andro Mathewson.

Publishing a book is an adventure of a different kind, and I've been fortunate to have the right guides for the journey. My friend and shipmate Greg Melville provided wise counsel along the way. My agent Andrew Stuart read a book review I wrote almost a decade ago, kept in touch in the years since, and managed my many calls and questions as he delivered a tremendous opportunity. Sacha Zimmerman has been a good friend and copyeditor. And the team at Liveright, a division of W.W. Norton, including Phil Marino, Gina Iaquinta, Peter Miller, and in particular Katie Adams, have been the right partners to get this ready and, hopefully, read.

A few friends have done more for this project than I deserve. Mike Casey answered every call, read every word, and believed in me and this project despite it all. Josh Earnest made countless introductions and talked endlessly about this book. Brian Hallisay, along with his wife, Jennifer, hosted the research trips that led to so many of this book's endnotes, but it was their friendship and support that helped me fill the rest of the pages. Jeremy Ventuso, Ashley Elliot, Will Herter, John Harper, Aaron Sherman, Derek Chollet, James Wilson, Brian McKeon, Alexandra Evans, Hal Brands, and Ylber Bajraktari, and more have read drafts and provided never-ending encouragement. They and many other dear friends have done more than I can ever repay.

As I wrote these staff stories, my family has also helped me figure out my own story, and to live it as well as I can. My parents, John and Eileen, have encouraged every word since my first, and my mother, who loves politics, Washington, and a good tale in equal measure, has done more for this project than can ever be explained. My other parents Vinod and Sita have kept me loved and fed along the way. And all my siblings, Allison and Charlie, and Erin and Rit, have listened and helped me live and laugh through these pages and many of the past few years' ups and downs. I owe them all.

Of course, the White House warriors have kept my new and growing family company (and occasionally crazy) in its first few years. Jack, who was born just as this project began, and Henry, who was born three days after the penultimate edits were submitted, are a reminder of what is at stake in these pages. Their arrivals are just two of the many changes we have been blessed by these past few years. Thanks to my wife Anjuli, we have all made it through it all and these pages, in good form. If this story, my story, and our story, is centered, if it has any heart at all, it is thanks to her. I owe Anji everything.

NOTE ON SOURCES

The legendary British double agent Kim Philby wrote: "Just because a document is a document it has a glamour which tempts the reader to give it more weight than it deserves.... An hour's serious discussion with a trustworthy informant is often more valuable than any number of original documents. Of course, it is best to have both."[1] In writing this history and learning about the NSC, I have been fortunate to "have both" and more.

Over eighty public servants—trustworthy informants all—have spent many hours answering my questions, correcting me, and flattering this project, and me, with their attention and patience. The full list of interviewees reflects many of the individuals who have shaped American foreign policy over the last fifty years, but it does not include everyone who spoke to me about this book, as some preferred to remain anonymous. In particular, I must thank the NSC staffers, Mort Halperin, Phil Dur, Richard Haass, Sandy Vershbow, Meghan O'Sullivan, and Doug Lute, who dealt with me, and my queries, with patience and kindness. Howard Teicher, Geoff Kemp, Sandy Drew, and Peter Feaver also deserve special thanks.

In addition to these conversations, this book is built on the work of others. It would not exist but for those who have served, and written, in government, and had their work end up at an archive. It would not exist but for all those who have ever FOIA'ed a document to free it from overly onerous secrecy requirements. And it would not exist but for the enthusiastic support of the librarians at Johns Hopkins University, as well as the staff at the Truman, Eisenhower, Kennedy, Johnson, Nixon, Ford, Carter, Reagan, George Bush, and Clinton libraries, the National Security Archives at George Washington University, and the National Archives.

Generations of authors, journalists, scholars, editors, and publishers have also helped us all understand this history. In particular, David Rothkopf, Ivo Daalder, and I. M. Destler have exposed the NSC to the little sunlight it has ever seen. Their books introduced the world to the staff, even if the staffers occasionally got lost in the shadows of presidents and national security advisors. This book exists in part because of Rothkopf's, Daalder's, and Destler's work.

In addition, Anna Nelson and Alfred Sander are the reasons we know what we know about the Truman years and the NSC's early history, and David Halberstam is the only reason we can write knowingly about the Kennedy presidency and so-called Camelot. Walter Isaacson and Seymour Hersh exposed the Nixon-Kissinger-NSC psychodrama. Lou Cannon got inside Ronald Reagan's head. Bob Woodward has done more than anyone else for Americans to understand the wars fought in their names over the past four decades, including the Gulf War, the Balkans (further illuminated by Elizabeth Drew, Derek Chollet, and Daalder), and the wars in Iraq and Afghanistan (with context added by Tom Ricks, Fred Kaplan, and Michael Gordon and Bernard Trainor). No one can write about these presidencies without following in these authors' considerable footsteps and footnotes.

Still, trying to tell the heretofore untold story of the people and power of the NSC required, as Philby could attest, a lucky break or two. Good fortune helped me catch out of one bleary eye a small handwritten note at the Reagan archive. I have also run into sources on the streets of Washington and harangued them into an interview. And folks, like the unpaid intern at *The Atlantic* who took an interest and tracked down an old article, have helped me connect a dot or two.

I could not have written this book without any of these predecessors or breaks. Any errors are my own.

NOTES

Introduction: The President's "Personal Band of Warriors"

1. Peter Baker, *Days of Fire: Bush and Cheney In the White House* (New York: Doubleday, 2013), 524.
2. George W. Bush, *Decision Points* (New York: Crown Publishers, 2010). Kindle Edition, locations: 6544, 6620.
3. Meghan O'Sullivan, interview with author, August 30, 2017.
4. "The Men Who Guard the Nation's Security," *New York Times*, August 29, 1948, SM10.
5. Ivo H. Daalder and I. M. Destler, *In the Shadow of the Oval Office: Profiles of the National Security Advisers and the Presidents They Served: From JFK to George W. Bush* (New York: Simon & Schuster, 2009), 4; Anna Kasten Nelson, "President Truman and the Evolution of the National Security Council," *Journal of American History* 72, no. 2 (September 1985): 387; Director, Memorandum for the President, August 8, 1947, 1; Clark Clifford Papers, Box 11, Harry S. Truman Presidential Library (HSTL).
6. Director, Memorandum for the President, August 8, 1947, 2; Clark Clifford Papers, Box 11.
7. Richard E. Neustadt, *Presidential Power and the Modern Presidents: The Politics of Leadership from Roosevelt to Reagan* (New York: Free Press, 1990), 7.
8. Baker, *Days of Fire*, 525.

Chapter One: "The Bright, Young Men" on the NSC

1. Andrew Preston, "The Soft Hawks' Dilemma in Vietnam: Michael V. Forrestal at the National Security Council, 1962–1964," *International History Review* 25, no. 1 (March 2003), 63; Robert S. McNamara, *In Retrospect: The Tragedy and Lessons of Vietnam* (New York: Vintage Books, 1996), 83.

2. Arthur M. Schlesinger Jr., *A Thousand Days: John F. Kennedy in the White House* (New York: Houghton Mifflin, 1965), 997.

3. Robert Dallek, *Franklin D. Roosevelt and American Foreign Policy, 1932–1945* (New York: Oxford University Press, 1979), 29.

4. Warren F. Kimball, *The Juggler: Franklin Roosevelt as Wartime Statesman* (Princeton, NJ: Princeton University Press, 1991), 7.

5. Alfred D. Sander, "Truman and the National Security Council: 1945–1947," *Journal of American History* 59, issue 2 (September 1, 1972): 371.

6. Ferdinand Eberstadt, "Postwar Organization for National Security," in *Fateful Decisions: Inside the National Security Council*, ed. Karl F. Inderfurth and Loch K. Johnson (New York: Oxford University Press, 2004), 18.

7. Ibid.

8. Anna Kasten Nelson, "President Truman and the Evolution of the National Security Council," *Journal of American History* 72, no. 2 (September 1985): 363.

9. Ibid., 362–64.

10. Ibid.; Charles S. Murphy, Richard E. Neustadt, David H. Stowe, and James E. Webb interviewed by Hugh Heclo and Anna Nelson, "Oral History Interview with The Truman White House," HSTL, February 20, 1980.

11. Sander, "Truman and the National Security Council: 1945–1947," 380–81.

12. Ibid., 387.

13. Director, Memorandum for the President, August 8, 1947, Box 11, Clark Clifford Papers, HSTL, 1–2, 8–9.

14. "Minutes of the First Meeting of the National Security Council," September 26, 1947, Document 225, *Foreign Relations of the United States* (FRUS) 1945–1950, Retrospective Volume, Emergence of the Intelligence.

15. Charles S. Murphy, Richard E. Neustadt, David H. Stowe, and James E. Webb, "Oral History Interview with The Truman White House," interviewed by Hugh Heclo and Anna Nelson, HSTL, February 20, 1980.

16. "The Men Who Guard the Nation's Security," *New York Times*, August 29, 1948, SM10.

17. Daalder and Destler, *In the Shadow*, 4.

18. Anthony Levierow, "Coordinator of Security," *New York Times*, April 24, 1949, SM60.

19. Sidney W. Souers, "Policy Formulation for National Security," *American Political Science Review* 43, no. 3 (June 1949): 537.

20. Ibid.

21. Nelson, "President Truman and the Evolution of the National Security Council," 370.

22. Souers, "Policy Formulation for National Security," 537.

23. "Ambassador Max Waldo Bishop," February 26, 1993, *Foreign Affairs Oral History Collection*, Association for Diplomatic Studies and Training, Arlington, VA, www.adst.org.

24. Ibid.

25. Ibid.

26. "Six Truman Plans Shuffle Agencies," *New York Times*, August 21, 1949, 32; James Reston, "Hoover Group Asks Truman Unify Home-Foreign Plans," *New York Times*, December 13, 1948, 1.

27. Robert A. Lovett, "Perspective on the Policy Process," in *The National Security Council: Jackson Subcommittee Papers on Policy-Making at the Presidential Level*, ed. Henry M. Jackson (New York: Frederick A. Praeger, 1965), 78.

28. National Security Council Report 68 (NSC-68), 66, HSTL, http://www .trumanlibrary.org/whistlestop/study_collections/coldwar/documents/ pdf/10-1.pdf.

29. Ibid; "Organization for Coordinating National Security Policies and Programs," NSC-68/1.3 Annex 9, Records of the National Security Council, 11-13, HSTL; Nelson, "President Truman and the Evolution of the National Security Council," 375–76.

30. Richard A. Best Jr., "The National Security Council: An Organizational Assessment," Congressional Research Service, 7-5700, RL30840, December 28, 2011, 8.

31. Nelson, "President Truman and the Evolution of the National Security Council," 373.

32. James Reston, "President Orders Harriman to Brace Security Policies," *New York Times*, July 31, 1950, 1.

33. Dwight D. Eisenhower, "Text of Eisenhower Speech at Party Rally in Baltimore," *Washington Post*, September 26, 1952, 14.

34. Fred I. Greenstein and Richard H. Immerman, "Effective National Security Advising: Recovering the Eisenhower Legacy," *Political Science Quarterly* 115, no. 3 (Autumn 2000): 339.

35. "Memorandum for the President by the Special Assistant to the President for National Security Affairs (Cutler)," subject: "Recommendations Regarding the National Security Council," March 16, 1953, Document 49, FRUS, 1952–1954, vol. 2, part 1, National Security Affairs; Robert Cutler, "The Development of the National Security Council," *Foreign Affairs* 34, no. 3 (April 1956); Robert Cutler, "Use of the NSC Mechanism," Dillon Anderson-Robert Cutler (2), Box 1, series 1: General Correspondence, 1947–1976, Gordon Gray Papers, Dwight D. Eisenhower Presidential Library, Museum and Boyhood Home (EPL), 2.

36. Dwight D. Eisenhower: "White House Statement Concerning Steps Taken To Strengthen and Improve the Operations of the National Security Council," March 23, 1953, online by Gerhard Peters and John T. Woolley, The American Presidency Project, http://www.presidency.ucsb.edu/ws/?pid=9800; "Memorandum for the President by the Special Assistant to the President for National Security Affairs (Cutler)."

37. Dillon Anderson, "The President and National Security," *The Atlantic*, January 1956, 44.

38. Robert D. McFadden, "Robert Bowie, 104, Adviser to Truman, Eisenhower, Johnson and Carter, Dies," *New York Times*, November 20, 2013.

39. "State, Spa CD Directors to Attend Board Meeting," *Schenectady Gazette*, July 6, 1963.

40. "Memorandum for the President by the Special Assistant to the President for National Security Affairs (Cutler)."

41. See for example: "Report to the National Security Council by the Executive Secretary (Lay)," NSC 162/2, October 30, 1953, Document 101, FRUS, 1952–1954, National Security Affairs, vol. 2, part 1; and National Security Council Report, "U.S. Action in Event of Unprovoked Communist Attack against U.S. Aircraft," April 23, 1956, Document 76, FRUS, 1955–1957, vol. 19, National Security Policy.

42. Greenstein and Immerman, "Effective National Security Advising: Recovering the Eisenhower Legacy," 343.

43. Dale Smith, "What is O.C.B.?" *Foreign Service Journal* (November 1955): 48.

44. "Ambassador Max Waldo Bishop," Association for Diplomatic Studies and Training.

45. Robert Bowie and Richard H. Immerman, *Waging Peace: How Eisenhower Shaped an Enduring Cold War Strategy* (New York: Oxford University Press, 1998), 139.

46. "Report to the National Security Council by the Executive Secretary (Lay)."

47. Ibid.

48. Robert Cutler, "The Development of the National Security Council," 444–48.

49. Ibid., 448–49.

50. See "Note by the President's Special Assistant for National Security Affairs (Cutler)," April 2, 1958, Document 15, FRUS, 1958–1960, vol. 3, Document 15; "Memorandum From the President's Special Assistant for National Security Affairs (Cutler) to President Eisenhower," April 7, 1958, Document 17, FRUS, 1958–1960, vol. 3; and Robert Cutler, "The National Security Council under President Eisenhower," *The National Security Council: Jackson Subcommittee Papers on Policy-Making at the Presidential Level*, ed. Henry M. Jackson (New York: Frederick A. Praeger, 1965), 111–39.

51. Senator Henry M. Jackson, "How Shall We Forge a Strategy of Survival?," address before the National War College, Washington, DC, April 16, 1959, reprinted in *Fateful Decisions*, ed. Inderfurth and Johnson, 53.

52. Henry M. Jackson, ed., *The National Security Council: Jackson Subcommittee Papers on Policy-Making at the Presidential Level* (New York: Frederick A. Praeger, 1965), 25.

53. Dean Acheson, "Recorded Interview by Lucius D. Battle," April 27, 1964, Oral Histories, John F. Kennedy Presidential Library (JFKPL), 6.

54. Richard Reeves, *President Kennedy: Profile of Power* (New York: Simon & Schuster, 1993), 23; Jack Raymond, "U.S. Security Council Assailed; Senators Report Time-Wasting," *New York Times*, December 20, 1960, 1.

55. Richard Neustadt, "Memo 2: Attachment A: Roosevelt's Approach to Staffing the White House," in *Preparing to Be President: The Memos of Richard E. Neustadt*, ed. Charles O. Jones (Washington, DC: AEI Press, 2000), 40 and 58.

56. Richard Neustadt, "Memo 6: The National Security Council: First Steps," in *Preparing to Be President*, 77–78.

57. I. M. Destler, "National Security Management: What Presidents Have Wrought," *Political Science Quarterly* 95, no. 4 (Winter 1980–1981): 579.

58. Office of the Historian, History of the National Security Council, 1947–1997, U.S. Department of State; August 1997; Bromley K. Smith, *Organizational History of the National Security Council during the Kennedy and Johnson Administrations* (Washington, DC: National Security Council, 1988); Michael V. Forrestal, recorded interview by Joseph Kraft, April 8, 1964, (1), JFKPL, 57.

59. Forrestal, (1), JFKPL, 41.

60. Ibid., 4–5.

61. Stanley Karnow, *Vietnam: A History* (New York: Viking Press, 1983), 249.

62. Andrew Preston, *The War Council* (Cambridge, MA: Harvard University Press, 2010), 78–81.

63. Charles Bartlett, "Executive Team Changes Coming," *Battle Creek Enquirer*, February 20, 1961, 6.

64. Amy B. Zegart, *Flawed by Design: The Evolution of the CIA, JCS, and NSC* (Stanford, CA: Stanford University Press, 1999), 97.

65. Paige E. Mulhollan, "Bromley Smith Oral History Interview I," transcript, internet copy, Lyndon B. Johnson Library (LBJL), July 29, 1969.

66. James Reston, "How Cambridge Flunked the First Test," *New York Times*, April 28, 1961, 30.

67. Daalder and Destler, *In the Shadow*, 24.

68. Andrew Preston, "The Little State Department: McGeorge Bundy and the National Security Council Staff, 1961–65," *Presidential Studies Quarterly* 31, no. 4 (December 2001): 646.

69. Smith, *Organizational History of the National Security Council*, 12.

70. "Memorandum for President Kennedy, June 22, 1961," Document 31, FRUS 1961–1963, vol. 8, National Security Policy, 1961–1963.

71. Forrestal, (1), JFKPL, 7.

72. David Halberstam. *The Best and the Brightest* (New York: Random House, 2001), 39.

73. Ibid., 93.

74. Gordon M. Goldstein, *Lessons in Disaster: McGeorge Bundy and the Path to War in Vietnam* (New York: Henry Holt, 2009), 77.

75. "Memorandum for the Record of the White House Daily Staff Meeting," March 30, 1964, Document 99, FRUS, 1964–1968, vol. 1.

76. Paige E. Mulhollan, "Michael Forrestal Oral History Interview I," transcript, internet copy, LBJL, November 3, 1969.

77. Forrestal, (1), JFKPL, 58–59.

78. Preston, "The Soft Hawks' Dilemma in Vietnam," 74.

79. Ibid., 71.

80. *The Pentagon Papers: The Defense Department History of United States Decision-making on Vietnam*. Senator Gravel edition (Boston: Beacon Press, 1971), 203.

81. "Telegram From the Department of State to the Embassy in Vietnam," August 24, 1963, 9:36 p.m., Document 281, FRUS, 1961–1963, vol. 3, Vietnam, January–August 1963.

82. "Telegram From Michael V. Forrestal of the National Security Council Staff to the President, at Hyannis Port, Massachusetts," August 24, 1963, 4:50 p.m., Document 280, FRUS, 1961–1963, vol. 3, Vietnam, January–August 1963.

83. "Telegram From the Department of State to the Embassy in Vietnam."

84. David M. Barrett, *Uncertain Warriors: Lyndon Johnson and His Vietnam Advisers* (Lawrence: University Press of Kansas, 1993), 15; Maxwell D. Taylor, *Swords and Plowshares* (New York: W. W. Norton, 1972), 292.

85. David E. Kaiser, *American Tragedy: Kennedy, Johnson, and the Origins of the Vietnam War* (Cambridge, MA: Belknap Press of Harvard University Press, 2000), 264.

86. Goldstein, *Lessons in Disaster*, 94.

87. Michael V. Forrestal, recorded interview by Joseph Kraft, August 14, 1964 (3), JFKPL; and Goldstein, *Lessons in Disaster*, 94.

88. Kahin, *Intervention*, 183.

89. "Memorandum for the Record of Discussion at the Daily White House Staff Meeting," November 1, 1963, 8 a.m., Document 263, FRUS, 1961–1963, vol. 4, August–December 1963.

90. Kai Bird, *The Color of Truth: McGeorge Bundy and William Bundy: Brothers In Arms: A Biography* (New York: Simon & Schuster, 1998), 263.

91. Mulhollan, "Michael Forrestal Oral History Interview I," 25.

92. Forrestal, (3), JFKPL.

93. Goldstein, *Lessons in Disaster*, 101.

94. Paige E. Mulhollan, "McGeorge Bundy Oral History Interview I," transcript, internet copy, LBJPL, January 30, 1969, 36.

95. Mulhollan, "Michael Forrestal Oral History Interview I," 25.

96. "Memorandum From Michael V. Forrestal of the National Security Council Staff to the President's Special Assistant for National Security Affairs (Bundy)," March 30, 1964, Document 100, FRUS 1964–1968, vol. 1.

97. See note 1; also, "Memorandum From Michael V. Forrestal of the National Security Council Staff to the President," subject: "South Vietnam," May 29, 1964, Document 183, FRUS 1964–1968, vol. 1, Vietnam.

98. Mulhollan, "Michael Forrestal Oral History Interview I," 25.

99. Ibid., 21.

100. Chester Cooper, *The Lost Crusade* (New York: Dodd, Mead, 1970), 249.

101. "Memorandum From the President's Special Assistant for National Security Affairs (Bundy) to Secretary of State Rusk," December 1, 1965, Document 158,

FRUS, 1964–1968, vol. 33, Organization and Management of Foreign Policy; United Nations.

102. National Security File, Country File, Vietnam, "Volume 23," Box 11, Document 161 and 161a, Thompson to Bundy, attachment, Forrestal to The Secretary, December 4, 1964, LBJ Library; National Security File, Country File, Vietnam, "Volume 23," Box 11, Document 161a, attachment, Forrestal to The Secretary, December 2, 1964, LBJPL.

103. "Memorandum From Chester L. Cooper of the National Security Council Staff to the President's Special Assistant for National Security Affairs (Bundy)," subject: "Vietnam," March 1, 1965, Document 173, FRUS 1964–1968, vol. 2, Vietnam, January–June 1965.

104. National Security File, Country File, Vietnam, "Volume 29," Box 14, Document 147, Thomson to Bundy, 2/19/1965, LBJPL.

105. Kai Bird, *The Color of Truth*, 297.

106. Ibid.

107. The National Archives, "Vietnam War U.S. Military Fatal Casualty Statistics," Electronic Records Reference Report, https://www.archives.gov/research/military/vietnam-war/casualty-statistics.

108. Richard M. Nixon, "October 25, The security gap. Radio broadcast. 101:38," originally broadcast October 24, 1968, Richard Nixon Presidential Library & Museum (RNPL), speech file (PPS 208 (1946)), 7; James Yuenger, "LBJ Calls Nixon Charges 'Ugly, Unfair,'" *Chicago Tribune*, October 28, 1968, 8.

109. Cooper, *The Lost Crusade*, 305.

110. Lyndon B. Johnson: "The President's News Conference," September 21, 1964, online by Gerhard Peters and John T. Woolley, The American Presidency Project, http://www.presidency.ucsb.edu/ws/?pid=26517.

111. Ted Gittinger, "Walt W. Rostow Oral History Interview II," transcript, internet copy, LBJPL, January 9, 1981, 19.

112. Jack Valenti, "Memorandum From the President's Special Assistant (Valenti) to President Johnson, March 1, 1966," Document 163, FRUS, 1964–1968, vol. 33, Organization and Management of Foreign Policy.

Chapter Two: The "Center of the Foreign Policy Universe in America"

1. Robert B. Semple Jr., "Nixon Explains Cambodia Policy to 45 Governors," *New York Times,* May 12, 1970, 1; Robert M. Smith, "4 More Leaving Kissinger's Staff," *New York Times*, May 23, 1970, 22.

2. R. W. Apple Jr., "Kissinger Named a Key Nixon Aide in Defense Policy," *New York Times*, December 3, 1968, 1.

3. Henry A. Kissinger, *White House Years* (Boston: Little, Brown, 1979), 11.

4. Mort Halperin, interview with author, August 16, 2017.

5. Ibid.

6. Robert B. Semple Jr., "Nixon Vows to End War with a 'New Leadership,'" *New York Times*, March 6, 1968, 1, 11; Jeffrey P. Kimball, *Nixon's Vietnam War* (Lawrence: University Press of Kansas, 1998), 40.

7. Roger Morris, *Uncertain Greatness: Henry Kissinger and American Foreign Policy* (New York: Harper & Row, 1977), 4.

8. Robert Dallek, *Nixon and Kissinger: Partners in Power* (New York: HarperCollins, 2007), 80–83.

9. "Kissinger Conducts His Last Seminar in Government Before Joining It," *New York Times*, December 17, 1968, 39.

10. Halperin, interview with author, August 16, 2017.

11. Ibid.

12. Ibid.

13. Walter Isaacson, *Kissinger: A Biography* (New York: Simon & Schuster, 1992), 155.

14. Seymour M. Hersh, *The Price of Power: Kissinger in the Nixon White House* (New York: Summit Books, 1983), 30.

15. Morris, *An Uncertain Greatness*, 46.

16. Robert B. Semple Jr., "Nixon Meets His Top Aides and Orders Vietnam Study," *New York Times*, December 29, 1968, 1.

17. Henry A. Kissinger, "Memorandum From the President's Assistant for National Security Affairs-Designate to President-Elect Nixon," January 7, 1969, Document 3, FRUS, 1969–1976, vol. 2, Organization and Management of U.S. Foreign Policy, 1969–1972.

18. Henry A. Kissinger, "Memorandum From the President's Assistant for National Security Affairs-Designate to President-Elect Nixon," December 27, 1968, Document 1, FRUS, 1969–1976, vol. 2, Organization and Management of U.S. Foreign Policy, 1969–1972.

19. Isaacson, *Kissinger*, 203.

20. Winston Lord, interview with author, April 15, 2013.

21. Isaacson, *Kissinger*, 184–85.

22. James Reston, "Mr. Nixon's First Whiff of Trouble," *New York Times*, February 9, 1969, E12.

23. Mark Gillespie, "Americans Look Back at Vietnam," Gallup News, November 17, 2000, http://news.gallup.com/poll/2299/americans-look-back-vietnam-war.aspx.

24. Freedom House advertisement, "For Peace . . . with Freedom," printed in *New York Times*, December 5, 1965, E6.

25. Larry Berman, *No Peace, No Honor* (New York: Simon & Schuster, 2001), 47.

26. Daniel Ellsberg, *Secrets: A Memoir of Vietnam and the Pentagon Papers* (New York: Viking, 2002), 234–35.

27. Henry A. Kissinger, "Bureaucracy and Policy Making: The Effect of Insiders and Outsiders on the Policy Process," in "Bureaucracy, Politics and Strategy," ed. Kissinger and Bernard Brodie, Security Studies Project, University of California, Los Angeles, paper number 17 (Los Angeles: UCLA, 1968), 8.

28. "Minutes of National Security Council Meeting," January 25, 1969, Document 10, FRUS 1969–1976, vol. 6, January 1969–July 1970.

29. Kimball, *Nixon's Vietnam*, 125; Kissinger, *White House Years*, 241.

30. Kimball, *Nixon's Vietnam*, 94; Hersh, *The Price of Power*, 50.

31. Isaacson, *Kissinger*, 164; Hersh, *The Price of Power*, 50.

32. "National Security Study Memorandum 1," subject: "The Situation in Vietnam," January 21, 1969, Document 4, FRUS 1969–1976, vol. 6, January 1969–July 1970.

33. Isaacson, *Kissinger*, 164.

34. Paper, "Summary of Responses to NSSM 1: The Vietnam Situation," attached to Memorandum, subject: "Revised Summary of Responses to NSSM 1: The Situation in Vietnam," Jeanne W. Davis (NSC Secretariat) to Office of the Vice President, Office of the Secretary of State, Office of the Secretary of Defense, Office of the Director, Office of Emergency Preparedness, March 22, 1969, folder NSSM 1 Response (State) [2 of 2], Box H-122; NSC Institutional Files (H-Files), National Security Study Memoranda (NSSMs); RNPL; Kissinger, *White House Years*, 238–39.

35. Attachment, "Summary of Response to NSSM 1," 29.

36. "Memorandum of Meeting Between the President's Assistant for National Security Affairs (Kissinger), Secretary of Defense Laird, and the Chairman of the Joint Chiefs of Staff (Wheeler)," January 30, 1969, 3 p.m., Document 12, FRUS 1969–1976, vol. 6, January 1969–July 1970.

37. See notes 2 and 4; "Telegram From the Department of State to the Embassy in the United Kingdom," February 25, 1969, Document 26, FRUS 1969–1976, vol. 6, January 1969–July 1970; "Telegram From the Department of State to the Embassy in Vietnam," Document 30, FRUS 1969–1976, vol. 6, January 1969–July 1970; "Message From Secretary of Defense Laird to President Nixon," February 25, 1969, Document 25, FRUS 1969–1976, vol. 6, January 1969–July 1970.

38. H. R. Haldeman, *The Haldeman Diaries: Inside the Nixon White House* (New York: G. P. Putnam's, 1994), 36.

39. Kissinger, *White House Years*, 141–42, 169.

40. Richard Nixon, "Asia After Viet Nam," *Foreign Affairs*, October 1, 1967; Richard M. Nixon, *RN: The Memoirs of Richard Nixon* (New York: Grosset & Dunlap, 1978), 369–70.

41. Lydia Saad, "Gallup Vault: Hawks vs. Doves on Vietnam," Gallup News, May 25, 2016, http://news.gallup.com/vault/191828/gallup-vault-hawks-doves-vietnam.aspx.

42. Isaacson, *Kissinger*, 160.

43. Dale Van Atta, *With Honor: Melvin Laird In War, Peace, and Politics* (Madison: University of Wisconsin Press, 2008), 173.

44. Halperin, interview with author, August 16, 2017.

45. Seymour M. Hersh, "Kissinger and Nixon in the White House," *The Atlantic*, May 1982.

46. Hersh, *The Price of Power*, note on 87.

47. *Military Times*, "Alexander Meigs Haig, Jr.," Hall of Valor, https://valor
.militarytimes.com/recipient.php?recipientid=4574.

48. Alexander M. Haig, *Inner Circles: How America Changed the World: A Memoir*
(New York: Warner Books, 1992), 188.

49. "Memorandum From the President's Military Assistant (Haig) to the President's
Assistant for National Security Affairs (Kissinger)," February 7, 1969, Document
22, FRUS 1969–1976, vol. 2, 1969–1972.

50. "Memorandum From the President's Military Assistant (Haig) to the President's
Assistant for National Security Affairs (Kissinger)," subject: "Organization of
National Security Council Staff and White House Office of the Assistant to the
President for National Security Affairs," February 11, 1969, Document 24, FRUS
1969–1976, vol. 2, 1969–1972.

51. Haig, *Inner Circles*, 200.

52. Ibid., 188.

53. Kimball, *Nixon's Vietnam*, 145.

54. Taylor Owen and Ben Kiernan, "Bombs over Cambodia," *The Walrus*, October
2006, 63, http://www.taylorowen.com/Articles/Walrus_CambodiaBombing_
OCT06.pdf.

55. Hersh, *Price of Power*, 63.

56. Halperin, interview with author, August 16, 2017.

57. Isaacson, *Kissinger*, 189.

58. Haig, *Inner Circles*, 199.

59. Lord, interview with author, April 15, 2013.

60. Haig, *Inner Circles*, 199.

61. Hersh, *The Price of Power*, 100.

62. Ibid., 99–100.

63. "Memorandum From the Military Assistant (Haig) to the President's Assistant
for National Security Affairs (Kissinger)," subject: "Staff Meeting," May 2, 1969,
Document 37, FRUS, 1969–1976, vol. 2, 1969–1972.

64. Ibid.

65. Ibid.

66. Morris, *An Uncertain Greatness*, 156.

67. Ibid.

68. "Minutes of National Security Council Meeting," March 28, 1969, Document 49,
FRUS 1969–1976, vol. 6, January 1969–July 1970.

69. National Security Study Memorandum 36, subject: "Vietnamizing the War,"
April 10, 1969, Document 58, FRUS 1969–1976, vol. 6, January 1969–July
1970.

70. Lord, Oral History: "The Nixon Administration National Security Council,"
moderated by I. M. "Mac" Destler and Ivo Daalder, in *The National Security Council Project*, December 8, 1998.

71. Kissinger, *White House Years*, 33, 276.

72. William Beecher, "Raids in Cambodia by U.S. Unprotested," *New York Times*, May 9, 1969.

73. Ibid.

74. Isaacson, *Kissinger*, 212–13.

75. Dallek, *Nixon and Kissinger*, 121.

76. Isaacson, *Kissinger*, 213.

77. Ibid., 214; Halperin, interview with author, August 16, 2017.

78. Haldeman, *The Haldeman Diaries*, 62.

79. Isaacson, *Kissinger*, 213.

80. Nixon, *RN*, 486.

81. Richard Nixon, "Letters of the President and President Ho Chi Minh of the Democratic Republic of Vietnam," November 3, 1969, online by Gerhard Peters and John T. Woolley, The American Presidency Project, http://www.presidency.ucsb.edu/ws/?pid=2304; Nixon, *RN*, 394; Kissinger, *White House Years*, 278.

82. Richard Nixon, "Letters of the President and President Ho Chi Minh of the Democratic Republic of Vietnam"; Nixon, *RN*, 394.

83. H. R. Haldeman, with Joseph DiMona, *The Ends of Power*, 82–83, excerpted in Jeffrey Kimball, *The Vietnam War Files* (Lawrence: University Press of Kansas, 2004), 54–55; Kimball, *Nixon's Vietnam*, 76.

84. Don Nicoll, "Lake, Anthony 'Tony' oral history interview" (2002), Edmund S. Muskie Oral History Collection, http://scarab.bates.edu/muskie_oh/202/.

85. Halperin, interview with author, August 16, 2017; Don Nicoll, "Lake, Anthony 'Tony' oral history interview/."

86. Nixon, *RN*, 487.

87. "Memorandum From the President's Assistant for National Security Affairs (Kissinger) to President Nixon," subject: "Meeting in Paris with North Vietnamese," August 6, 1969, report and memorandum of conversation, Document 106, FRUS 1969–1976, vol. 6, January 1969–July 1970.

88. Kissinger, *Ending the Vietnam War*, 89.

89. Isaacson, *Kissinger*, 243.

90. Ibid.

91. "Memorandum From the President's Assistant for National Security Affairs (Kissinger) to President Nixon," subject: "Response from Ho Chi Minh," August 30, 1969, Document 111, FRUS 1969–1976, vol. 6, January 1969–July 1970; Kissinger, *Ending the Vietnam War*, 91; Nixon, *RN*, 397.

92. Haig, *Inner Circles*, 227; George C. Herring, *America's Longest War: The United States and Vietnam, 1950–1975*, 4th edition (Boston: McGraw-Hill, 2002), 278.

93. Isaacson, *Kissinger*, 238.

94. Hersh, "Kissinger and Nixon in the White House."

95. Paper, "The NSC and New Initiatives," attached to Memorandum, Morton H. Halperin to Dr. Kissinger, August 5, 1969, folder [04]; Halperin, Morton H., Staff Memos [1969] [1 of 1], Box 817, NSC Name Files, RNPL.

96. Memo; Morton H. Halperin to Dr. Kissinger, September 10, 1969, folder Vietnamization, vol. 1, September 1967–December 1969 [2 of 2], Box 91, NSC Subject Files, RNPL.

97. Joseph Kraft, "Kissinger Staff Resignations Show Flaw in Nixon Method," *Washington Post, Times Herald*, September 16, 1969.

98. Morris, *An Uncertain Greatness*, 101, 99–100.

99. Ibid.; NSC Staff member Michael Guhin, Oral History: "The Nixon Administration National Security Council," December 8, 1998, moderated by I. M. "Mac" Destler and Ivo Daalder, The National Security Council Project.

100. Haldeman, *The Haldeman Diaries*, 103.

101. "Memorandum From the Staff Secretary, National Security Council (Watts) to the President's Assistant for National Security Affairs (Kissinger)," subject: "Revised NSC Staff Arrangements," September 14, 1969, Document 72, FRUS 1969–1976, vol. 2, 1969–1972; Memorandum, Robert E. Osgood to Dr. Kissinger, September 25, 1969, folder [01], National Security Council, vol. 3, 6/1/69–12/31/69 [2 of 2], Box H-300, National Security Council Institutional Files (H-Files), RNPL; and TelCon, Henry Kissinger with Stewart Loory, 6:50 p.m., September 11, 1969, folder [06] September 1–18, 1969 [2 of 2], Box 2; Henry A. Kissinger Telephone Conversation Transcripts (Telcons), RNPL .

102. "Memorandum From the President's Assistant for National Security Affairs (Kissinger) to President Nixon," subject: "Our Present Course on Vietnam," September 10, 1969, Document 117, FRUS 1969–1976, vol. 6, January 1969–July 1970.

103. Memo, Henry Kissinger and President Nixon, September 11, 1969, folder Vietnamization, vol. 1, September 1967–December 1969 [2 of 2], Box 91, NSC Subject Files, RNPL.

104. Memo, Tony Lake to Henry Kissinger, September 7, 1969, 9, folder [03] Tony Lake CHRON, September 1969–January 1970, Box 1047, National Security Council Lake Chron Files, RNPL.

105. See cover memorandum, Morton H. Halperin to Dr. Kissinger, August 5, 1969, folder [04] Halperin, Morton H., Staff Memos [1969] [1 of 1], Box 817, NSC Name Files, RNPL.

106. "Minutes of National Security Council Meeting," subject: "Vietnam," September 12, 1969, Document 120, FRUS 1969–1976, vol. 6, January 1969–July 1970.

107. Ibid.

108. Ibid.

109. Report, subject: "The Effects of the Imposition of a Quarantine on North Vietnam," CIA, July 16, 1969, folder Top Secret/Sensitive Vietnam Contingency Planning Henry A. Kissinger, October 2, 1969 [1 of 2], Box 89, National Security Council Subject Files, RNPL.

110. "Memorandum From the President's Assistant for National Security Affairs (Kissinger) to President Nixon," subject: "Analysis for Vietnam," September 5, 1969, Document 115, FRUS 1969–1976, vol. 6, January 1969–July 1970.

111. Memo, Tony Lake to Henry Kissinger, September 7, 1969, 8–9; Haldeman, *The Haldeman Diaries*, 90.

112. TelCon, Henry Kissinger with The President, 7:50 p.m., September 15, 1969, folder [06] September 1–18, 1969 [2 of 2], Box 2, Henry A. Kissinger Telephone Conversation Transcripts (Telcons), RNPL.

113. Hersh, *The Price of Power*, 123.

114. Isaacson, *Kissinger*, 247.

115. Hersh, *The Price of Power*, 126.

116. Morris, *An Uncertain Greatness*, 164.

117. Hersh, *The Price of Power*, 127.

118. "Cable, PRUNING KNIFE Status Report No. 1," September 15, 1969, attached to Cable, subject: "PRUNING KNIFE," MACV to CINCPAC, September 23, 1969, excerpted in *The Vietnam War Files*, ed. Kimball, 101; Kissinger, *White House Years*, 284.

119. Memorandum, subject: "Contingency Military Operations Against North Vietnam," Henry A. Kissinger to The President, October 2, 1969, folder Top Secret/Sensitive Vietnam Contingency Planning Henry A. Kissinger, October 2, 1969 [2 of 2], Box 89, National Security Council Vietnam Subject Files, RNPL; and Memorandum, Tony Lake to Kissinger, September 17, 1969, subject: "Initial comments on concept of operations, with attachment, 'Vietnam Contingency Planning,'" September 16, 1969, excerpted in *The Vietnam War Files*, ed. Kimball, 102–4.

120. Robert Dallek, *Nixon and Kissinger: Partners in Power* (New York: HarperCollins, 2007), 155; Isaacson, *Kissinger*, 246.

121. Haldeman, *The Haldeman Diaries*, 95.

122. Isaacson, *Kissinger*, 247.

123. "Notes of a Telephone Conversation Between President Nixon and his Assistant for National Security Affairs (Kissinger)," October 10, 1969, 7:30 p.m., Document 135, Document 136, FRUS 1969–1976, vol. 6, January 1969–July 1970.

124. "Memorandum for the Record," subject: "JCS Meeting with the President, Saturday, October 1969 (U)," October 11, 1969, 9:45 a.m.–12:45 p.m., Document 136, FRUS 1969–1976, vol. 6, January 1969–July 1970.

125. Ibid.

126. William Safire, *Before the Fall: An Inside View of the Pre-Watergate White House* (Garden City, NY: Doubleday, 1975), note 368; David Johnston, "Nixon's Big Regret: Bombing Delay," *New York Times*, April 11, 1988.

127. Memo, Roger Morris and Tony Lake to Henry Kissinger, 5 October 21, 1969, 1, folder [03] Tony Lake CHRON, September 1969–January 1970, Box 1047, National Security Council Lake Chron Files, RNPL; Isaacson, *Kissinger*, 247.

128. TelCon, Henry Kissinger with The President; 6:30 p.m., October 8, 1969, folder [08], October 1–13, 1969, Box 2; Henry A. Kissinger Telephone Conversation Transcripts (Telcons); RNPL.

129. The National Archives, "Vietnam War U.S. Military Fatal Casualty Statistics."

130. Isaacson, *Kissinger*, 263.

131. Don Nicoll, "Lake, Anthony 'Tony' oral history interview."

132. Haig, *Inner Circles*, 237.

133. Isaacson, *Kissinger*, 263.

134. Isaacson, *Kissinger*, 264; Kissinger, *White House Years*, note 285.

135. M. David Landau, "Kissinger Aide Resigns in Protest To Recent 'Invasion' of Cambodia," *Harvard Crimson*, May 14, 1970, http://www.thecrimson.com/article/1970/5/14/kissinger-aide-resigns-in-protest-to/.

136. See also note 1: "Draft Letter From W. Anthony Lake and Roger Morris of the National Security Council Staff to the President's Assistant for National Security Affairs (Kissinger)," undated, Document 106, FRUS 1969–1976, vol. 2, 1969–1972.

137. "Kissinger and Tho Win Nobel Prize for Vietnam Pact," *New York Times*, October 17, 1973.

138. Henry Kissinger, *Years of Upheaval* (Boston: Little, Brown, 1982), 1243–44.

139. Martin Tolchin, "Kissinger Issues Wiretap Apology," *New York Times*, November 13, 1992.

140. Haig, *Inner Circles*, 217, 220.

141. See note 3: "Draft Letter From W. Anthony Lake and Roger Morris of the National Security Council Staff to the President's Assistant for National Security Affairs (Kissinger)," undated, Document 106, FRUS 1969–1976, vol. 2, 1969–1972.

142. Winston Lord, interview with author, April 15, 2013.

143. Isaacson, *Kissinger*, 204.

144. James T. Wooten, "Carter Pledges an Open Foreign Policy," *New York Times*, June 24, 1976, 1; C. L. Sulzberger, "Plains Language from Truthful James," August 22, 1976, *New York Times*, 147.

145. Hedrick Smith, "Carter Reported Studying Plan for Reorganizing White House Staff," *New York Times*, December 9, 1976, 16; "Carter Names 4 Transition Aides on Foreign Policy," *New York Times*, November 12, 1976, 10.

146. "Transcript of a News Conference Held by President-Elect Carter," *New York Times*, November 16, 1976, 32.

147. Zbigniew Brzezinski, interview with author, April 12, 2013.

148. Bernard Gwertzman, "Brzezinski Revamps Security Unit Staff," *New York Times*, January 16, 1977, 1; Smith, "Carter Reported Studying Plan for Reorganizing White House Staff," 16; Charles Mohr, "Brzezinski Helping Carter Change the Way Foreign Policy Is Made," *New York Times*, May 23, 1977, 12.

149. Mohr, "Brzezinski Helping Carter Change the Way Foreign Policy Is Made," 12.

150. Gwertzman, "Brzezinski Revamps Security Unit Staff," 1.

151. Gary Sick, *All Fall Down: America's Tragic Encounter with Iran* (New York: Penguin Books, 1986), 290.

152. Zbigniew Brzezinski, Memorandum, "Getting the Hostages Free," April 10, 1980,

Zbigniew Brzezinski Collection, NSC Accomplishments Iran: 4/80–10/80, Container 34, Jimmy Carter Presidential Library.

153. Brzezinski, interview with author, April 12, 2013.

Chapter Three: "Reckless Cowboys, off on Their Own on a Wild Ride"

1. Cable, subject: "NSDD on Lebanon," from White House (John Poindexter) to Ambassador Robert McFarlane, September 11, 1983, at 0325Z, File: NSC 00088, September 10, 1983 (2) [START/Lebanon], Executive Secretariat, NSC: MEETING FILES, Box 91285, Ronald Reagan Presidential Foundation and Library (RRL).

2. Howard Teicher, interview with author, April 15, 2013.

3. Philip Dur, interview with author, August 11, 2017.

4. Ibid.

5. Lou Cannon, *President Reagan: The Role of a Lifetime* (New York: Simon & Schuster, 1991), 36.

6. Teicher, interview with author, April 15, 2013.

7. Howard Teicher, interview with author, July 21, 2017.

8. Dur, interview with author, August 11, 2017; Teicher, interview with author, July 21, 2017.

9. Steven Spiegel, *The Other Arab-Israeli Conflict: Making America's Middle East Policy, from Truman to Reagan* (Chicago: University of Chicago Press, 1985), 400.

10. Teicher, interview with author, July 21, 2017.

11. Alexander Haig, *Caveat: Realism, Reagan, and Foreign Policy* (New York: Macmillan, 1984), 74; and Leslie Gelb, "Foreign Policy System Criticized by U.S. Aides," *New York Times*, October 19, 1981, A1.

12. David Rothkopf, *Running the World: The Inside Story of the National Security Council and the Architects of American Power* (New York: PublicAffairs, 2005), 222; Hedrick Smith, "A Scaled-Down Version of Security Advisor's Task," *New York Times*, March 4, 1981, A2.

13. Richard Burt, "Reagan's Foreign Policy from Someone Who Knows," *New York Times*, June 29, 1980; and Miller Center, "Interview with Richard Allen," University of Virginia, May 28, 2002, http://millercenter.org/president/reagan/oralhistory/richard-allen.

14. Geoffrey Kemp, "My NSC Elephants Were Baby Ones, Not Rogues," *Washington Post*, December 7, 1986.

15. John Poindexter, interview with author, April 8, 2013.

16. Ibid.

17. Adam Clymer, "Reagan Evoking Rising Concern, New Poll Shows," *New York Times*, March 19, 1982, A1.

18. Judith Miller, "Senators Give Clark Angry Advice, But Still Consent," *New York Times*, February 8, 1981.

19. Kemp, "My NSC Elephants Were Baby Ones, Not Rogues."

20. Robert C. McFarlane with Zofia Smardz. *Special Trust* (New York: Cadell & Davies, 1994), 189.

21. Paul Kengor and Patricia Clark Doerner, *The Judge: William Clark, Ronald Reagan's Top Hand* (San Francisco: Ignatius Press, 2007), 105; Ronald Reagan, "National Security Decision Directive 2: National Security Council Structure," January 12, 1982, http://www.fas.org/irp/offdocs/nsdd; and Office of the Historian, "History of the National Security Council, 1947–1997."

22. Kemp, "My NSC Elephants Were Baby Ones, Not Rogues."

23. Leslie H. Gelb, "The Bureaucracy; Status Move," *New York Times*, June 22, 1983, A22.

24. Kengor and Doerner, *The Judge*, 231.

25. Constantine Christopher Menges, *Inside the National Security Council: The True Story of the Making and Unmaking of Reagan's Foreign Policy* (New York: Simon and Schuster, 1988), 55; Miller Center, "Interview with William Clark," August 17, 2003; and Dur, interview with author, May 1, 2013.

26. Kemp, "Lessons in Lebanon," 58.

27. Jack Redden, "The 800 U.S. Marines who came to Lebanon," UPI, September 10, 1982.

28. Kemp, interview with author, July 18, 2017.

29. Dur, interview with author, August 11, 2017.

30. Ronald Reagan, "President's Press Conference," The American Presidency Project, September 28, 1982, http://www.presidency.ucsb.edu/ws/index.php?pid=43062&st=lebanon&st1=#axzz1klzb59mE.

31. Ronald Reagan, "Address to the Nation on United States Policy for Peace in the Middle East," September 1, 1982, The American Presidency Project, http://www.presidency.ucsb.edu/ws/index.php?pid=42911&st=seize&st1=Lebanon#ixzz11qkRxGgD.

32. Ronald Reagan, "Text of Reagan's Letter to Congress on Marines in Lebanon," *New York Times*, September 29, 1982; The Long Commission, "The Report of the DoD Commission on Beirut International Airport Terrorist Act: October 23, 1983," December 20, 1983, 39; and Memorandum, subject: "U.S. Responsibilities Concerning the Protection of Civilians in the Beirut Area," from Davis R. Robinson to the Deputy Secretary, October 22, 1982, The John Boykin Collection, the National Security Archives (George Washington University), Box 4, accessed August 2012.

33. Dur, interview with author, August 11, 2017; Armitage, interview with author, September 26, 2017.

34. The Long Commission, 49–50.

35. Ronald Reagan, "Address to the Veterans of Foreign Wars Convention in Chicago," August 18, 1980, online by Gerhard Peters and John T. Woolley, The American Presidency Project, http://www.presidency.ucsb.edu/ws/?pid=85202.

36. Gallup, "Military and National Defense," In-depth Topics, A-Z, http://news .gallup.com/poll/1666/military-national-defense.aspx.

37. Reagan, "Address to the Veterans of Foreign Wars Convention in Chicago."

38. Kemp, "Lessons in Lebanon," 60.

39. Teicher, interview with author, July 21, 2017.

40. Ibid.

41. Ibid.

42. Kemp, interview with author, July 18, 2017.

43. Dur, interview with author, April 23, 2014.

44. Reagan, "Address to the Veterans of Foreign Wars Convention in Chicago."

45. Colin Powell, *My American Journey: An Autobiography* (New York: Random House, 1995), 291.

46. James Fallows, "The Spend-Up," *The Atlantic*, July 1986, https://www.theatlantic .com/magazine/archive/1986/07/the-spend-up/308325/.

47. Armitage, interview with author, September 26, 2017.

48. Dur, interview with author, August 11, 2017.

49. David Crist, *The Twilight War: The Secret History of America's Thirty-Year Conflict with Iran* (Penguin Publishing Group, Kindle Edition), 142.

50. Caspar Weinberger, *Fighting for Peace: Seven Critical Years at the Pentagon* (London: Michael Joseph, 1990), 159.

51. Howard Teicher and Gayle Radley Teicher, *Twin Pillars to Desert Storm: America's Flawed Vision in the Middle East from Nixon to Bush* (New York: William Morrow, 1993), 218.

52. Thomas Friedman, *From Beirut to Jerusalem: One Man's Middle Eastern Odyssey* (London: Fontana, 1990), 198.

53. Memorandum, subject: "US Vulnerability in Lebanon," from Graham E. Fuller to the Director of Central Intelligence, May 6, 1984, 1–2, CIA Records Research Tool (CREST), downloaded December 2012.

54. Graham E. Fuller, Memorandum for Acting Director of Central Intelligence, subject: "Downward Spiral in Lebanon," August 16, 1983, 1. CREST, downloaded December 2012.

55. Cable, Subject: "Habib/Draper Mission: Where We Stand After Initial Rounds in Lebanon and Israel." (Phil) Habib to SECSTATE, February 15, 1983, 18:17Z, Section One of Three; 3 of 3; Folder "Lebanon," Clark, William Patrick: Files, 1982–1983; Box 4. RRL.

56. Michael Getler, "For NSC Staff, It's Heady to Be the Hub of Activity," *Washington Post*, May 16, 1983, A9; and John M. Goshko and Michael Getler, "Shultz no longer perceived as driving force in foreign policy," *Washington Post,* August 15, 1983, A1.

57. Dur, interview with author, May 1, 2013; Howard Teicher, interview with author, April 15, 2013.

58. Dur, interview with author, May 1, 2013.
59. Memorandum, subject: "Comments on Lebanon Draft NSDD," from Charles Hill to William Clark, September 8, 1983, folder: NSDD 103 (Strategy for Lebanon) (2), Executive Secretariat, NSC: NSDDs, Box RAC, Box 6, RRL.
60. Weinberger, *Fighting for Peace*, 157–58.
61. Draft Paper, subject: "Near-Term Lebanon Strategy," September 6, 1983, 1, attached to Memorandum, from Jack N. Merritt to John Poindexter, September 8, 1983, file: NSDD 103 (Strategy for Lebanon) [1], Executive Secretariat, NSC: NSDDs, Box 91285, RRL.
62. Ronald Reagan's marked-up copy. Cable, subject: "McFarlane/Fairbanks Mission: Worst Case Strategy for Lebanon," from Ambassador (Robert C.) McFarlane to SECSTATE, September 9, 1983, Section 1 at 0104Z and Section 2 at 0109Z. File: Lebanon, CLARK, WILLIAM PATRICK: Files, Box 4, RRL.
63. Dur, interview with author, August 11, 2017.
64. Ibid.
65. Ronald Reagan, *The Reagan Diaries*, ed. Douglas Brinkley (New York: Harper-Collins, 2007), 178; handwritten notes, "NSC mtg 10Sept83, Lebanon," September 10, 1983, file: Lebanon III [3/5] FORTIER, DONALD R.: files, Box RAC Box 7, RRL.
66. Reagan, *The Reagan Diaries*, 178.
67. Ronald Reagan, National Security Decision Directive 103, "Strategy for Lebanon," September 10, 1983, http://www.reagan.utexas.edu/archives/reference/Scanned%20NSDDS/NSDD103.pdf.
68. Cable, subject: "NSDD on Lebanon," from White House (John Poindexter) to Ambassador Robert McFarlane, September 11, 1983, at 0325Z, File: NSC 00088, September 10, 1983 (2) [START/Lebanon], Executive Secretariat, NSC: MEETING FILES, Box 91285, RRL.
69. Eric Hammel, *The Root: The Marines in Beirut August 1982–February 1984* (San Diego: Harcourt Brace Jovanovich, 1999), 216; Friedman, *From Beirut to Jerusalem*, 200.
70. McFarlane, *Special Trust*, 250.
71. Kemp, interview with author, July 18, 2017.
72. Kemp, interview with author, July 18, 2017.
73. Charles R. Babcock and Don Oberdorfer, "The NSC Cabal How Arrogance and Secrecy Brought on Scandal," *Washington Post*, June 21, 1987.
74. Cannon, *Role of a Lifetime*, 368–69; Dur, interview with author, August 11, 2017.
75. Reagan, *The Reagan Diaries*, 178.
76. Ronald Reagan, National Security Decision Directive 103, "Addendum to NSDD 103 on Lebanon of September 19, 1983," September 11, 1983, http://www.reagan.utexas.edu/archives/reference/Scanned%20NSDDS/NSDD103.pdf.
77. Ibid.
78. Dur, interview with author, August 11, 2017.

79. Reagan, *The Reagan Diaries,* 178.
80. White House News Summary, "Tuesday, September 13, 1983," file: Lebanon, Clark, William Patrick: files, Box 4, RRL; Lou Cannon and George C. Wilson, "Reagan Authorizes Marines to Call in Beirut Air Strikes," *Washington Post,* September 13, 1983; editorial: "The Stakes in Beirut," *New York Times,* September 15, 1983, 26.
81. Long Commission, 32.
82. Ibid., 46.
83. Ibid., 32, 40, and 42.
84. Memorandum, subject: "Movement of the USS NEW JERSEY (BB-62) to Lebanon," from Cap (Caspar Weinberger) to the President (Ronald Reagan), undated (attached to September 20, 1983, cover memorandum), file: NSDD 103 (Strategy for Lebanon) [1], Executive Secretariat, NSC: NSDDs, Box 91285, RRL; Memorandum, William Clark to Caspar W. Weinberger, September 20, 1982 [*sic*] (attached to September 20, 1983, cover memorandum), file: NSDD 103 (Strategy for Lebanon) [1], Executive Secretariat, NSC: NSDDs, Box 91289, RRL.
85. Robert "Bud" McFarlane, interview with author, September 5, 2013.
86. Teicher, interview with author, July 21, 2017.
87. Don Oberdorfer, "The Beirut Massacre," *Washington Post,* October 24, 1983.
88. Jane Mayer, "Ronald Reagan's Benghazi," *The New Yorker,* May 5, 2014.
89. Teicher and Teicher, *Twin Pillars,* 258.
90. Robert Timberg, *The Nightingale's Song* (New York: Simon and Shuster, 1995), 337.
91. Ronald Reagan, "Address to the Nation on Events in Lebanon and Grenada," The American Presidency Project, October 27, 1983, http://www.presidency.ucsb.edu/ws/index.php?pid=40696&st=beirut&st1=october#ixzz1ljh7skX4.
92. Memorandum, Subject: "US Policy in Lebanon and the Middle East," From Cap (Caspar Weinberger) to Bud (Robert C. McFarlane), October 21, 1983, 1. File: Lebanon III [3/5] Fortier, Donald R.: Files, Box RAC Box 7, RRL; Paper, Subject: "Our Strategy in Lebanon and the Middle East: Operational Issues," October 17, 1983, 1. Folder: NSDD 111 [Next Steps Toward Progress in Lebanon and the Middle East] (2), Executive Secretariat, NSC: NSDDs, Box 91291 (006R-NSDDs), RRL.
93. Memorandum, subject: "National Security Decision Directive on Lebanon and the Middle East," from Robert C. McFarlane to George Shultz, Caspar W. Weinberger, William J. Casey, and John W. Vessey, October 29, 1983, folder: NSDD 111 [Next Steps Toward Progress in Lebanon and the Middle East] (1), Executive Secretariat, NSC: NSDDs, Box 91291 (006R-NSDDs), RRL.
94. Handwritten notes on Memorandum, "NSDD: Lebanon and the Middle East," from Geoffrey Kemp to Robert C. McFarlane, October 25, 1983, folder: NSDD 111 [Next Steps Toward Progress in Lebanon and the Middle East] (1), Executive Secretariat, NSC: NSDDs, Box 91291, RRL; and Memorandum, subject: "Lebanon and the Middle East," from Robert C. McFarlane to the President (Ronald Reagan), October 28,

1983, 1, folder: NSDD 111 [Next Steps Toward Progress in Lebanon and the Middle East] (2), Executive Secretariat, NSC: NSDDs, Box 91289 (006R-NSDDs), RRL.

95. Memorandum, subject: "National Security Decision Directive on Lebanon and the Middle East," from Robert C. McFarlane to George Shultz, Caspar W. Weinberger, William J. Casey, and John W. Vessey, October 29, 1983, folder: NSDD 111 [Next Steps Toward Progress in Lebanon and the Middle East] (1), Executive Secretariat, NSC: NSDDs, Box 91289 (006R-NSDDs), RRL.

96. Armitage, interview with author, September 26, 2017.

97. Memorandum, subject: "NSDD-111 on Lebanon and the Middle East," from John A. Wickham Jr. to the Secretary of Defense (Caspar Weinberger), November 4, 1983, folder: NSDD 111 [Next Steps Toward Progress in Lebanon and the Middle East] (1), Executive Secretariat, NSC: NSDDs, Box 91289 (006R-NSDDs), RRL; and Memorandum, subject: "NSDD-111 on Lebanon and the Middle East," from Cap (Caspar Weinberger) to the Assistant to the President for National Security Affairs (Robert McFarlane), November 7, 1983, folder: NSDD 111 [Next Steps Toward Progress in Lebanon and the Middle East] (1), Executive Secretariat, NSC: NSDDs, Box 91289 (006R-NSDDs), RRL.

98. Memorandum, subject: "Security in Lebanon," from Philip A. Dur to Robert C. McFarlane, November 25, 1983, 1, folder: NSDD 111 [Next Steps Toward Progress in Lebanon and the Middle East] (3), Executive Secretariat, NSC: NSDDs, Box 91291 (006R-NSDDs), RRL.

99. McFarlane, *Special Trust*, 268.

100. McFarlane, interview with author, September 5, 2013; David Crist, *The Twilight War*, 147.

101. Reagan, *The Reagan Diaries*, 205.

102. Dur, interview with author, August 11, 2017.

103. Armitage, interview with author, September 26, 2017.

104. Ronald Reagan, "Statement on the Situation in Lebanon," February 7, 1984, http://www.presidency.ucsb.edu/ws/?pid=39433.

105. Kemp, "Lessons in Lebanon," 65.

106. Dur, interview with author, August 11, 2017.

107. Kemp, "Lessons in Lebanon," 64.

108. Dur, interview with author, August 11, 2017.

109. Teicher, interview with author, July 21, 2017.

110. Ibid.

111. Powell, *My American Journey*, 291.

112. Ibid., location 4970–4971.

113. Dur, interview with author, August 11, 2017.

114. Brock Brower, "Bud McFarlane: Semper Fi," *New York Times Magazine*, January 22, 1989.

115. Charles R. Babcock and Don Oberdorfer, "The NSC Cabal: How Arrogance and Secrecy Brought on Scandal," *Washington Post*, June 21, 1987.

116. John Tower, Edmund Muskie, and Brent Scowcroft, *The Tower Commission Report* (New York: Bantam Books, 1987), 70 and 66.

117. See graph. The National Security Council Project, the Brookings Institution and the University of Maryland Center for International and Security Studies (CISSM), http://www.brookings.edu.

118. Kemp, "My NSC Elephants Were Baby Ones, Not Rogues."

119. Rothkopf, *Running the World*, 244.

120. United Press International, "Blame the Cake on Ollie North, McFarlane Says," *Los Angeles Times*, January 22, 1987.

121. Teicher and Teicher, *Twin Pillars*, 358.

122. Ronald Reagan, "Address to the Nation on the Iran Arms and Contra Aid Controversy," March 4, 1987, online by Gerhard Peters and John T. Woolley, The American Presidency Project, http://www.presidency.ucsb.edu/ws/?pid=33938.

123. Maureen Dowd, "The White House Crisis: McFarlane Suicide Attempt," *New York Times*, March 2, 1987.

124. McFarlane, *Special Trust*, 189.

125. R. W. Apple, "Introduction," in Tower, Muskie, and Scowcroft, "The Tower Commission Report," xv.

126. Powell, *My American Journey*, 332.

127. Bartholomew H. Sparrow, *The Strategist: Brent Scowcroft and the Call of National Security* (New York: PublicAffairs, 2015), 255.

128. Hadley, interview with author, March 28, 2018.

129. Tower, Muskie, and Scowcroft, *The Tower Commission Report*, 4.

130. Powell, *My American Journey*, 331.

131. Ibid.

132. Fred Hiatt, "Role of National Security Council Again Uncertain," *Washington Post*, January 6, 1986.

133. See discussion in Michael R. Gordon, "At Foreign Policy Helm: Shultz vs. White House," *New York Times*, August 26, 1987.

134. Dur, interview with author, August 11, 2017.

Chapter Four: "What No Other Part of the Government Did"

1. George H. W. Bush, "Remarks and an Exchange with Reporters on the Iraqi Invasion of Kuwait," The American Presidency Project, August 5, 1990, http://www.presidency.ucsb.edu/ws/?pid=18741.

2. Powell, *My American Journey*, 466; Colin Powell, "The Gulf War," *Frontline: Oral History*, http://www.pbs.org/wgbh/pages/frontline/gulf/oral/powell/1.html.

3. Richard Haass, "Commencement Address," Oberlin College, May 25, 2009, https://www.huffingtonpost.com/richard-n-haass/dissent-is-as-american-as_b_207430.html.

4. Richard Haass Interview, May 27, 2004, George H. W. Bush Oral History Project, Miller Center, University of Virginia, https://millercenter.org/the-presidency/

presidential-oral-histories/richard-haass-oral-history-special-assistant-president.

5. Daalder and Destler, *In the Shadow*, 165.

6. Brent Scowcroft, interview with author, January 31, 2013.

7. Richard Haass, "Reassessing the NSC," *Harvard Crimson*, December 3, 1986.

8. Richard Haass, interview with author, August 14, 2017.

9. Ibid.

10. R. N. Haass, "Filling the Vacuum: U.S. Foreign Policy towards Southwest Asia, 1969–1976," diss., University of Oxford, 1982.

11. Richard Haass, "Reassessing the NSC."

12. Ibid.

13. Richard Haass Interview, Miller Center.

14. Alfonso Chardy, "Bush Aides Drafting New Contra Policy," *Miami Herald*, November 16, 1988, 1A.

15. Richard Haass Interview, Miller Center.

16. George Bush, "Transcript of Bush News Conference on Choice of Scowcroft," November 24, 1999, B12.

17. Scowcroft, interview with author, January 31, 2013.

18. Richard Haass Interview, Miller Center.

19. Ibid.

20. Scowcroft, interview with author, January 31, 2013.

21. Richard Haass Interview, Miller Center.

22. Richard Haass, *War of Necessity, War of Choice* (New York: Simon & Schuster, 2009), 33, 36.

23. David Welch, interview with author, September 9, 2013.

24. Bernard Weinraub, "Bush Backs Plan to Enhance Role of Security Staff," *New York Times*, February 2, 1989, A1.

25. Haass, interview with author, January 10, 2013.

26. Scowcroft, interview with author, January 31, 2013.

27. Daalder and Destler, "The Role of the National Security Advisor," 2.

28. Ibid.

29. Colin Powell, *My American Journey*, 408.

30. Richard Haass Interview, Miller Center.

31. Daniel Patrick Moynihan, "The Peace Dividend," *New York Review of Books* 37, no. 11 (June 28, 1990).

32. George Bush, National Security Directive 3, "U.S. Policy Toward Afghanistan," February 13, 1989, https://fas.org/irp/offdocs/nsd/nsd3.pdf.

33. Richard Haass Interview, Miller Center; George Bush, National Security Directive 3.

34. Michael R. Gordon and Bernard Trainor, *The Generals' War: The Inside Story of the Conflict in the Gulf* (Boston: Little, Brown, 1995), 7–8.

35. Gordon and Trainor, *The Generals' War*, 9.
36. Defense Department, "Conduct of the Persian Gulf War: Final Report to Congress," April 1992, xxi.
37. George Bush, National Security Directive 26, "U.S. Policy Toward the Persian Gulf," October 2, 1989, https://bush41library.tamu.edu/archives/nsd.
38. Brent Scowcroft, "The Gulf War," *Frontline*, Oral History, PBS, http://www.pbs.org/wgbh/pages/frontline/gulf/oral/scowcroft/1.html.
39. George Bush, National Security Directive 26.
40. Gordon and Trainor, *The Generals' War*, 13; Richard Haass, *War of Necessity, War of Choice*, 50.
41. *U.S. News & World Report*, June 1990.
42. Haass, *War of Necessity, War of Choice*, 53.
43. Richard Haass Interview, Miller Center.
44. Ibid.
45. Yousseff M. Ibrahim, "Iraq Threatens Emirates and Kuwait on Oil Glut," *New York Times*, July 18, 1990, D1; April Glaspie, Cable: "Iraqi Threats to Kuwait and UAE," 181454z, July 1990, Haass, Richard N., Files, Working Files, GHWB-Haass-BoxCF01937-003, Folder: "Iraq—Pre 8/2/90 [3]," George Bush Presidential Library and Museum (GBPLM), 2, 4.
46. Richard Haass Interview, Miller Center.
47. April Glaspie, Cable: "Ambassador's Meeting with Saddam Husayn," 251104z, July 1990, Haass, Richard N., Files, Working Files, GHWB-Haass-BoxCF01937-003, Folder: "Iraq—Pre 8/2/90 [3]," GBPLM, 1–2; Richard Haass, *War of Necessity, War of Choice*, 57; Richard Haass, "The Gulf War," *Frontline*, Oral History, PBS, https://www.pbs.org/wgbh/pages/frontline/gulf/oral/haass/1.html.
48. April Glaspie, Cable: "Iraq Blinks—Provisionally," 261230z, July 1990, Haass, Richard N., Files, Working File, GHWB-Haass-BoxCF01585-f001, Folder: "Iraq Pre 8/2/90 [1]," GBPLM.
49. Gordon and Trainor, *The Generals' War*, 5, 25–26.
50. Richard Haass Interview, Miller Center.
51. Ibid.
52. George Bush and Brent Scowcroft, *A World Transformed* (New York: Knopf; Vintage, 1998), 302.
53. Richard Haass Interview, Miller Center; Haass, *Frontline*.
54. Richard Haass Interview, Miller Center.
55. George Bush, "Remarks and an Exchange with Reporters on the Iraqi Invasion of Kuwait," August 2, 1990, The American Presidency Project, http://www.presidency.ucsb.edu/ws/?pid=18726; "Minutes of NSC/Deputy Committee Meeting," August 2, 1990, Haass, Richard N., Files, Presidential Meeting Files, BoxCF01618-019, Folder: "NSC Meeting—August 2, 1990 Re: Iraqi Invasion of Kuwait," GBPLM.

56. Gordon and Trainor, *The Generals' War*, 7–8.
57. Defense Department, "Conduct of the Persian Gulf War: Final Report to Congress," xxi; Gordon and Trainor, *The Generals' War*, 46.
58. Haass, *Frontline*.
59. Ibid.
60. Dick Cheney, interview with author, August 9, 2013.
61. "Minutes of NSC Meeting on Iraqi Invasion of Kuwait," August 3, 1990, Haass, Richard N., Files, Working Files, GHWB-Haass-BoxCF01478-030, Folder: "Iraq—August 2, 1990–December 1990 [8]," GBPLM.
62. Powell, *My American Journey*, 451.
63. Sparrow, *The Strategist*, 385.
64. Haass, *War of Necessity, War of Choice*, 62.
65. Bush and Scowcroft, *A World Transformed*, 322.
66. Lawrence Freedman and Efraim Karsh, *The Gulf Conflict, 1990–1991: Diplomacy and War in the New World Order* (London: Faber and Faber, 1993), 180, 85; Jaoa Resende-Santos, "The Persian Gulf Crisis: A Chronology of Events," in *After the Storm: Lessons from the Gulf War*, ed. Joseph S. Nye Jr. and Roger K. Smith (Lanham, MD: Madison Books, 1992), 301–6, 317; CIA, Report, subject: "Oil Market Situation," August 8, 1990, Melby, Eric, Files, Subject File, Box CF01434, Folder: 003, "Energy—Gulf Crisis [3]," GBPLM.
67. "Minutes of NSC Meeting on Iraqi Invasion of Kuwait," August 4, 1990, Haass, Richard N., Files, Working Files, GHWB-Haass-BoxCF01478-030, Folder: "Iraq—August 2, 1990–December 1990 [8]," GBPLM, 2.
68. David Halberstam, *War in a Time of Peace* (New York: Scribner, 2001), 70; Powell, *Frontline*.
69. Richard Haass Interview, Miller Center.
70. Ibid.
71. Ibid.
72. Sparrow, *The Strategist*, 276–77.
73. Richard Haass Interview, Miller Center.
74. Haass, *Frontline*.
75. Jon Meacham, *Destiny and Power: The American Odyssey of George Herbert Walker Bush* (New York: Random House, 2015), 744, note 432.
76. George Bush, "Remarks and an Exchange With Reporters on the Iraqi Invasion of Kuwait," August 5, 1990, online by Gerhard Peters and John T. Woolley, The American Presidency Project, http://www.presidency.ucsb.edu/ws/?pid=18741.
77. Meacham. *Destiny and Power*, 434.
78. Thomas L. Friedman, "Bush Hinting Force, Declares Assault 'Will Not Stand,'" *New York Times*, August 6, 1990.
79. Dick Cheney, "The Gulf War," *Frontline*, Oral History, PBS, https://www.pbs.org/wgbh/pages/frontline/gulf/oral/cheney/1.html. Cheney, interview with author, August 9, 2013; Powell, *Frontline*.

80. Richard Haass Interview, Miller Center.

81. Gordon and Trainor, 72; Richard Haass Interview, Miller Center.

82. David Jeremiah, George H. W. Bush Oral History Project, Miller Center, University of Virginia, November 15, 2010.

83. Richard Haass Interview, Miller Center.

84. "Presidential Calls During Iraq-Kuwait Crisis," n.d., Poadiuk, Roman, Files, Subject Files, GHWB-BoxCF00703-003, Folder: "Kuwait-Iraq, Middle East [3]," GBPLM.

85. Haass, interview with author, January 10, 2013; "8/24 to do," August 24, 1990, Haass, Richard N., Files, Working Files, GHWB-Haass-BoxCF01478-026, Folder: "Iraq—August 2, 1990–December 1990 [4]," GBPLM.

86. Richard Haass Interview, Miller Center.

87. Ibid.

88. Sparrow, *The Strategist*, 392; Rothkopf, *Running the World*, 297–98.

89. Miller Center, "Interview with Brent Scowcroft," University of Virginia, November 12–13, 1999, http://millercenter.org/president/bush/oralhistory/brent-scowcroft.

90. Scowcroft, *Frontline*.

91. Powell, *My American Journey*, 457; Bob Woodward, *The Commanders* (New York: Simon & Schuster, 1991), 248–49; Powell, *Frontline*.

92. "Minutes of NSC Meeting on Iraqi Invasion of Kuwait," August 4, 1990, Haass, Richard N., Files, Working Files, GHWB-Haass-BoxCF01478-030, Folder: "Iraq—August 2, 1990–December 1990 [8]," GBPLM, 7; and Freedman and Karsh, *The Gulf Conflict*, 140–41.

93. Miller Center, "Interview with Robert M. Gates," University of Virginia, July 23–24, 2000, http://millercenter.org/president/bush/oralhistory/robert-gates; James Baker, "The Gulf War," *Frontline*, Oral History, https://www.pbs.org/wgbh/pages/frontline/gulf/oral/baker/1.html; Baker, interview with author, April 8, 2013.

94. Richard N. Haass, Memorandum for Brent Scowcroft, "What next in the Gulf?," August 27, 1990, Haass, Richard N., Files, Working Files, GHWB-Haass-BoxCF01478-030, Folder: "Iraq—August 2, 1990–December 1990 [8]," GBPLM.

95. Richard Haass, "Draft: The Gulf Crisis: Thoughts, Scenarios & Options," August 19, 1990, Haass, Richard N., Files, Working Files, GHWB-Haass-BoxCF01478-024, Folder: "Iraq—August 2, 1990–December 1990 [2]," GBPLM, 1.

96. "Minutes of NSC Meeting on Iraqi Invasion of Kuwait," August 3, 1990, Haass, Richard N., Files, Working Files, GHWB-Haass-BoxCF01478-030, Folder: "Iraq—August 2, 1990–December 1990 [8]," GBPLM.

97. Haass, Memorandum for Brent Scowcroft, "What next in the Gulf?," 3.

98. David W. Moore, "Americans Believe U.S. Participation in Gulf War a Decade Ago Worthwhile," Gallup News Service, February 26, 2001, http://news.gallup.com/poll/1963/americans-believe-us-participation-gulf-war-decade-ago-worthwhile.aspx.

99. Michael R. Gordon and Special to the New York Times, "Mideast Tensions; Nunn, Citing 'Rush' to War, Assails Decision to Drop Troop Rotation Plan," *New York Times*, November 12, 1990, A15.

100. Powell, *My American Journey*, 457; Woodward, *The Commanders*, 248–49; Powell, *Frontline*.

101. "Iraq And The World's Biggest Armies," *Los Angeles Times*, March 6, 1991, http://articles.latimes.com/1991-03-06/news/mn-359_1_north-korea.

102. Powell, *Frontline*.

103. Baker, *Frontline*.

104. Cheney, interview with author, August 9, 2013.

105. Powell, *My American Journey*, 427.

106. Cheney, interview with author, August 9, 2013.

107. Richard Haass Interview, Miller Center.

108. Haass, "What next in the Gulf?"

109. Haass, interview with author, August 14, 2017; see also handwritten notes on Richard Haass, "Themes for call to PM Thatcher," October 18, 1990, 11 a.m., Haass, Richard N., Files, Working File, GHWB-Haass-BoxCF01584-031, Folder: "Iraq—October 1990 [1]," GBPLM, 3.

110. Richard Haass Interview, Miller Center; Haass, *War of Necessity, War of Choice*, 92.

111. Richard Haass, "Draft: The Gulf Crisis: Thoughts, Scenarios & Options," August 19, 1990, and "The Gulf Crisis: Possible Futures," October 30, 1990, Haass, Richard N., Files, Presidential Meeting File, GHWB-Haass-BoxCF01584-033; Folder: "Iraq—October 1990 [3]," GBPLM, 1.

112. Richard Haass, "Oct 4, 90—Bob: Some issues/questions for today's 6pm small group session," Gates, Robert M., Files, GHWB-Gates-BoxCF00946-NotesAug90, Folder: "Notes—August 90—Saudi Arabia/Iraq/Kuwait [1]," GBPLM.

113. Woodward, *The Commanders*, 305; Gordon and Trainor, *The Generals' War*, 129.

114. Powell, *My American Journey*, 485.

115. Bush and Scowcroft, *A World Transformed*, 381.

116. Haass, *Frontline*.

117. Scowcroft, *Frontline*.

118. Haass, interview with author, August 14, 2017.

119. Cheney, interview with author, August 9, 2013.

120. Gordon and Trainor, *The Generals' War*, 144–45, 149.

121. Richard Haass Interview, Miller Center.

122. "Minutes of DC Meeting on Gulf Crisis," October 18, 1990, Haass, Richard N., Files, Working File, GHWB-Haass-BoxCF01585-001, Folder: "Minutes for DC Meetings on [1]," GBPLM, 1–2.

123. Ibid., 1–2.

124. James A. Baker III with Thomas M. DeFrank, *The Politics of Diplomacy: Revolution, War, and Peace, 1989–1992* (New York: G. P. Putnam's Sons, 1995), 303; Dick

Cheney with Liz Cheney, *In My Time: A Personal and Political Memoir* (New York: Threshold Editions, 2011), 203; Woodward, *The Commanders*, 311.

125. Bush and Scowcroft, *A World Transformed*, 381; Gordon and Trainor, *The Generals' War*, 138–39.

126. Powell, *My American Journey*, 467; Bush and Scowcroft, *A World Transformed*, 382; Cheney, interview with author, August 9, 2013; Gordon and Trainor, *The Generals' War*, 130–31.

127. David Jeremiah, Memorandum for Richard Haass, "subject: The Gulf Crisis: 4 Futures," October 24, 1990, Haass, Richard N., Files, Presidential Meeting File, GHWB-Haass-BoxCF01584-033, Folder: "Iraq—October 1990 [3]," GBPLM, 1.

128. Ibid., 1.

129. David Jeremiah, interview with author, April 12, 2013; Haass, interview with author, January 10, 2013.

130. Memorandum: "subject: The Gulf Crisis: 4 Futures," from David Jeremiah for Richard Haass, October 24, 1990, 2–3.

131. Gates, interview with author, July 31, 2013.

132. Haass, interview with author, August 14, 2017.

133. Powell, *Frontline*, 457, 467; Woodward, *The Commanders*, 42, 301.

134. Gates, interview with author, July 31, 2013.

135. Ibid.; Gordon and Trainor, *The Generals' War*, 139.

136. Richard Haass, "Memorandum for Brent Scowcroft," subject "October 30, 3:30 p, Mini-NSC on the Gulf," October 29, 1990, Gates, Robert M., Files, GHWB-Gates-BoxCF00946-006, Folder: "Persian Gulf Conflict—Pre-1991," GBPLM.

137. Bush and Scowcroft, *A World Transformed*, 393.

138. Ibid., 395.

139. Powell, *My American Journey*, 488.

140. Resende-Santos, "The Persian Gulf Crisis," 323, 325.

141. Bob Gates Interview, Miller Center.

142. Bush and Scowcroft, *A World Transformed*, 449.

143. George Bush, National Security Directive 54, "Responding to Iraqi Aggression in the Gulf," January 15, 1991, https://bush41library.tamu.edu/archives/nsd.

144. Woodward, *The Commanders*, 371.

145. "Working Paper/Dec 31, 1990, Pre-January 15/Use of Force Checklist, Gates, Robert M., Files, GHWB-Gates-BoxCF00946-006, Folder: "Persian Gulf Conflict—Pre-1991]," Bush PLM.

146. Brent Scowcroft, Memorandum for the President, "subject: Ending the Gulf War," February 25, 1991, Haass, Richard N., Files, Working Files, GHWB-Haass-BoxCF01584-005, Folder: "Iraq—February 1991 [3]," Bush PLM.

147. Ibid.

148. Haass, interview with author, August 14, 2017; Brent Scowcroft, "Ending the Gulf War."

149. Haass, interview with author, August 14, 2017.

150. Scowcroft, "Ending the Gulf War."

151. Taylor and Blackwell, "The Ground War in the Gulf," 16; Gordon and Trainor, *The Generals' War*, xii.

152. Scowcroft, "Ending the Gulf War"; Haass, *Frontline*.

153. George Bush, "Remarks to the American Legislative Exchange Council," March 1, 1991, online by Gerhard Peters and John T. Woolley, The American Presidency Project, http://www.presidency.ucsb.edu/ws/?pid=19351.

154. Frank Newport, David W. Moore, and Jeffrey M. Jones, "Special Release: American Opinion on the War," Gallup News, March 21, 2003, http://news.gallup.com/poll/8068/special-release-american-opinion-war.aspx; David W. Moore, "Americans Believe U.S. Participation in Gulf War a Decade Ago Worthwhile," Gallup News, February 26, 2001, http://news.gallup.com/poll/1963/americans-believe-us-participation-gulf-war-decade-ago-worthwhile.aspx.

155. Powell, *My American Journey*, 480.

156. Richard Haass interview, Miller Center; Bush, Remarks to the American Legislative Exchange Council.

157. Richard Haass Interview, Miller Center.

158. Haass, "Reassessing the NSC."

159. Richard Haass Interview, Miller Center.

160. Paul Wolfowitz, interview with author, September 5, 2013.

161. Haass, interview with author, August 14, 2017.

Chapter Five: A "Policy Person First and Foremost"

1. Derek Chollet, *The Road to the Dayton Accords: A Study of American Statecraft* (New York: Palgrave Macmillan, 2005), 1.

2. Bob Woodward, *The Choice: How Clinton Won* (New York: Simon & Schuster, 1996), 261.

3. William J. Clinton, "Address Accepting the Presidential Nomination at the Democratic National Convention in New York," July 16, 1992, The American Presidency Project, http://www.presidency.ucsb.edu/ws/?pid=25958.

4. Jason DeParle, "The Man Inside Bill Clinton's Foreign Policy," *New York Times Magazine*, August 20, 1995.

5. S. Nelson Drew, "NATO from Berlin to Bosnia: Trans-Atlantic Security in Transition," Institute for National Security Studies, McNair Paper 35 (Washington: National Defense University, January 1995), 8.

6. Anthony Lake, interview with author, August 30, 2013.

7. Alexander Vershbow, interview with author, August 16, 2017.

8. S. Nelson Drew, "NATO from Berlin to Bosnia."

9. Intelligence Memorandum, subject: "Yugoslavia Military Dynamics of A Potential Civil War," March 1991, 7, Document Number: 5235e80d993294098d517528, CIA Bosnia Documents.

10. National Intelligence Estimate, 15-90, subject: "Yugoslavia Transformed,"

October 1990, iii, Document Number: 5235e80c993294098d5174dd, CIA Bosnia Documents.

11. Laura Silber and Alan Little. *Yugoslavia: Death of a Nation* (New York: Penguin Books, 1997), 30.

12. Vershbow, interview with author, August 16, 2017.

13. Ibid.

14. Interview with Sandra Drew, September 10, 2017.

15. Major Christopher L. Christon, Fitness Report for Samuel Nelson Drew, January 2, 1979 to September 17, 1979, signed October 1, 1979, courtesy of Sandra Drew, photographed September 2017.

16. Stephen Engelberg, "Brutal Impasse: The Yugoslav War A Special Report; Yugoslav Ethnic Hatreds Raise Fears of a War Without an End," *New York Times*, December 23, 1991, A1.

17. "Clinton Campaign Promises," Files: Speechwriting-Boorstin, Box OA/ID Number 415, Folder: "NSC—1995 Accomplishments," William J. Clinton Presidential Library and Museum (WJCL).

18. I. M. Destler and Ivo Daalder (moderators), "The Role of the National Security Advisor," October 25, 1990, The National Security Council Project, The Brookings Institution, and the University of Maryland Center for International and Security Studies (CISSM), 11, https://www.brookings.edu/wp-content/uploads/2016/07/19991025.pdf.

19. Daalder and Destler, *In the Shadow*, 212.

20. Steven Mufson, "Clinton to Send Message with Economic Choices," *Washington Post*, November 8, 1992; Daalder and Destler, "The Role of the National Security Advisor," 11.

21. DeParle, "The Man Inside Bill Clinton's Foreign Policy."

22. Samuel Berger, interview with author, May 1, 2013.

23. Ibid.; Rothkopf, *Running the World*, 323; Thomas Friedman, "Clinton Trimming Lower-Level Aides," *New York Times*, February 10, 1993, A1.

24. Anthony Lake, *Somoza Falling* (Boston: Houghton Mifflin, 1989), 280, 282.

25. Berger, interview with author, May 1, 2013.

26. Ibid.

27. Foreign Affairs Oral History Project, "Ambassador Jenonne Walker," interviewed by Raymond Ewing, May 26, 2004, The Association for Diplomatic Studies and Training; Barbara Crossette, "Failure of the New Order; Yugoslav Carnage Poses Painful Questions For Western Alliance and United Nations," *New York Times*, May 15, 1992.

28. Jenonne Walker, interview with author, April 22, 2014.

29. Notes or draft minutes, subject: "Principals Committee Meeting on The Former Yugoslavia, February, 5, 1993," 1, 2, Document number: 523c39e5993294098d51762e, CIA Bosnia Documents.

30. Lake, *Somoza Falling*, 276.

31. CIA, "Reponses To Clinton Transition Team Questions on The Balkans," December 28, 1992, 14, Document Number: 5235e80d993294098d51752d, CIA Bosnia Documents; Bill Clinton, "The President's News Conference With Prime Minister Kiichi Miyazawa of Japan," April 16, 1993, The American Presidency Project, http://www.presidency.ucsb.edu/ws/?pid=46438.

32. Chollet, *The Road to the Dayton Accords*, 5.

33. Ivo Daalder, *Getting to Dayton: The Making of America's Bosnia Policy* (Washington, DC: Brookings Institution Press, 2000), 14–15.

34. Ibid.; Drew, *On the Edge*, 154; Memorandum for the National Security Advisor, subject: "Options for Bosnia," April 14, 1993, p.1, Document Number: 523c39e5993294098d51763f, CIA Bosnia Documents.

35. Woodward, *The Choice*, 257.

36. Anthony Lake, May 21, 2002, William J. Clinton Presidential History Project, Miller Center, University of Virginia; Daalder and Destler, "The Role of the National Security Advisor," 80.

37. Anthony Lake, Miller Center (2002).

38. Drew, *On the Edge*, 156; Kaplan, *Balkan Ghosts: A Journey Through History* (New York: St. Martin's Press, 1993).

39. Drew, *On the Edge*, 155.

40. Walker, interview with author, April 22, 2014.

41. Vershbow, interview with author, August 16, 2017.

42. Mark Matthews, "State Dept. resignations reflect dissent on Bosnia U.S. policy called weak, 'dangerous,'" *Baltimore Sun*, August 24, 1993.

43. Vershbow, interview with author, August 16, 2017.

44. Daniel Williams, "A Third State Dept. Official Resigns over Balkan Policy," *Washington Post*, August 24, 1993; Vershbow, interview with author, August 16, 2017.

45. Drew, *On the Edge*, 275.

46. Donald Kerrick, interview with author, April 8, 2013.

47. Powell, *My American Journey*, Kindle Locations 4970–4971.

48. Vershbow, interview with author, August 16, 2017.

49. Walter Slocombe, interview with author, February 13, 2013.

50. Drew, *On the Edge*, 45.

51. Halberstam, *War in a Time of Peace*, 168.

52. Andrew Kohut, "American International Engagement on the Rocks," Pew Research Center, July 11, 2013, http://www.pewglobal.org/2013/07/11/american-international-engagement-on-the-rocks/.

53. Drew, *On the Edge*, 359.

54. Elaine Sciolino, "Washington Talk; A Shake-Up Of Advisers: Who's Next?," *New York Times*, June 16, 1994, A7.

55. Ibid.

56. Walker, interview with author, April 22, 2014; Sciolino, "Washington Talk."

57. Vershbow, interview with author, August 2017.

58. Berger, interview with author, May 1, 2013.

59. Vershbow, interview with author, March 21, 2013.

60. Vershbow, interview with author, August 16, 2017.

61. Daalder, *Getting to Dayton*, 84.

62. Vershbow, interview with author, August 16, 2017.

63. Ibid.

64. Intelligence Report, subject: "Grave Humanitarian Conditions Loom in Bihac region," November 3, 1994, Document Number: 5235e80d993294098d51759e, CIA Bosnia Documents.

65. David Halberstam, *War in a Time of Peace* (New York: Scribner, 2001), 285.

66. Alexander Vershbow, interview with author, March 21, 2013; Memorandum for the President, subject: "Bosnia Policy After the Fall of Bihac," November 27, 1994, 1, Document Number: 523c39e5993294098d517664, CIA Bosnia Documents.

67. Memorandum for the President, subject: "Bosnia Policy After the Fall of Bihac."

68. Michael Kelly, "Surrender and Blame," *The New Yorker*, December 19, 1994, 51.

69. Anthony Lake, Miller Center (2002).

70. Woodward, *The Choice*, 17.

71. Anthony Lake, Miller Center (2002).

72. Ibid.

73. Chollet, *The Road to the Dayton Accords*, 6.

74. National Intelligence Council Special Estimate, SE 94-5, subject: "Prospects for UNPROFOR Withdrawal from Bosnia," December 1994, Document Number: 5235e80d993294098d517592, CIA Bosnia Documents.

75. "Proposed US Policy Principles During NATO-led UNPROFOR Withdrawal," handwritten: "OSD/JCS Paper," May 12, 1995, Document Number: 5235e80c993294098d5174be; Daalder, *Getting to Dayton*, 50.

76. Coaster, courtesy of Sandra Drew, photographed September 2017.

77. Vershbow, interview with author, August 16, 2017; interview with Sandra Drew, September 10, 2017.

78. Drew, interview with author, September 2017.

79. Fitness Report for Samuel Nelson Drew, October 26, 1987 to October 25, 1988, courtesy of Sandra Drew, photographed September 2017.

80. Lake, interview with author, August 30, 2013.

81. Berger, interview with author, May 1, 2013.

82. "Former Yugoslavia Policy Review," February 27, 1995; unsigned but in-meeting minutes confirm Vershbow wrote it, Document Number: 5235e80d 993294098d517584, CIA Bosnia Documents.

83. Chollet, *The Road to the Dayton*, 1.

84. Memorandum (and attachments) for Anthony Lake from Rob Malley, subject: "Washington Post Article on Serb atrocities in Srebrenica," November 6, 1995, Box OA/ID Number 613, Document ID 9508100, WJCL.

85. Woodward, *The Choice*, 255.

86. Derek Chollet and Bennet Freeman. *The Secret History of Dayton: U.S. Diplomacy and the Bosnia Peace Process 1995*, National Security Archive Electronic Briefing Book No. 171, National Security Archive, Washington, 1995, 11–12.

87. Ibid., 11.

88. Anthony Lake, Miller Center (2002).

89. See note 1, "Draft Letter From W. Anthony Lake and Roger Morris of the National Security Council Staff to the President's Assistant for National Security Affairs (Kissinger)," undated, Document 106, FRUS 1969–1976, vol. 2, 1969–1972.

90. Lake, *Somoza Falling*, 276.

91. Vershbow, interview with author, March 21, 2013; Woodward, *The Choice*, 258.

92. Vershbow, interview with author, August 2017.

93. Woodward, *The Choice*, 258.

94. Nancy Soderberg, interview with author, April 17, 2013; Chollet and Freeman, *The Secret History of Dayton*, 13–15.

95. Woodward, *The Choice*, 258.

96. Vershbow, interview with author, August 2017; Daalder, *Getting to Dayton*, 93–95.

97. Elaine Sciolino, "Clinton Rules Out a Quick Response to Bosnia Attack," *New York Times*, February 7, 1994; Berger, interview with author, May 1, 2013.

98. Silber and Little, *Yugoslavia*, 345.

99. Woodward, *The Choice*, 260; Soderberg, interview with author, April 17, 2013.

100. Vershbow, interview with author, August 16, 2017.

101. Memorandum for Madeleine Albright, Strobe Talbott, et al., subject: "Bosnia Strategy," from Sandy Berger, July 20, 1995, Document Number: 5235e80d993294098d51754c, CIA Bosnia Documents.

102. NSC Discussion Paper, "Schematic of Endgame Strategy," July 25, 1995, 1, Document Number: 5235e80d993294098d517533, CIA Bosnia Documents.

103. Chollet and Freeman, *The Secret History of Dayton*, 19.

104. Memorandum for Madeleine Albright, Strobe Talbott, et al., subject: "Bosnia Strategy," from Sandy Berger, July 20, 1995, Document Number: 5235e80d993294098d51754c, CIA Bosnia Documents.

105. Vershbow, interview with author, August 16, 2017.

106. Chollet and Freeman, *The Secret History of Dayton*, 37–38.

107. Memorandum for the National Security Advisor from Ambassador Albright, subject: "Why America Must Lead," August 3, 1995, 2, Document Number: 5235e80c993294098d5174b3, CIA Bosnia Documents.

108. Chollet and Freeman, *The Secret History of Dayton*, 39; Daalder, *Getting to Dayton*, see note 51, 104–6.

109. Daalder, *Getting to Dayton*, 110.

110. Chollet and Freeman, *The Secret History of Dayton*, 41; Daalder, *Getting to Dayton*, see note 64, 110.

111. Tim Weiner, "Clinton's Balkan Envoy Finds Himself Shut Out," *New York Times*, August 12, 1995.

112. Halberstam, *War in a Time of Peace*, 340.

113. Chollet and Freeman, *The Secret History of Dayton*, 47.

114. Vershbow, interview with author, August 16, 2017.

115. Mike O'Connor, "3 U.S. Diplomats Killed in Bosnia," *New York Times*, August 20, 1995.

116. Drew, interview with author, September 10, 2017; Vershbow, interview with author, August 16, 2017.

117. William J. Clinton, "Remarks at a Memorial Service in Arlington, Virginia, for the American Diplomats Who Died in Bosnia-Herzegovina," August 23, 1995, The American Presidency Project, http://www.presidency.ucsb.edu/ws/?pid=51761.

118. Richard C. Holbrooke, *To End A War* (New York: Modern Library, 1999), 87.

119. Kerrick, interview with author, April 8, 2013.

120. Woodward, *The Choice*, 270.

121. William J. Clinton, "Address to the Nation on Implementation of the Peace Agreement in Bosnia-Herzegovina," November 27, 1995, The American Presidency Project, http://www.presidency.ucsb.edu/ws/?pid=50808.

122. David W. Moore, "Americans Divided on U.S. Troops in Bosnia," Gallup News, December 24, 1997.

123. Gallup News, "Presidential Approval Ratings—Bill Clinton," http://news.gallup.com/poll/116584/presidential-approval-ratings-bill-clinton.aspx.

124. Vershbow, interview with author, March 21, 2013.

125. Anthony Lake, Miller Center (2002).

126. Karen DeYoung, "Rice Favors 'Mean but Lean' National Security Council," *Washington Post*, January 17, 2017.

127. Rothkopf, *Running the World*, 323.

128. "Presidential Decision Directive/statutory NSC-56: Managing Complex Contingency Operations," May 1997. http://www.fas.org/irp/offdocs/pdd56.htm; Office of the Press Secretary, "Fact Sheet: Combatting Terrorism: Presidential Decision Directive 62," The White House, May 22, 1998, http://www.fas.org/irp/offdocs/pdd-62.htm.

129. Vershbow, interview with author, August 2017.

Chapter Six: A "Wartime" Staff

1. Peter Baker, *Days of Fire: Bush and Cheney in the White House* (New York: Doubleday, 2013), 527–28.

2. James Traub, "W.'s World," *New York Times Magazine*, January 14, 2001, 28.

3. "Exchanges Between the Candidates in the Third Presidential Debate," *New York Times*, October 18, 2000, A26.

4. Bob Woodward, *Bush At War* (New York: Simon & Schuster, 2002), 168.

5. Meghan O'Sullivan, interview with author, January 23, 2014.

6. Condoleezza Rice, interview with author, June 24, 2014.

7. Meghan O'Sullivan, interview with author, August 30, 2017.

8. George W. Bush, "Organization of the National Security Council System," National Security Presidential Directive-1, February 13, 2001.

9. Jane Perlez, "Bush Team's Counsel Is Divided on Foreign Policy," *New York Times*, March 27, 2001.

10. Rice, interview with author, June 24, 2014.

11. Condoleezza Rice, *No Higher Honor: A Memoir of My Years In Washington* (New York: Crown Publishers, 2011), 14; Derek Chollet, "The National Security Council: Is It Effective, or Is It Broken?," in Derek S. Reveron, Nikolas K. Gvosdev, and John A. Cloud, *The Oxford Handbook of U.S. National Security* (New York: Oxford University Press, 2018), 114.

12. Stephen Hadley, interview with author, September 6, 2013.

13. Rothkopf, *Running the World*, 421; Rice, *No Higher Honor*, 17.

14. Donald Rumsfeld, interview with author, April 9, 2014; and Donald Rumsfeld, *Known and Unknown: A Memoir* (New York: Sentinel, 2011), Kindle Edition, location 5647.

15. Cheney, interview with author, August 9, 2013.

16. Rice, interview with author, June 24, 2014.

17. Donald Rumsfeld to Condoleezza Rice, "Snowflake," subject: "Chain of Command," December 2, 2002, in *The Rumsfeld Papers*, http://papers.rumsfeld.com/library/.

18. O'Sullivan, interview with author, August 30, 2017.

19. Fred M. Kaplan, *The Insurgents: David Petraeus and the Plot to Change the American Way of War* (New York: Simon & Schuster, 2013), 76–77.

20. O'Sullivan interview with author, August 30, 2017; Meghan L. O'Sullivan, "Iraq: Time for a Modified Approach," Brookings Institution Report, February 21, 2001, https://www.brookings.edu/research/iraq-time-for-a-modified-approach/.

21. Ibid.

22. Ibid.

23. Michael R. Gordon and Bernard E. Trainor, *The Endgame: The Inside Story of the Struggle for Iraq, From George W. Bush to Barack Obama* (New York: Pantheon Books, 2012), 14–15; Baker, *Days of Fire*, 298; Kaplan, *The Insurgents*, 82.

24. O'Sullivan, interview with author, August 30, 2017.

25. Baker, *Days of Fire*, 251.

26. Elisabeth Bumiller, "Adviser Has President's Ear as She Keeps Eyes on Iraq," *New York Times*, June 12, 2006.

27. Rice, *No Higher Honor*, 242.

28. Ibid., 15.

29. David Sanger, "White House to Overhaul Iraq and Afghan Missions," *New York Times*, October 6, 2003, A7; Gordon and Trainor, *The Endgame*, 28.

30. Baker, *Days of Fire*, 292; Bob Woodward, *State of Denial* (New York: Simon & Schuster, 2006), 266.

31. In-Depth Topics, "Iraq," Gallup, http://news.gallup.com/poll/1633/iraq.aspx.

32. Kaplan, *The Insurgents*, 3.

33. Bumiller, "Adviser Has President's Ear as She Keeps Eyes on Iraq."

34. Gordon and Trainor, *The Endgame*, 28.

35. The White House, "The Road to Freedom," June 28, 2004. https://georgewbush-whitehouse.archives.gov/infocus/elections/freedomessay/index.html#.

36. Gordon and Trainor, *The Endgame*, 28–29; Rumsfeld, interview with author, April 9, 2014.

37. O'Sullivan, second interview with author, February 10, 2014.

38. Glenn Kessler and Al Kamen, "Ex-Adviser Reportedly Hurt Embassy Aide; Kuwait Airport Incident Disputed," *Washington Post*, November 12, 2004, A6.

39. Bumiller, "Adviser Has President's Ear as She Keeps Eyes on Iraq."

40. Ibid.; Bob Woodward, *The War Within: A Secret White House History, 2006–2008* (New York: Simon & Schuster, 2008), 101.

41. Meghan O'Sullivan, interview with author, January 23, 2014.

42. Ibid.

43. MNF-I: "Campaign Plan: Operation Iraqi Freedom, from Occupation to Constitutional Elections," August 5, 2004, 7–8, General George Casey Papers (GGCP), National Defense University Archives, declassified September 29, 2009; MNF-I Red Team: "Building Legitimacy and Confronting Insurgency in Iraq," July 15, 2004, 1, 3, GGCP, declassified September 29, 2009.

44. MNF-I: "Campaign Plan: Operation Iraqi Freedom, From Occupation to Constitutional Elections," August 5, 2004, 16, GGCP, declassified September 29, 2009.

45. Gordon and Trainor, *The Endgame*, 129.

46. Hadley, interview with author, September 6, 2013.

47. Hadley, interview with author, September 6, 2013; Feaver, interview with author, December 3, 2013.

48. Peter Feaver, interview with author, December 3, 2013.

49. Peter Feaver, interview with author, October 10, 2017.

50. Woodward, *War Within*, 12.

51. Gordon and Trainor, *The Endgame*, 182; MNF-I Campaign Action Plan for 2005—Transition to Self Reliance," April 22, 2005, 2, GGCP, declassified September 29, 2009.

52. Francis J. West, *The Strongest Tribe: War, Politics, and the Endgame In Iraq* (New York: Random House, 2008), 108–9.

53. Woodward, *War Within*, 79.

54. Ibid.

55. George W. Bush, "Address to the Nation on the War on Terror from Fort Bragg, North Carolina," June 28, 2005, The American Presidency Project, http://www.presidency.ucsb.edu/ws/?pid=64989; Brett McGurk, interview with author, June 2, 2014; Philip Zelikow, interview with author, May 6, 2014.

56. Condoleezza Rice, "Opening Remarks before the Senate Foreign Relations Committee," State Department, October 19, 2005, http://2001-2009.state.gov/secretary/

rm/2005/55303.htm; "News Briefing with Secretary of Defense Donald Rumsfeld and Gen. Peter Pace," Defense Department, November 29, 2005, 1:20 p.m. EDT, http://archive.defense.gov/Transcripts/Transcript.aspx?TranscriptID=1492; Kaplan, *The Insurgents*, 195.

57. Kaplan, *The Insurgents*, 195.
58. Hadley, interview with author, September 6, 2013.
59. Ibid.
60. MNF-I: "Campaign Progress Review," December 20, 2005, 1, GGCP, declassified September 29, 2009.
61. Edward Wong, "Turnout in the Iraqi Election Is Reported at 70 Percent," *New York Times*, December 22, 2005.
62. Bush, *Decision Points*, Kindle Edition, Locations 6374–6375.
63. Casey, interview with author, April 21, 2014.
64. Baker, *Days of Fire*, 448.
65. Hadley, interview with author, September 6, 2013.
66. George W. Bush, "The President's Radio Address," March 18, 2006, online by Gerhard Peters and John T. Woolley, The American Presidency Project, http://www.presidency.ucsb.edu/ws/?pid=65416.
67. U.S. Mission Iraq and MNF-I: "Joint Campaign Plan, Operation Iraqi Freedom: Transition to Iraqi Self-Reliance," April 28, 2006, 17, GGCP, declassified September 29, 2009; Woodward, *The War Within*, 5.
68. Feaver, interview with author, December 3, 2013.
69. O'Sullivan, interview with author, January 23, 2014.
70. George Packer, "The Lesson of Tal Afar," *The New Yorker*, April 10, 2006.
71. CQ Transcripts, "President Bush Discusses the War in Iraq," *Washington Post*, March 20, 2006, http://www.washingtonpost.com/wp-dyn/content/article/2006/03/20/AR2006032000762.html.
72. Feaver, interview with author, December 3, 2013.
73. Peter D. Feaver, "The Right to be Right," *International Security*, vol. 35, no. 4, Spring 2011, 101.
74. Baker, *Days Of Fire*, 466.
75. Ibid., 466–67.
76. Feaver, interview with author, December 3, 2013.
77. Gordon and Trainor, *The Endgame*, 287–88.
78. Ibid., 288; Woodward, *The War Within*, 61.
79. Hadley, interview with author, September 6, 2013.
80. Baker, *Days of Fire*, 474; Woodward, *The War Within*, 72–73.
81. Woodward, *The War Within*, 68–70.
82. Ibid., 72.
83. Ibid., 73.
84. Casey, interview with author, April 21, 2014.
85. Woodward, *The War Within*, 78.

86. Ibid., 94.

87. In-Depth Topics, "Iraq," Gallup, http://news.gallup.com/poll/1633/iraq.aspx; "Presidential Approval Ratings—George W. Bush," Gallup, http://news.gallup.com/poll/116500/presidential-approval-ratings-george-bush.aspx.

88. Crouch, interview with author, April 23, 2014; Rice, interview with author, June 24, 2014; Zelikow, interview with author, May 6, 2014.

89. Zelikow, interview with author, May 6, 2014; Woodward, *The War Within*, 235.

90. Feaver, "The Right to Be Right," 102.

91. Baker, *Days of Fire*, 495.

92. Feaver, "The Right to Be Right," 103.

93. Thomas E. Ricks. *The Gamble: General David Petraeus and the American Military Adventure In Iraq, 2006–2008* (New York: Penguin Press, 2009), 103.

94. Woodward, *The War Within*, 190–92.

95. Baker, *Days of Fire*, 487.

96. See chart, "Enemy-Initiated Attacks by Month, May 2003 to May 2008," Figure 1, Government Accountability Office (GAO), "Securing, Stabilizing and Rebuilding Iraq," GAO-08-837, June 2008, 12; Politics, "Bush transcript, part 3: Election loss a 'thumping,'" CNN.com, November 8, 2006.

97. Baker, *Days of Fire*, 510–11.

98. Ibid., 510–11.

99. Feaver, "The Right to be Right," 103.

100. Hadley, interview with author, September 6, 2013.

101. Woodward, *The War Within*, 240.

102. Kaplan, *The Insurgents*, 237.

103. Casey, interview with author, April 21, 2014; Woodward, *The War Within*, 232, 242; George W. Casey, *Strategic Reflections: Operation Iraqi Freedom, July 2004–February 2007* (Washington, DC: National Defense University Press, 2012), 124.

104. Ricks, *The Gamble*, 93.

105. Woodward, *The War Within*, 249.

106. David E. Sanger, *Confront and Conceal: Obama's Secret Wars and Surprising Use of American Power* (New York: Crown Publishers, 2012), 17; Associated Press, "A timeline of U.S. troop levels in Afghanistan since 2001," *Military Times*, July 6, 2016, https://www.militarytimes.com/news/your-military/2016/07/06/a-timeline-of-u-s-troop-levels-in-afghanistan-since-2001/.

107. Woodward, *The War Within*, 266–67.

108. Baker, *Days of Fire*, 511.

109. Peter Baker, Michael A. Fletcher, and Michael Abramowitz, "25 Minutes in the Oval Office: President Bush on Iraq, Elections and Immigration," *Washington Post*, December 20, 2006, http://www.washingtonpost.com/wp-dyn/content/article/2006/12/19/AR2006121900886.html.

110. In-Depth Topics, "Iraq," Gallup, http://news.gallup.com/poll/1633/iraq.aspx; Fred Barnes, "How Bush Decided on the Surge," *Weekly Standard*, February 4, 2008.

111. Rice, *No Higher Honor*, 544–45; Baker, *Days of Fire*, 515; Gates, *Duty*, 37; Gordon and Trainor, *The Endgame*, 306–7.

112. Ricks, *The Gamble*, 105.

113. George W. Bush, "Background Briefing by Senior Administration Officials," January 10, 2007, The American Presidency Project, http://www.presidency.ucsb.edu/ws/?pid=60328.

114. Baker, *Days of Fire*, 524.

115. See chart, "Enemy-Initiated Attacks by Month, May 2003 to May 2008," Figure 1, Government Accountability Office (GAO), "Securing, Stabilizing and Rebuilding Iraq," GAO-08-837, June 2008, 12.

116. Background conversation; Jeff Zeleny, "Leading Democrat in Senate Tells Reporters, 'This War Is Lost,'" *New York Times*, April 20, 2017.

117. Joint Hearing of U.S. House of Representatives Foreign Affairs and Armed Services Committees, "Transcript of Iraq hearing statements," CNN.com, September 10, 2007.

118. Doug Lute, interview with author, September 30, 2017.

119. Baker, *Days of Fire*, 520.

120. Hadley, interview with author, March 28, 2018.

121. Thomas E. Ricks, "Meghan O'Sullivan enthroned at Harvard," *Foreign Policy*, September 2, 2009; Jack Kelly, "Managerial Incompetence and the 'War Czar,'" *Real Clear Politics*, April 17, 2007; Bumiller, "Adviser Has President's Ear as She Keeps Eyes on Iraq."

122. CQ Press, *2005 Federal Staff Directory* (Washington, DC: CQ Press, Fall 2005), 18–23.

123. Baker, *Days of Fire*, 541.

124. Martha Raddatz, "Bush Taps New 'War Czar,'" *ABC News*, May 15, 2017.

125. Peter Baker and Thomas E. Ricks, "3 Generals Spurn the Position of War 'Czar,'" *Washington Post*, April 11, 2007.

126. Robert Gates, *Duty: Memoirs of a Secretary at War* (New York: Alfred A. Knopf, 2014), 67.

127. DeYoung, "Rice Favors 'mean but lean' National Security Council."

128. Transcript, Hearing, U.S. Committee on Armed Services, June 7, 2007.

129. Gates, *Duty*, 67.

130. David Petraeus, interview with author, March 11, 2018.

131. O'Sullivan, interview with author, January 23, 2014.

Chapter Seven: "When You Work for the President, You Work for the President"

1. Bob Woodward, *Obama's Wars* (New York: Simon & Schuster, 2010), 322.

2. Doug Lute, interview with author, September 30, 2017.

3. Transcript, Hearing, U.S. Committee on Armed Services, June 7, 2007.

4. GovTrack, "On the Nomination PN599: Lt. Gen. Douglas E. Lute, in the Army, to be Lieutenant General," 110th Congress, June 28, 2007.

5. Lute, interview with author, September 30, 2017.

6. Woodward, *Obama's War*, 41.

7. Transcript, Hearing, U.S. Committee on Armed Services, June 7, 2007.

8. Woodward, *War Within*, 398.

9. Gates, *Duty*, 67.

10. Ibid.; Mullen, interview with author, December 20, 2017.

11. Sanger, *Confront and Conceal*, 17.

12. Tom Bowman, "U.S. Military Falls Short of Afghan Training Goal," NPR, January 25, 2008.

13. Alan McLean and Archie Tse, "American Forces in Afghanistan and Iraq," *New York Times*, June 22, 2011.

14. Cartwright, interview with author, October 23, 2017.

15. Frank Newport, "More Americans Now View Afghanistan War as a Mistake," Gallup, February 19, 2014.

16. Ian S. Livingston and Michael O'Hanlon, "Afghanistan Index," The Brookings Institution, March 31, 2016, 6.

17. Doug Lute, interview with author, September 30, 2017.

18. Woodward, *Obama's Wars*, 43.

19. Ibid., 44.

20. Richard Skinner, "9/11 Improved Presidential Transitions," October 10, 2016.

21. Jim Mann, *The Obamians: The Struggle Inside the White House to Redefine American Power* (New York: Viking, 2012), 79.

22. Barack Obama, "Transcript: Obama's Speech Against The Iraq War," NPR, January 20, 2009.

23. Barack Obama, Remarks: "A New Beginning," DePaul University, Chicago, Illinois, October 2, 2007.

24. Rosie Gray, "Iraq War Hangs Over a Top White House Appointment," *Buzzfeed*, January 25, 2013.

25. Barack Obama, "Press Release: Key Members of Obama-Biden National Security Team Announced," December 1, 2008, online by Gerhard Peters and John T. Woolley, The American Presidency Project, http://www.presidency.ucsb.edu/ws/?pid=84936.

26. Todd Purdum, "Team of Mascots," *Vanity Fair*, July 2012, https://www.vanityfair.com/news/2012/07/obama-cabinet-team-rivals-lincoln.

27. Mann, *The Obamians*, 9; Woodward, *Obama's Wars*, 37.

28. Woodward, *Obama's Wars*, 37.

29. Denis McDonough, interview with author, October 18, 2017.

30. James Jones, interview with author, October 18, 2017.

31. Ibid.

32. Ibid.; James Jones, "The 21st Century Interagency Process," March 18, 2009; Ed

Luce and Daniel Dombey, "US foreign policy: Waiting on a sun king," *Financial Times*, March 30, 2010, http://www.ft.com/intl/cms/s/0/df53a396-3c2a-11df-b40c-00144feabdc0.html#axzz2NRt2UbkB.

33. Spencer S. Hsu, "Obama Integrates Security Councils, Adds New Offices," *Washington Post*, May 27, 2009, http://articles.washingtonpost.com/2009-05-27/news/36814987_1_homeland-security-frank-j-cilluffo-national-security.

34. Jones, interview with author, October 18, 2017.

35. Jason Horowitz, "Politics and policy: Tom Donilon's rise to national security adviser," *Washington Post*, December 7, 2010, https://www.washingtonpost.com/style/politics-and-policy-tom-donilons-rise-to-national-security-adviser/2010/12/07/ABVBIjD_story_3.html.

36. McDonough, interview with author, October 18, 2017; Michael Crowley, "The Decider," *The New Republic*, August 12, 2009.

37. Woodward, *Obama's Wars*, 79.

38. Sanger, *Confront and Conceal*, 15.

39. Woodward, *Obama's Wars*, 88.

40. Barack Obama, Speech: "The War We Need to Win," August 1, 2007, The Woodrow Wilson International Center for Scholars.

41. Woodward, *Obama's Wars*, 90; Lute, interview with author, September 30, 2017.

42. Woodward, *Obama's Wars*, 90, 99–100.

43. Barack Obama, "The War We Need to Win."

44. Woodward, *Obama's Wars*, 105.

45. Lute, interview with author, September 30, 2017; Woodward, *Obama's Wars*, 95.

46. Woodward, *Obama's Wars*, 95.

47. The White House Press Office, "Statement by the President on Afghanistan," February 17, 2009.

48. Woodward, *Obama's Wars*, 96.

49. Barack Obama, "Remarks by the President on a New Strategy for Afghanistan and Pakistan," The White House, March 27, 2009.

50. Lute, interview with author, September 30, 2017.

51. John Tien, interview with author, October 30, 2017.

52. Woodward, *Obama's Wars*, 145.

53. Ibid., 146.

54. Lute, interview with author, March 9, 2018.

55. Woodward, *Obama's Wars*, 118.

56. Ben Rhodes, *The World As It Is: A Memoir of the Obama White House* (New York: Random House, 2018), 77.

57. Jon Meacham, "Q&A: Obama on Dick Cheney, War and Star Trek," *Newsweek*, May 15, 2009.

58. Tien, interview with author, October 30, 2017.

59. Press Conference: "Secretary Gates and Adm. Mullen on Leadership Changes in Afghanistan From the Pentagon," US Defense Department, May 11, 2009.

60. "Hearing of The Senate Armed Services Committee," June 2, 2009, https://votesmart.org/public-statement/429055/hearing-of-the-senate-armed-services-committee-nomination-of-admiral-james-stavridis-usn-for-reappointment-to-the-grade-of-admiral-and-to-be-commander-us-european-command-and-supreme-allied-commander-europe.

61. Bob Woodward, "Key in Afghanistan: Economy, Not Military," *Washington Post*, July 1, 2009.

62. Woodward, *Obama's Wars*, 183.

63. Gates, *Duty*, 350; multiple background interviews.

64. Gates, *Duty*, 368.

65. Ann Scott Tyson, "U.S. Commander in Afghanistan Calls Situation 'Serious,'" *Washington Post*, September 1, 2009, http://www.washingtonpost.com/wp-dyn/content/article/2009/08/31/AR2009083101100.html.

66. Commander, NATO International Security Assistance Force, Afghanistan, "Commander's Initial Assessment," August 30, 2009, 1–2.

67. Woodward, *Obama's Wars*, 184.

68. Ibid., 160.

69. Ibid., 251.

70. Jon Meacham, "Q&A: Obama on Dick Cheney, War and Star Trek," *Newsweek*, May 15, 2009.

71. Background interview.

72. Richard Holbrooke, "Gordon Goldstein's 'Lessons in Disaster,'" *New York Times*, November 27, 2008; and Woodward, *Obama's Wars*, 97.

73. Gates, *Duty*, 385; Mullen, interview with author, December 20, 2017.

74. Woodward, *Obama's Wars*, 244.

75. Mark Landler, *Alter Egos: Hillary Clinton, Barack Obama, and the Twilight Struggle Over American Power* (New York: Random House, 2016), 70.

76. Woodward, *Obama's Wars*, 264.

77. Rajiv Chandrasekaran, "'Little America': Infighting on Obama team squandered chance for peace in Afghanistan," *Washington Post*, June 24, 2012.

78. Background interview.

79. Woodward, *Obama's Wars*, 281.

80. Landler, "The Afghan War and the Evolution of Obama."

81. Woodward, *Obama's Wars*, 277.

82. Ibid., 231.

83. Ibid., 331 and 335; Barack Obama, "Remarks by the President in Address to the Nation on the Way Forward in Afghanistan and Pakistan," The White House, December 1, 2009, https://obamawhitehouse.archives.gov/the-press-office/remarks-president-address-nation-way-forward-afghanistan-and-pakistan.

84. Peter Baker, "How Obama Came to Plan for 'Surge' in Afghanistan," *New York Times*, December 5, 2009.

85. Woodward, *Obama's Wars*, 302.

86. Woodward, *Obama's Wars*, 313.

87. Leaked copy of "Terms Sheet," in Woodward, *Obama's Wars*, 385.

88. Tien, interview with author, October 30, 2017.

89. Woodward, *Obama's Wars*, 320–21.

90. Ibid., 311.

91. Gates, *Duty*, 383.

92. Ibid..

93. Mann, *The Obamians*, 68.

94. David Samuels, "The Aspiring Novelist Who Became Obama's Foreign-Policy Guru," *New York Times Magazine*, May 5, 2016.

95. Barack Obama, "Nobel Lecture," Oslo, Norway, December 10, 2009, https://www.nobelprize.org/nobel_prizes/peace/laureates/2009/obama-lecture_en.html.

96. Sheryl Gay Stolberg, "Obama Defends Strategy in Afghanistan," *New York Times*, August 17, 2009.

97. Woodward, *Obama's Wars*, 375.

98. Lute, interview with author, March 9, 2018.

99. Mullen, interview with author, December 20, 2017.

100. Gates, *Duty*, 385.

101. McDonough, interview with author, October 18, 2017; Gates, *Duty*, 500.

102. Gates, *Duty*, 482; Carrie Dann, "Hagel's Predecessors Decried White House 'Micromanaging,'" *NBC News*, November 24, 2014, https://www.nbcnews.com/politics/first-read/hagels-predecessors-decried-white-house-micromanaging-n255231.

103. Sanger, *Confront and Conceal*, 49.

104. Helene Cooper and Thom Shanker, "U.S. Redefines Afghan Success Before Conference," *New York Times*, May 17, 2012.

105. Sanger, *Confront and Conceal*, 55.

106. Brian McKeon, interview with author, October 13, 2017.

107. US Representative Jackie Walorski, "House Approves Walorski Amendment to Restore Transparency to National Security Council," press release, May 17, 2016, http://walorski.house.gov/house-approves-walorski-amendment-to-restore-transparency-to-national-security-council/; Karen DeYoung, "How the Obama White House Runs Foreign Policy," *Washington Post*, August 4, 2015, https://www.washingtonpost.com/world/national-security/how-the-obama-white-house-runs-foreign-policy/2015/08/04/2befb960-2fd7-11e5-8353-1215475949f4_story.html.

108. Vali Nasr, "The Inside Story of How the White House Let Diplomacy Fail in Afghanistan," *Foreign Policy*, March 4, 2013.

109. McDonough, interview with author, October 18, 2017.

110. Landler, *Alter Egos*, xii.

111. Rice, interview with author, January 17, 2018.

112. Ibid.

113. Ibid.

114. Barack Obama, "Changing the Name of the National Security Staff to the National Security Council Staff," Executive Order 13657, White House Press Office, February 10, 2014, http://www.presidency.ucsb.edu/ws/index.php?pid=104736.

115. Michael D. Shear, "Security Staff Getting Its Old Name Back," *New York Times*, February 10, 2014, https://www.nytimes.com/2014/02/11/us/politics/security-staff-getting-its-old-name-back.html.

116. Suzy George, "Fine-Tuning NSC Staff Processes and Procedures," *White House Blog*, June 22, 2015, https://obamawhitehouse.archives.gov/blog/2015/06/22/fine-tuning-nsc-staff-processes-and-procedures.

117. Kathleen J. McInnis, "Fact Sheet: FY2017 National Defense Authorization Act (NDAA) DOD Reform Proposals," Congressional Research Service, R44508, May 18, 2017, https://fas.org/sgp/crs/natsec/R44508.pdf.

118. David E. Sanger, Eric Schmitt, and Peter Baker, "Turmoil at the National Security Council, From the Top Down," *New York Times*, February 12, 2017.

119. Comedian Sarah Silverman wrote, "Call 202-224-4751 My name is _____ I am from ____ I am an American citizen & I oppose Steve Bannon being confirmed 2 sit on our NSC," and film director Judd Apatow tweeted, "Former Obama adviser calls Trump decision on Nat Sec panel 'stone cold crazy.'" Sarah Silverman, @sarahksilverman, Twitter, February 10, 2017, https://twitter.com/SarahKSilverman/status/830170694814011392; Judd Apatow, @juddapatow, Twitter, January 30, 2017, https://twitter.com/JuddApatow/status/826093268614180865.

120. Stephen Braun and Robert Burns, "Flynn, fired once by a president, now removed by another," Associated Press, February 14, 2017.

121. Michael Shear, "Obama Warned Trump About Hiring Flynn, Officials Say," *New York Times*, May 8, 2017.

122. NBC News, "Meet the Flynn Stones: Holdovers From Mike Flynn's Brief Term as National Security Adviser," March 10, 2017, https://www.nbcnews.com/card/meet-flynn-stones-holdovers-mike-flynn-s-reign-nsa-n731746.

123. Rosie Gray, "An NSC Staffer Is Forced Out Over a Controversial Memo," *The Atlantic*, August 2, 2017.

124. H. R. McMaster, interview with author, June 25, 2018.

125. Ibid.; background interview.

126. McMaster, interview with author, June 25, 2018.

127. Spencer Ackerman, "White House Aide's Plan to Stop Leaks: Spy on His Co-Workers," *The Daily Beast*, May 13, 2018; Rosie Gray, "An NSC Staffer Is Forced Out Over a Controversial Memo," *The Atlantic*, August 2, 2017.

128. McMaster, interview with author, June 25, 2018.

129. Donald Trump, @RealDonaldTrump, Twitter, March 1, 2013, https://twitter.com/realdonaldtrump/status/307568422789709824.

130. McMaster, interview with author, June 25, 2018.

131. Donald Trump, "Remarks by President Trump on the Strategy in Afghanistan

and South Asia," The White House, August 21, 2017, https://www.whitehouse
.gov/briefings-statements/remarks-president-trump-strategy-afghanistan-
south-asia/.

132. McMaster, interview with author, June 25, 2018.

133. Eliana Johnson, Nahal Toosi, and Kenneth P. Vogel, "McMaster rolls back
Flynn's changes at NSC," Politico, March 1, 2017; Karen DeYoung and Greg Jaffe,
"McMaster ousts senior official on National Security Council," Washington Post,
July 27, 2017.

134. McMaster, interview with author, June 25, 2018.

135. National Security Strategy Archive, The Taylor Group, http://nssarchive.us/.

136. Eliana Johnson, "Trump dumped Abrams over his criticisms during the campaign, sources say." Politico, February 10, 2017; Elliot Abrams, "The Trump
National Security Strategy," Blog Post, Council on Foreign Relations, December
26, 2017, https://www.cfr.org/blog/trump-national-security-strategy.

137. Greg Jaffe and Josh Dawsey, "Trump and McMaster have seemed anxious to part
but so far remain together," Washington Post, March 1, 2018.

138. Lena H. Sun, "Top White House official in charge of pandemic response exits
abruptly," Washington Post, May 10, 2018; and Eric Geller, "White House elimi-
nates top cyber adviser post," Politico, May 15, 2018.

139. Nahal Toosi, Bryan Bender, and Eliana Johnson, "Cabinet chiefs feel shut out of
Bolton's 'efficient policy process,'" Politico, July 25, 2018; and Josh Rogin, "John
Bolton's new deputy is a hawk with sharp elbows, just like him," Washington Post,
April 23, 2018.

140. Mark Landler and Helene Cooper, "White House Wants Pentagon to Offer More
Options on North Korea," New York Times, February 1, 2018.

141. Donald Trump, @RealDonaldTrump, Twitter, September 26, 2017, https://twitter
.com/realDonaldTrump/status/912836917296877569.

Epilogue: What the NSC's Warriors Have Won

1. Michael Nelson, ed., Guide to the Presidency and Executive Branch (5th edition),
vol. 1 (Thousand Oaks, CA: CQ Press, 2013), 1345.

2. Matthew Dickinson, "Is The Loneliest Job In the World Getting Lonelier?" Presidential Power Blog, August 16, 2014.

3. Rice, No Higher Honor, 14.

4. The Vows Column, "Richard Haass, Assistant to President, Weds Ms. Mer-
candetti, TV Producer," New York Times, November 18, 1990, http://www
.nytimes.com/1990/11/18/style/richard-haass-assistant-to-president-weds-ms-
mercandetti-tv-producer.html.

5. Richard Haass Interview, Miller Center.

6. Ibid.

7. Niccolò Machiavelli, The Prince, trans. Luigi Ricci (London: Grant Richards,
1903), 95.

8. Rhodes, *The World As It Is*, 200.

9. Eliot A. Cohen, "Civil-military relations," *Orbis* 41, no. 2 (Spring 1997): 177.

10. Gates, *Duty*, 482.

11. David J. Rothkop, *National Insecurity: American Leadership in an Age of Fear* (New York: PublicAffairs, 2016); Walorski, "House Approves Walorski Amendment"; and DeYoung, "How the Obama White House Runs Foreign Policy."

12. Donald Trump, @RealDonaldTrump, Twitter, July 14, 2018, https://twitter.com/realdonaldtrump/status/1018072081676865536.

13. Anonymous, "I Am Part of the Resistance Inside the Trump Administration," *New York Times*, September 5, 2018.

14. Monmouth University Polling Institute, "Public Troubled by 'Deep State'," March 19, 2018, https://www.monmouth.edu/polling-institute/reports/monmouthpoll_us_031918/.

15. Allan Bloom, *The Republic of Plato* (New York: Basic Books, 1968), Book 2, 375a–d, 52–53.

Debts

1. Bruce Springsteen, Atlantic City, Nebraska, © September 30, 1982 by Columbia Records.

Notes on Sources

1. Kai Bird, *The Good Spy: The Life and Death of Robert Ames* (New York: Crown Publishers, 2014), Kindle Edition, location 640–45.

SOURCES

Interviews

Salman Ahmed, interview with author, November 30, 2017.

Richard Armitage, interview with author, September 26, 2017.

James A. Baker III, interview with author, April 8, 2013.

James Baker, interview with author, September 4, 2013.

Samuel "Sandy" Berger, interview with author, May 1, 2013.

Tony Blinken, interview with author, October 26, 2017.

Paul Bremer, interview with author, April 18, 2013.

Shawn Brimley, interview with author, April 11, 2013.

Zbigniew Brzezinski, interview with author, April 12, 2013.

James Cartwright, interview with author, October 23, 2017.

George Casey, interview with author, April 21, 2013.

Sandra Charles, interview with author, September 19, 2013.

Tarun Chhabra, interview with author, November 16, 2017.

Dick Cheney, interview with author, August 9, 2013.

Derek Chollet, interview with author, December 21, 2011.

J. D. Crouch, interview with author, April 23, 2014.

Ivo Daalder, interview with author, March 21, 2013.

Sandra Drew, interview with author, September 10, 2017.

Phillip Dur, interviews with author, May 1, 2013; April 23, 2014; and August 11, 2017.

Peter Feaver, interviews with author, December 3, 2013; and October 10, 2017.

Michèle Flournoy, interview with author, October 22, 2017.

Leon Fuerth, interview with author, May 2, 2014.

Robert Gates, interview with author, July 31, 2013.

Suzy George, interview with author, February 12, 2018.

Richard Haass, interviews with author, January 10, 2013; and August 14, 2017.

Stephen Hadley, interviews with author, September 6, 2013; and March 28, 2018.

Mort Halperin, interviews with author, April 12, 2013; and August 16, 2017.

David Jeremiah, interview with author, April 12, 2013.

James Jones, interview with author, October 18, 2017.

Geoff Kemp, interviews with author, April 17, 2013; and July 18, 2017.

Donald Kerrick, interview with author, April 8, 2013.

Robert Kimmitt, interview with author, April 11, 2013.

Anthony Lake, interview with author, August 30, 2013.

Winston Lord, interview with author, April 15, 2013.

Doug Lute, interview with author, September 30, 2017.

William Luti, interview with author, April 5, 2014.

Laurence Lynn, interview with author, May 15, 2013.

Kelly Magsamen, interview with author, October 21, 2017.

Denis McDonough, interview with author, October 18, 2017.

Robert "Bud" McFarlane, interview with author, September 5, 2013.

Brett McGurk, interview with author, June 2, 2014.

Brian McKeon, interview with author, October 13, 2017.

H. R. McMaster, interview with author, June 25, 2018.

Michael Mullen, interview with author, December 20, 2017.

Vali Nasr, interview with author, April 15, 2013.

John Negroponte, interview with author, September 6, 2013.

James O'Brien, interview with author, September 20, 2013.

Meghan O'Sullivan, interviews with author, January 23, 2014; February 10, 2014; and August 30, 2017.

David Petraeus, interview with author, March 11, 2018.

John Poindexter, interview with author, April 8, 2013.

Colin Powell, interview with author, April 4, 2013.

Condoleezza Rice, interview with author, June 24, 2014.

Susan Rice, interview with author, January 17, 2018.

Donald Rumsfeld, interview with author, April 9, 2014.

Brent Scowcroft, interview with author, January 31, 2013.

George Shultz, interview with author, December 19, 2012.

Gary Sick, interview with author, April 25, 2013.

Walter Slocombe, interview with author, February 13, 2013.

Nancy Soderberg, interview with author, April 17, 2013.

John Sununu, interview with author, April 11, 2013.

Howard Teicher, interviews with author, April 15, 2013; and July 21, 2017.

John Tien, interview with author, October 30, 2017.

Strobe Talbott, interview with author, January 28, 2013.

Nate Tibbitts, interview with author, April 18, 2013.

Alexander Vershbow, interviews with author, March 21, 2013; and August 16, 2017.

Tommy Vietor, interview with author, September 28, 2017.
Jenonne Walker, interview with author, April 22, 2014.
David Welch, interview with author, September 9, 2013.
Francis "Bing" West, interview with author, July 9, 2013.
Paul Wolfowitz, interview with author, September 5, 2013.
Phillip Zelikow, interview with author, May 6, 2014.

Original Document Sources

Central Intelligence Agency. "Bosnia, Intelligence, and the Clinton Presidency," accessed May 2014, http://www.foia.cia.gov/collection/bosnia-intelligence-and-clinton-presidency.

Central Intelligence Agency, CIA Records Research Tool (CREST).

Drew Family Archives, courtesy of Sandra Drew.

Eisenhower Presidential Library, Museum, and Boyhood Home, Abilene, Kansas (EPL).

Federation of American Scientists (FAS). https://www.fas.org/.

Foreign Relations of the United States (FRUS).

General George Casey Papers, National Defense University Archives (GGCP).

George Bush Presidential Library and Museum, College Station, Texas (GBPLM).

Gerald R. Ford Presidential Library, Ann Arbor, Michigan (GFPL).

Harry S. Truman Library and Museum, Independence, Missouri (HSTL).

The Jimmy Carter Presidential Museum, Atlanta, George (JCPM).

The John Boykin Collection, The National Security Archives (George Washington University).

John F. Kennedy Presidential Library, Boston, Massachusetts (JFKPL).

Lyndon B. Johnson Library, Austin, Texas (LBJL).

The National Archives.

The National Security Archives at George Washington University.

Papers of Donald Rumsfeld. http://papers.rumsfeld.com/library/.

Peters, Gerhard, and John T. Woolley. The American Presidency Project. http://www.presidency.ucsb.edu.

Richard Nixon Presidential Library and Museum, Yorba Linda, California (RNPL).

Ronald Reagan Presidential Foundation and Library, Simi Valley, California (RRL).

William J. Clinton Presidential Library, Little Rock, Arkansas (WJCL).

Oral Histories

Destler, I. M., and Ivo Daalder (moderators). "The Clinton Administration National Security Council." September 27, 2000. The National Security Council Project, The Brookings Institution and the University of Maryland Center for International and Security Studies (CISSM). http://www.brookings.edu/about/projects/archive/nsc/oralhistories.

———. "The Nixon Administration National Security Council." December 8, 1998. The National Security Council Project, The Brookings Institution and the University

of Maryland Center for International and Security Studies (CISSM). http://www
.brookings.edu/about/projects/archive/nsc/oralhistories.

———. "The Role of the National Security Advisor." October 25, 1990. The National
Security Council Project, The Brookings Institution and the University of Maryland Center for International and Security Studies (CISSM). http://www.brookings
.edu/about/projects/archive/nsc/oralhistories.

Edmund S. Muskie Oral History Collection. https://scarab.bates.edu/muskie_oh/.

Foreign Affairs Oral History Collection, Association for Diplomatic Studies and
Training, Arlington, VA, www.adst.org.

Frontline, "Oral History," "The Gulf War," PBS. http://www.pbs.org/wgbh/pages/
frontline/gulf/oral/.

Library of Congress, "The Foreign Affairs Oral History Collection." http://www.loc
.gov/collection/foreign-affairs-oral-history/about-this-collection/.

Miller Center, "Presidential Oral History Program," University of Virginia. http://
millercenter.org/oralhistory.

Oral Histories, Eisenhower Presidential Library, Museum, and Boyhood Home,
Abilene, Kansas (EPL).

Oral Histories, Harry S. Truman Library and Museum, Independence, Missouri
(HSTL).

Oral Histories, Lyndon B. Johnson Library, Austin, Texas (LBJL).

Oral Histories, John F. Kennedy Presidential Library, Boston, Massachusetts
(JFKPL).

Books

Acheson, Dean. *Present at the Creation: My Years in the State Department*. New York:
Norton, 1969.

Allison, Graham T. *Conceptual Models and the Cuban Missile Crisis: National Policy,
Organization Process, and Bureaucratic Politics*. Santa Monica, CA: RAND Corporation, 1968.

Baker, James A. III, with Thomas M. DeFrank. *The Politics of Diplomacy: Revolution,
War, and Peace, 1989–1992*. New York: G. P. Putnam's Sons, 1995.

Baker, James A. III, and Lee H. Hamilton. "The Iraq Study Group Report." United
States Institute of Peace, December 6, 2006.

Baker, Peter. *Days of Fire: Bush and Cheney in the White House*. New York: Doubleday, 2013.

Barrett, David M. *Uncertain Warriors: Lyndon Johnson and His Vietnam Advisers*.
Lawrence: University Press of Kansas, 1993.

Berman, Larry. *No Peace, No Honor*. New York: Simon & Schuster, 2001.

———. *Planning a Tragedy: The Americanization of Vietnam*. New York: Norton, 1982.

Beschloss, Michael R. *Reaching for Glory: Lyndon Johnson's Secret White House Tapes,
1964–1965*. New York: Simon & Schuster, 2001.

——— . *Taking Charge: The Johnson White House Tapes, 1963–1964*. New York: Simon & Schuster, 1997.

Bird, Kai. *The Color of Truth: McGeorge Bundy and William Bundy, Brothers in Arms: A Biography*. New York: Simon & Schuster, 1998.

——— . *The Good Spy: The Life and Death of Robert Ames*. Kindle Edition. New York: Crown Publishers, 2014.

Bloom, Allan. *The Republic of Plato*. New York: Basic Books, 1968.

Bowie, Robert R., and Richard H. Immerman. *Waging Peace: How Eisenhower Shaped an Enduring Cold War Strategy*. Oxford: Oxford University Press, 1998.

Brzezinski, Zbigniew. *Power and Principle: Memoirs of the National Security Advisor, 1977–1981*. New York: Farrar, Straus, Giroux, 1983.

Bundy, William. *A Tangled Web: The Making of Foreign Policy in the Nixon Presidency*. New York: Hill and Wang, 1998.

Burke, John. *Honest Broker: The National Security Advisor and Presidential Decision Making*. College Station: Texas A & M University Press, 2009.

Burke, John, and Fred I. Greenstein. *How Presidents Test Reality*. New York: Russell Sage Foundation, 1989.

Bush, George, and Brent Scowcroft. *A World Transformed*. New York: Knopf; Vintage, 1998.

Bush, George W. *Decision Points*. Kindle Edition. New York: Crown Publishers, 2010.

Cannon, Lou. *President Reagan: The Role of a Lifetime*. New York: Simon & Schuster, 1991.

Caro, Robert A. *Passage of Power: The Years of Lyndon Johnson*. New York: Alfred A. Knopf, 2012.

Casey, George W. *Strategic Reflections: Operation Iraqi Freedom, July 2004–February 2007*. Washington, DC: National Defense University Press, 2012.

Cheney, Dick, with Liz Cheney. *In My Time: A Personal and Political Memoir*. New York: Threshold Editions, 2011.

Chollet, Derek. *The Road to the Dayton Accords: A Study of American Statecraft*. New York: Palgrave Macmillan, 2005.

Chollet, Derek, and Bennet Freeman. *The Secret History of Dayton: U.S. Diplomacy and the Bosnia Peace Process 1995*. National Security Archive Electronic Briefing Book No. 171. Washington: National Security Archive, 1995.

Christopher, Warren. *In the Stream of History: Shaping Foreign Policy for a New Era*. Stanford, CA: Stanford University Press, 1998.

Clausewitz, Carl von. *On War*. Revised edition. Princeton, NJ: Princeton University Press, 1984.

Cooper, Chester. *The Lost Crusade*. New York: Dodd, Mead, 1970.

CQ Press. *2005 Federal Staff Directory*. Washington, DC: CQ Press, Fall 2005.

Crist, David. *The Twilight War: The Secret History of America's Thirty-Year Conflict with Iran*. Kindle Edition, 142. Penguin Publishing Group.

Daalder, Ivo H. *Getting to Dayton: The Making of America's Bosnia Policy.* Washington, DC: Brookings Institution Press, 2000.

Daalder, Ivo H., and I. M. Destler. *In the Shadow of the Oval Office: Profiles of the National Security Advisers and the Presidents They Served: From JFK to George W. Bush.* New York: Simon & Schuster, 2009.

Dallek, Robert. *Franklin D. Roosevelt and American Foreign Policy, 1932–1945.* New York: Oxford University Press, 1979.

———. *Nixon and Kissinger: Partners in Power.* New York: Harper Collins, 2007.

Deaver, Michael, with Mickey Herkowitz. *Behind the Scenes.* New York: William Morrow and Company, 1987.

Destler, I. M. *Presidents, Bureaucrats, and Foreign Policy: The Politics of Organizational Reform.* Princeton, NJ: Princeton University Press, 1972.

Destler, I. M., Les Gelb, and Anthony Lake. *Our Own Worst Enemy: The Unmaking of American Foreign Policy.* New York: Simon & Schuster, 1984.

Drew, Elizabeth. *On the Edge: The Clinton Presidency.* New York: Simon & Schuster, 1994.

———. *Showdown: The Struggle Between the Gingrich Congress and the Clinton White House.* New York: Simon & Schuster, 1996.

Ellsberg, Daniel. *Secrets: A Memoir of Vietnam and the Pentagon Papers.* New York: Viking, 2002.

Freedman, Lawrence, and Efraim Karsh. *The Gulf Conflict, 1990–1991: Diplomacy and War in the New World Order.* London: Faber and Faber, 1993.

Friedman, Thomas. *From Beirut to Jerusalem: One Man's Middle Eastern Odyssey.* London: Fontana, 1990.

Gans, John A. *The Midnight Watch: The NSC Staff, Drift, and Decision in Conflict.* Baltimore: Johns Hopkins University Press, 2014.

Gates, Robert M. *Duty: Memoirs of a Secretary at War.* New York: Alfred A. Knopf, 2014.

Gelb, Leslie H., with Richard K. Betts. *The Irony of Vietnam: The System Worked.* Washington, DC: Brookings Institution, 1979.

Gettleman, Marvin E., Jane Franklin, Marilyn B. Young, and H. Bruce Franklin, eds. *Vietnam and America.* New York: Grove Press, 1995.

Gittinger, Ted, ed. *The Johnson Years.* Austin: University of Texas Press, 1993.

Goldstein, Gordon M. *Lessons in Disaster: McGeorge Bundy and the Path to War in Vietnam.* New York: Henry Holt, 2009.

Goodwin, Doris Kearns. *Lyndon Johnson and the American Dream.* New York: New American Library, 1977.

Gordon, Michael R., and Bernard E. Trainor. *Cobra II: The Inside Story of the Invasion and Occupation of Iraq.* New York: Pantheon Books, 2006.

———. *The Endgame: The Inside Story of the Struggle for Iraq, From George W. Bush to Barack Obama.* New York: Pantheon Books, 2012.

———. *The Generals' War: The Inside Story of the Conflict in the Gulf.* Boston: Little, Brown, 1995.

Haass, Richard. *War of Necessity, War of Choice*. New York: Simon & Schuster, 2009.

Habeeb, William Mark. *The Middle East in Turmoil: Conflict, Revolution, and Change*. Santa Barbara, CA: Greenwood, 2012.

Haig, Alexander Meigs. *Caveat: Realism, Reagan, and Foreign Policy*. New York: Macmillan, 1984.

Haig, Alexander M. Jr., with Charles McCarry. *Inner Circles: How America Changed the World: A Memoir*. New York: Warner Books, 1992.

Halberstam, David. *The Best and the Brightest*. 20th edition. New York: Random House, 2001.

——. *The Making of a Quagmire: America and Vietnam During the Kennedy Era*. New York: Knopf, 1988.

——. *War in a Time of Peace*. New York: Scribner, 2001.

Haldeman, H. R. *The Haldeman Diaries: Inside the Nixon White House*. New York: G. P. Putnam's, 1994.

Haldeman, H. R, and Joseph DiMona. *The Ends of Power*. New York: Times Books, 1978.

Halperin, Morton H., and Priscilla A. Clapp, with Arnold Kanter. *Bureaucratic Politics and Foreign Policy*. 2nd edition. Washington, DC: Brookings Institution Press, 2006.

Hammel, Eric. *The Root: The Marines in Beirut August 1982–February 1984*. San Diego, CA: Harcourt Brace Jovanovich, 1999.

Herring, George C. *America's Longest War: The United States and Vietnam, 1950–1975*. 4th edition. Boston: McGraw-Hill, 2002.

Hersh, Seymour M. *The Price of Power: Kissinger in the Nixon White House*. New York: Summit Books, 1983.

Hilsman, Roger. *The Politics of Policy Making in Defense and Foreign Affairs*. New York: Harper & Row, 1971.

Holbrooke, Richard C. *To End A War*. New York: Modern Library, 1999.

Iklé, Fred. *Every War Must End*. New York: Columbia University Press, 1991.

Inderfurth, Karl F., and Loch K. Johnson, eds. *Fateful Decisions: Inside the National Security Council*. New York: Oxford University Press, 2004.

Isaacson, Walter. *Kissinger: A Biography*. New York: Simon & Schuster, 1992.

Jackson, Henry M., ed. *The National Security Council: Jackson Subcommittee Papers on Policy-Making at the Presidential Level*. New York: Frederick A. Praeger, 1965.

Johnson, Lyndon B. *The Vantage Point*. New York: Holt, Rinehart and Winston, 1971.

Johnson, Richard Tanner. *Managing the White House*. New York: Harper & Row, 1974.

Jones, Charles O., ed. *Preparing to be President: The Memos of Richard E. Neustadt*. Washington, DC: AEI Press, 2000.

Kahin, George McTurnan. *Intervention: How America Became Involved In Vietnam*. New York: Knopf, 1986.

Kagan, Frederick W. "Choosing Victory: A Plan for Success in Iraq: Phase I Report." A Report of the Iraq Planning Group, American Enterprise Institute (AEI), 2006. http://www.aei.org/events/2006/12/14/choosing-victory-a-plan-for-success-in-iraq-event/.

Kaiser, David E. *American Tragedy: Kennedy, Johnson, and the Origins of the Vietnam War*. Cambridge, MA: Belknap Press of Harvard University Press, 2000.

Kaplan, Fred M. *The Insurgents: David Petraeus and the Plot to Change the American Way of War*. Kindle Edition. New York: Simon & Schuster, 2013.

Kaplan, Robert D. *Balkan Ghosts: A Journey Through History*. New York: St. Martin's Press, 1993.

Karnow, Stanley. *Vietnam: A History*. New York: Viking Press, 1983.

Kengor, Paul, and Patricia Clark Doerner. *The Judge: William Clark, Ronald Reagan's Top Hand*. San Francisco: Ignatius Press, 2007.

Kimball, Jeffrey P. *Nixon's Vietnam War*. Lawrence: University Press of Kansas, 1998.

———, ed. *The Vietnam War Files*. Lawrence: University Press of Kansas, 2004.

Kimball, Warren F. *The Juggler: Franklin Roosevelt As Wartime Statesman*. Princeton, NJ: Princeton University Press, 1991.

Kissinger, Henry A. *Ending the Vietnam War*. New York: Simon & Schuster, 2003.

———. *The Necessity for Choice: Prospects of American Foreign Policy*. New York: Harper, 1961.

———. *White House Years*. Boston: Little, Brown, 1979.

———. *Years of Upheaval*. Boston: Little, Brown, 1982.

Lake, Anthony. *Somoza Falling*. Boston: Houghton Mifflin, 1989.

Landler, Mark. *Alter Egos: Hillary Clinton, Barack Obama, and the Twilight Struggle Over American Power*. New York: Random House, 2016.

Logevall, Fredrik. *Choosing War: The Lost Chance for Peace and the Escalation of War in Vietnam*. Berkeley: University of California Press, 1999.

Machiavelli, Niccolò. *The Prince*. Translated by Luigi Ricci. London: Grant Richards, 1903.

Mann, James. *The Obamians: The Struggle Inside the White House to Redefine American Power*. New York: Viking, 2012.

Mansoor, Peter. *Surge: My Journey with General David Petraeus and the Remaking of the Iraq War*. New Haven, CT: Yale University Press, 2013.

Mazarr, Michael J., Don M. Snider, and James A Blackwell Jr. *Desert Storm: The Gulf War and What We Learned*. Boulder, CO: Westview Press, 1993.

McCausland, Jeffrey. *The Gulf Conflict: A Military Analysis*. Adelphi papers no. 282. London: Brassey's for The International Institute for Strategic Studies, 1993.

McDermott, Anthony, and Kjell Skjelsbaek, eds. *The Multinational Force in Beirut, 1982–1984*. Miami: Florida International University Press, 1991.

McFarlane, Robert C., with Zofia Smardz. *Special Trust*. New York: Cadell & Davies, 1994.

McMaster, H. R. *Dereliction of Duty: Lyndon Johnson, Robert McNamara, the Joint Chiefs of Staff, and the Lies that Led to Vietnam*. New York: Harper Collins, 1997.

McNamara, Robert S. *In Retrospect: The Tragedy and Lessons of Vietnam*. New York: Vintage Books, 1996.

McNamara, Robert S., James G. Blight, and Robert K. Brigham. *Argument with-*

out End: In Search of Answers to the Vietnam Tragedy. New York: PublicAffairs, 1999.

Meacham, Jon. *Destiny and Power: The American Odyssey of George Herbert Walker Bush*. New York: Random House, 2015.

Menges, Constantine Christopher. *Inside the National Security Council: The True Story of the Making and Unmaking of Reagan's Foreign Policy*. New York: Simon and Schuster, 1988.

Metz, Steven. *Decisionmaking in Operation Iraqi Freedom: The Strategic Shift of 2007*. Carlisle, PA: Strategic Studies Institute, US Army War College, May 2010.

Morris, Roger. *An Uncertain Greatness: Henry Kissinger and American Foreign Policy*. New York: Harper & Row, 1977.

Nelson, Michael, ed. *Guide to the Presidency and Executive Branch*. 5th edition. Vol. 1. Thousand Oaks, CA: CQ Press, 2013.

Neustadt, Richard. *Presidential Power and the Modern Presidents: The Politics of Leadership from Roosevelt to Reagan*. New York: Free Press, 1990.

Nixon, Richard M. *RN: The Memoirs of Richard Nixon*. New York: Grosset & Dunlap, 1978.

The Pentagon Papers: The Defense Department History of United States Decisionmaking On Vietnam. Senator Gravel edition. Boston: Beacon Press, 1971.

Powell, Colin, with Joseph E. Persico. *My American Journey*. New York: Ballantine Books, 1995.

Prados, John. *Keepers of the Keys: A History of the National Security Council from Truman to Bush*. New York: William Morrow, 1991.

Preston, Andrew. *The War Council: McGeorge Bundy, the NSC and Vietnam*. Cambridge, MA: Harvard University Press, 2006.

Reagan, Ronald. *The Reagan Diaries*. Edited by Douglas Brinkley. New York: HarperCollins, 2007.

Reeves, Richard. *President Kennedy: Profile of Power*. New York: Simon & Schuster, 1993.

———. *President Nixon: Alone In the White House*. New York: Simon & Schuster, 2001.

Rhodes, Ben. *The World As It Is: A Memoir of the Obama White House*. New York: Random House, 2018.

Rice, Condoleezza. *No Higher Honor: A Memoir of My Years In Washington*. Kindle Edition. New York: Crown Publishers, 2011.

Ricks, Thomas E. *The Gamble: General David Petraeus and the American Military Adventure in Iraq, 2006–2008*. New York: Penguin Press, 2009.

Rothkopf, David. *National Insecurity: American Leadership in an Age of Fear*. New York: PublicAffairs, 2016.

———. *Running the World: The Inside Story of the National Security Council and the Architects of American Power*. New York: PublicAffairs, 2005.

Rumsfeld, Donald. *Known and Unknown: A Memoir*. Kindle Edition. New York: Sentinel, 2011.

Rusk, Dean, as told to Richard Rusk. *As I Saw It*. New York: Norton, 1990.

Safire, William. *Before the Fall: An Inside View of the Pre-Watergate White House*. Garden City, NY: Doubleday, 1975.

Sanger, David E. *Confront and Conceal: Obama's Secret Wars and Surprising Use of American Power*. New York: Crown Publishers, 2012.

Schlesinger, Arthur M. *A Thousand Days: John F. Kennedy in the White House*. Boston: Houghton Mifflin, 1965.

Schmitz, David. *Richard Nixon and the Vietnam War: The End of the American Century*. E-book edition. New York: Rowman & Littlefield Publishers, 2014.

Shoemaker, Christopher. *The Decisional Dilemma: Structure, Function, and the NSC Staff*. Carlisle Barracks, PA: US Army War College, 1989.

———. *The NSC Staff: Counseling the Council*. Boulder, CO: Westview Press, 1991.

Shultz, George Pratt. *Turmoil and Triumph: My Years As Secretary of State*. New York: Scribner's, 1993.

Sick, Gary. *All Fall Down: America's Tragic Encounter with Iran*. New York: Penguin Books, 1986.

Sparrow, Bartholomew H. *The Strategist: Brent Scowcroft and the Call of National Security*. New York: PublicAffairs, 2015.

Silber, Laura, and Alan Little. *Yugoslavia: Death of a Nation*. New York: Penguin Books, 1997.

Smith, Bromley K. *Organizational History of the National Security Council during the Kennedy and Johnson Administrations*. Washington, DC: National Security Council, 1988.

Spiegel, Steven. *The Other Arab-Israeli Conflict: Making America's Middle East Policy, from Truman to Reagan*. Chicago: University of Chicago Press, 1985.

Strober, Gerald S., and Deborah H Strober. *Nixon, an Oral History of His Presidency*. New York: HarperCollins, 1994.

Taylor, Maxwell D. *Swords and Plowshares*. New York: Norton, 1972.

Teicher, Howard, and Gayle Radley Teicher. *Twin Pillars to Desert Storm: America's Flawed Vision in the Middle East from Nixon to Bush*. New York: William Morrow, 1993.

Thompson, Kenneth W. *The Nixon Presidency: Twenty-Two Intimate Perspectives of Richard M. Nixon*. Lanham, MD: University Press of America, 1987.

Tower, John, Edmund Muskie, and Brent Scowcroft. *The Tower Commission Report*. New York: Bantam Books, 1987.

US News & World Report Staff. *Triumph without Victory: The Unreported History of the Persian Gulf War*. New York: Times Books, 1992.

Van Atta, Dale. *With Honor: Melvin Laird in War, Peace and Politics*. Madison: University of Wisconsin Press, 2008.

Weigley, Russell F. *The American Way of War: A History of United States Military Strategy and Policy*. Bloomington: Indiana University Press, 1977.

Weinberger, Caspar. *Fighting for Peace: Seven Critical Years at the Pentagon*. London: Michael Joseph, 1990.

West, Francis J. *The Strongest Tribe: War, Politics, and the Endgame In Iraq*. New York: Random House, 2008.

Woodward, Bob. *Bush At War*. New York: Simon & Schuster, 2002.

——. *The Choice: How Clinton Won*. New York: Simon & Schuster, 1996.

——. *The Commanders*. New York: Simon & Schuster, 1991.

——. *Obama's Wars*. New York: Simon & Schuster, 2010.

——. *State of Denial*. New York: Simon & Schuster, 2006.

——. *The War Within: A Secret White House History, 2006–2008*. New York: Simon & Schuster, 2008.

Yetiv, Steve A. *Explaining Foreign Policy: U.S. Decision-making in the Gulf Wars*. 2nd edition. Baltimore: Johns Hopkins University Press, 2011.

Zegart, Amy B. *Flawed by Design: The Evolution of the CIA, JCS, and NSC*. Stanford, CA: Stanford University Press, 1999.

Book Chapters

Apple, R. W. "Introduction." In John Tower, Edmund Muskie, and Brent Scowcroft, *The Tower Commission Report*. New York: Bantam Books, 1987.

Auerswald, David. "The Evolution of the Statutory NSC Process." In *The National Security Enterprise: Navigating the Labyrinth*. Edited by Roger Z. George and Harvey Rishikof, 31–54. Washington, DC: Georgetown University Press, 2011.

Brodie, Bernard. "The Tet Offensive." In *Decisive Battles of the Twentieth Century: Land, Sea, Air*. Edited by Noble Frankland and Christopher Dowling, 320–34. London: Sidgwick & Jackson, 1976.

Chollet, Derek. "The National Security Council: Is It Effective, or Is It Broken?" In *The Oxford Handbook of U.S. National Security*. Edited by Derek S. Reveron, Nikolas K. Gvosdev, and John A. Cloud, 111–22. New York: Oxford University Press, 2018.

Cutler, Robert. "The National Security Council under President Eisenhower." In *The National Security Council: Jackson Subcommittee Papers on Policy-Making at the Presidential Level*. Edited by Henry M. Jackson. New York: Frederick A. Praeger, 1965.

Eberstadt, Ferdinand. "Postwar Organization for National Security." Reprinted in *Fateful Decisions: Inside the National Security Council*. Edited by Karl F. Inderfurth and Loch K. Johnson, 17–20. New York: Oxford University Press, 2004.

Hudson, Valerie M. "Foreign Policy Decision-Making: A Touchstone for International Relations Theory in the Twenty-First Century." In *Foreign Policy Decision-Making* (Revisited). Edited by Valerie M. Hudson, Derek H. Chollet, and James M. Goldgeier, 1–20. New York: Palgrave Macmillan, 2002.

Hunter, Robert. "Working Hard, Having Fun at the NSC." In *Zbig: The Strategy and Statecraft of Zbigniew Brzezinski*. Edited by Charles Gati, 116–19. Baltimore: Johns Hopkins University Press, 2013.

Jackson, Henry M. "How Shall We Forge a Strategy of Survival?" Address before the National War College, Washington, DC, April 16, 1959. Reprinted in *Fateful*

Decisions: Inside the National Security Council. Edited by Karl F. Inderfurth and Loch K. Johnson. New York: Oxford University Press, 2004.

Kemp, Geoffrey. "The American Peacekeeping Role." In *The Multinational Force in Beirut, 1982–1984.* Edited by Anthony McDermott and Kjell Skjelsbaek, 131–42. Miami: Florida International University Press, 1991.

Kissinger, Henry A. "Bureaucracy and Policy Making: The Effect of Insiders and Outsiders on the Policy Process." In *Bureaucracy, Politics and Strategy.* Edited by Henry A. Kissinger and Bernard Brodie. Security Studies Project, University of California, Los Angeles, Paper Number 17. Los Angeles, CA: UCLA, 1968.

Lovett, Robert A. "Perspective on the Policy Process." In *The National Security Council: Jackson Subcommittee Papers on Policy-Making at the Presidential Level.* Edited by Henry M. Jackson, 75–98. New York: Frederick A. Praeger, 1965.

Nelson, Anna Kasten. "The Importance of Foreign Policy Process: Eisenhower and the National Security Council." In *Eisenhower: A Centenary Assessment.* Edited by Stephen E. Ambrose and Gunter Bischoff, 111–24. Baton Rouge: Louisiana State University Press, 1995.

Nelson, Richard W. "Multinational Peacekeeping in the Middle East and the United Nations Model." In *The Multinational Force in Beirut, 1982–1984.* Edited by Anthony McDermott and Kjell Skjelsbaek, 3–36. Miami: Florida International University Press, 1991.

Pelcovits, Nathan. "What Went Wrong?" In *The Multinational Force in Beirut, 1982–1984.* Edited by Anthony McDermott and Kjell Skjelsbaek, 37–79. Miami: Florida International University Press, 1991.

Resende-Santos, Jaoa. "The Persian Gulf Crisis: A Chronology of Events." In *After the Storm: Lessons from the Gulf War.* Edited by Joseph S. Nye Jr. and Roger K. Smith, 3–30. Lanham, MD: Madison Books, 1992.

Rothkopf, David. "Setting the Stage for the Current Era." In *Zbig: The Strategy and Statecraft of Zbigniew Brzezinski.* Edited by Charles Gati, 63–84. Baltimore: Johns Hopkins University Press, 2013.

Talbott, Strobe. "Status Quo Ante: The United States and Its Allies." In *After the Storm: Lessons from the Gulf War.* Edited by Joseph S. Nye Jr. and Roger K. Smith, 83–111. Lanham, MD: Madison Books, 1992.

Thomson, James. "The Evening Report." In *Zbig: The Strategy and Statecraft of Zbigniew Brzezinski.* Edited by Charles Gati, 120–24. Baltimore: Johns Hopkins University Press, 2013.

Journal Articles

Alvandi, Roham. "Nixon, Kissinger, and the Shah: The Origins of Iranian Primacy in the Persian Gulf." *Diplomatic History* 36, no. 2 (April 2012): 337–72.

Art, Robert J. "Bureaucratic Politics and American Foreign Policy: A Critique." *Policy Sciences* 4, no. 4 (December 1973): 467–90.

Biddle, Stephen, Jeffrey A. Friedman, and Jacob N. Shapiro. "Testing the Surge: Why

Did Violence Decline in Iraq in 2007?" *International Security* 37, no. 1 (Summer 2012): 7–40.

Bock, Joseph G., and Duncan L. Clarke. "The National Security Assistant and the White House Staff: National Security Policy Decisionmaking and Domestic Political Considerations, 1947–1984." *Presidential Studies Quarterly* 16, no. 2 (Spring 1986): 258–79.

Brzezinski, Zbigniew. "The NSC's Midlife Crisis." *Foreign Policy* 69 (Winter 1987–1988): 80–99.

Cohen, Eliot A. "Civil-Military Relations." *Orbis* 41, no. 2 (Spring 1997): 177–86.

Cutler, Robert. "The Development of the National Security Council." *Foreign Affairs* 34, no. 3 (April 1956): 441–58.

Destler, I. M. "A Job That Doesn't Work." *Foreign Policy*, no. 38 (Spring 1980): 80–88.

———. "National Security Advice to U.S. Presidents: Some Lessons from Thirty Years." *World Politics* 29, no. 2 (January 1977): 143–76.

———. "National Security Management: What Presidents Have Wrought." *Political Science Quarterly* 95, no. 4 (Winter 1980–1981): 577–83.

Dueck, Colin. "The Role of the National Security Advisor and the 2006 Iraq Strategy Review." *Orbis* 58, no. 1 (Winter 2014): 15–38.

Falk, Stanley L. "The National Security Council Under Truman, Eisenhower, and Kennedy." *Political Science Quarterly* 79, no. 3 (September 1964): 403–34.

Feaver, Peter. "The Right to Be Right: Civil-Military Relations and the Iraq Surge Decision." *International Security* 35, no. 4 (Spring 2011): 87–125.

George, Alexander L. "The Case for Multiple Advocacy in Making Foreign Policy." *The American Political Science Review* 66, no. 3 (September 1972): 751–95.

Greenstein, Fred. "A Journalist's Vendetta." *The New Republic* 189, no. 5 (August 1, 1983): 29.

Greenstein, Fred I., and Richard H. Immerman. "Effective National Security Advising: Recovering the Eisenhower Legacy." *Political Science Quarterly* 115, no. 3 (Autumn 2000): 335–45.

Hammond, Paul Y. "The National Security Council as a Device for Interdepartmental Coordination: An Interpretation and Appraisal." *American Political Science Review* 54, no. 4 (December 1960): 899–910.

Holbrooke, Richard. "America, a European Power." *Foreign Affairs* 74, no. 2 (March–April 1995): 38–51.

Horn, Murray J., and Kenneth A. Shepsle. "Commentary on 'Administrative Arrangements and the Political Control of Agencies: Administrative Process and Organizational Form as Legislative Responses to Agency Costs.'" *Virginia Law Review* 75 (1989): 499–508.

Humphrey, David C. "NSC Meetings during the Johnson Presidency." *Diplomatic History* 18, no. 1 (Winter 1994): 29–45.

Johnson, Robert H. "The National Security Council: The Relevance of its Past to its Future." *Orbis* (Fall 1969): 709–35.

Kemp, Geoffrey. "Lessons in Lebanon: A Guideline for Future U.S. Policy." *Middle East Insight* 6 (Summer 1988): 57–68.

Kissinger, Henry A. "The Viet Nam Negotiations." *Foreign Affairs* 47, no. 2 (January 1969): 211–34.

Lay, James S. Jr. "National Security Council's Role in the U.S. Security and Peace Program." *World Affairs* 115, no. 2 (Summer 1952): 37–39.

Macey, Jonathan R. "Organizational Design and Political Control of Administrative Agencies." *Journal of Law, Economics, & Organization* 8, no. 1 (March 1992): 93–110.

May, Ernest R. "The Development of Political-Military Consultation in the United States." *Political Science Quarterly* 70, no. 2 (June 1955): 161–80.

Nelson, Anna Kasten. "President Truman and the Evolution of the National Security Council." *Journal of American History* 72, no. 2 (September 1985): 360–78.

———. "The 'Top of Policy Hill': President Eisenhower and the National Security Council." *Diplomatic History* 7, no. 4 (October 1983): 307–26.

Nelson, Michael. "Neustadt's 'Presidential Power' at 50." *Chronicle of Higher Education*, March 28, 2010. http://chronicle.com/article/Neustadts-Presidential/64816/.

Nixon, Richard. "Asia After Viet Nam." *Foreign Affairs* 46, issue 1 (October 1967): 111–25.

Preston, Andrew. "The Little State Department: McGeorge Bundy and the National Security Council Staff, 1961–65." *Presidential Studies Quarterly* 31, no. 4 (December 2001): 635–59.

Preston, Andrew. "The Soft Hawks' Dilemma in Vietnam: Michael V. Forrestal at the National Security Council, 1962–1964." *The International History Review* 25, no. 1 (March 2003): 63–95.

Rusk, Dean. "The President." *Foreign Affairs* 38, no. 3 (April 1960): 353–69.

Sander, Alfred D. "Truman and the National Security Council: 1945–1947." *Journal of American History* 59, no. 2 (September 1972): 369–88.

Schlesinger, Arthur Jr. "Effective National Security Advising: A Most Dubious Precedent." *Political Science Quarterly* 115, no. 3 (Autumn 2000): 347–51.

Smith, Dale. "What is O.C.B.?" *Foreign Service Journal* (November 1955): 26–27, 48–56.

Souers, Sidney W. "Policy Formulation for National Security." *American Political Science Review* 43, no. 3 (June 1949): 534–43.

Taylor, William J. Jr., and James Blackwell. "The Ground War in the Gulf." *Survival* 33, no. 3 (1991): 230–45.

Government Reports

Best, Richard A. Jr. "The National Security Council: An Organizational Assessment." Congressional Research Service, 7-5700, RL30840, December 28, 2011.

Commander, NATO International Security Assistance Force, Afghanistan. "Commander's Initial Assessment." August 30, 2009, 1–2. http://www.washingtonpost.com/wp-dyn/content/article/2009/09/21/AR2009092100110.html.

Defense Department. "Conduct of the Persian Gulf War: Final Report to Congress."
April 1992.

Drew, S. Nelson. "NATO from Berlin to Bosnia: Trans-Atlantic Security in Transition." Institute for National Security Studies, McNair Paper 35. Washington, DC:
National Defense University, January 1995, 8.

George, Suzy. "Fine-Tuning NSC Staff Processes and Procedures." The White House
Blog. June 22, 2015.

Government Accountability Office (GAO). "Afghanistan: Key Oversight Issues." GAO-
13-218SP, February 2013.

Government Accountability Office (GAO). "Securing, Stabilizing and Rebuilding
Iraq." GAO-08-837, June 2008.

"Hearing Of The Senate Armed Services Committee." June 2, 2009. https://votesmart
.org/public-statement/429055/hearing-of-the-senate-armed-services-committee-
nomination-of-admiral-james-stavridis-usn-for-reappointment-to-the-grade-
of-admiral-and-to-be-commander-us-european-command-and-supreme-allied-
commander-europe.

Hoover, Herbert. "Letter from the Chairman, Commission on Organization of the
Executive Branch of the Government." February 28, 1949. Washington, DC: US
Government Printing Office, 1949.

Joint Chiefs of Staff. "Origin of Joint Concepts." Accessed May 2014. http://www.jcs
.mil/About/OriginofJointConcepts.aspx.

Kale, Katy A. "Executive Office of the President; Contingency Shutdown Plan; Operations in the Absence of Appropriations." The White House, September 26, 2013.
http://www.whitehouse.gov/sites/default/files/docs/eop_contingency_plan.pdf.

The Long Commission. "The Report of the DoD Commission on Beirut International
Airport Terrorist Act, October 23, 1983." December 20, 1983.

McInnis, Kathleen J. "Fact Sheet: FY2017 National Defense Authorization Act (NDAA)
DOD Reform Proposals." Congressional Research Service, R44508. May 18, 2017.
https://fas.org/sgp/crs/natsec/R44508.pdf.

Murphy, Robert D. "Report of the Commission on the Organization of the Government for the Conduct of Foreign Policy." Washington, DC: US Government Printing Office (GPO), 1975.

National Security Act of 1947. July 26, 1947. http://www.intelligence.senate.gov/
nsaact1947.pdf.

Obama, Barack. "Changing the Name of the National Security Staff to the National
Security Council Staff." Executive Order, White House Press Office. February
10, 2014.

——— . "Remarks by the President in Address to the Nation on the Way Forward in
Afghanistan and Pakistan." The White House. December 1, 2009.

——— . "Remarks by the President on a New Strategy for Afghanistan and Pakistan."
The White House. March 27, 2009.

Odeen, Philip. "The National Security Advisor: Role and Accountability." Hearing before the US Senate Committee on Foreign Relations. April 17, 1980. Washington, DC: US Government Printing Office (GPO), 1980.

Office of the Historian. "The Baghdad Pact (1955) and the Central Treaty Organization (CENTO)." State Department. http://history.state.gov/milestones/1953-1960/CENTO.

———. "History of the National Security Council, 1947–1997." U.S. Department of State. August 1997. Accessed May 2014. http://www.fas.org/irp/offdocs/NSChistory.htm.

Office of the Press Secretary. "Statement by the Press Secretary." The White House. October 13, 2004. http://georgewbush-whitehouse.archives.gov/news/releases/2004/10/20041013-4.html.

Press Conference: "Secretary Gates and Adm. Mullen on Leadership Changes in Afghanistan From the Pentagon." US Defense Department, May 11, 2009.

Reorganization Plan No. 4 of 1949, 5 U.S.C. § (1949). http://law.justia.com/codes/us/2010/title5/app/reorganiz/other/dup14/.

The White House, "The Road to Freedom." June 28, 2004, https://georgewbush-whitehouse.archives.gov/infocus/elections/freedomessay/index.html#.

The White House Press Office, "Statement by the President on Afghanistan." February 17, 2009.

Trump, Donald. "Remarks by President Trump on the Strategy in Afghanistan and South Asia." The White House. August 21, 2017.

US Representative Jackie Walorski. "House Approves Walorski Amendment to Restore Transparency to National Security Council." Press Release. May 17, 2016. http://walorski.house.gov/house-approves-walorski-amendment-to-restore-transparency-to-national-security-council/.

INDEX